D0294808

Thirty Years of Musical Life in London

From a daguerreotype owned by Mme. Patti

ADELINA PATTI AT THE AGE OF NINE

Thirty Years of Musical Life in London

1870–1900

By

Hermann Klein

With many Illustrations from Photographs

London
William Heinemann
1903

TO

SIGNOR MANUEL GARCIA

THE MOST ILLUSTRIOUS SINGING TEACHER
OF THE NINETEENTH CENTURY
THIS BOOK IS RESPECTFULLY DEDICATED
BY HIS GRATEFUL PUPIL
HERMANN KLEIN

CONTENTS

Contents

Contents

LIST OF ILLUSTRATIONS

List of Illustrations

List of Illustrations

List of Illustrations

PREFATORY NOTE

Not the least valuable asset of a life largely spent among artists is a good memory. From an early age I cultivated the faculty of making mental notes; and, like most faculties, innate or acquired, it grew until it developed into second nature. During my quarter of a century's work as a London musical critic, I seldom found it necessary to do more than jot down a word or two in the margin of a programme as a preliminary to the writing of an article. I accustomed my eye and ear to take records of what I saw and heard; and, where I happened to be sufficiently interested, those records assumed a more or less permanent form.

Most of the purely personal incidents related in these pages appear in print for the first time. So, also, do the letters which I have ventured to select for publication from a numerous autograph collection. Where the originals of these letters are in a foreign tongue, the English translation only is given. I have endeavored, save in one or two special instances, to avoid mere biographical details, particularly in the case of those musicians, dead and living, whose careers are in all essential matters familiar to the public.

My object is rather to furnish sketches of famous musical personages, and to set before the reader hitherto unrecorded scenes and events in their lives, together with slight studies of temperament and character, which may be of value in so far as they tend to throw a side-light upon the personality of the notable individuals with whom they deal. At the same time, by placing these as nearly as possible in chronological order, and supplementing them with brief accounts of all the prominent débuts and first performances that I have personally witnessed, the outcome is a tolerably complete picture of operatic and musical life in England during the last three decades of the nineteenth century.

By far the most important feature of these chronicles is the history of the remarkable renaissance of Opera effected through the ambitious spirit and energy of the late Sir Augustus Harris, impresario of the Royal Opera, Covent Garden; manager of Drury Lane; and sometime Sheriff of London. The inception, growth, and development of that interesting movement have not, so far as I am aware, been traced by any other writer; and the story acquires added value and significance from the fact that the scheme of fashionable Opera evolved by Augustus Harris in London is absolutely identical with that so ably carried on, until the spring of the present year, by Maurice Grau in New York.

I trust that I have succeeded in accomplishing my task without overstepping the border-line which should separate the friend from the critic. I have always watched that delicate yet important boundary with scrupulous care; and, happily, I have found it easy to observe and obey without loss of good-will or esteem on either side. Hence the existence of warm friendly ties with so many of the distinguished artists whom it has been my privilege to meet—ties very dear to me, yet the delight whereof, under less well-balanced conditions, I should regretfully have been compelled to deny myself.

Hermann Klein.

April, 1903.

THIRTY YEARS OF MUSICAL LIFE IN LONDON

CHAPTER I

Early Norwich days—A famous English festival—My schoolmaster describes Paganini — Jenny Lind — Spohr — Julius Benedict—Benedict and Beethoven—Theresa Tietjens—A great artist and a brave woman.

I WAS born in the musical city of Norwich. The epithet "musical" is not undeserved. Search the whole United Kingdom through, and you will scarcely find a place that can boast an older or more intimate connection with the "divine art" than the ancient capital of East Anglia. Its noble cathedral, its threescore churches, its chapels without number, are ever helping to create and sustain in the population a love of music. Above all, it is the scene, once in every three years, of a famous musical gathering. The "Norfolk and Norwich Musical Festival" (to give the full title) not only vies in age with those of the Three Choirs,—Gloucester, Worcester, and Hereford,—but very nearly ranks in importance with the triennial meetings of its richer sisters, Birmingham and Leeds.

My parents were not musical by profession; but the fact that both were engaged in professional vocations, coupled with their ardent love of the art, brought them into association with many of the operatic and vocal celebrities who visited the city from time to time. Our house on Elm Hill stood within sound of the cathedral chimes, and barely a stone's throw from St. Andrew's Hall, the quaint old Gothic building, half church, half concert-room, in which the festival rehearsals and performances were always held.

From the first I seemed to breathe the "festival atmosphere" of the place. On the very evening I was born (the date, I may mention, was July 23, 1856) there was a rehearsal of Sir Michael Costa's "Eli"; and as the voices of the choir were wafted through the windows on the hot summer air, the question arose whether it would not be appropriate to name me after the venerable priest who was the hero of the oratorio then being interpreted. However, it had been determined that in the event of my being a boy I should receive my father's name of Hermann. Fortunately, that decision was adhered to, and I was spared the fate of being addressed by my intimate friends for the whole of my life as "Eli."

The echoes of the festival proceedings penetrated even the thick walls of my school classrooms. For the worthy principal of Opie House School (so named after the gifted Norwich painter, John Opie, who had once occupied the red-bricked dwelling which still stands opposite St. Clement's Church) was a highly respected member of the

EXTERIOR

INTERIOR

ST. ANDREW'S HALL, NORWICH

From photographs by C. Brand & Co., Norwich

festival chorus. He owned a capital bass voice, and was a first-rate musician. What is more, he knew a good singer when he heard one. It was his delight to describe to us how superbly Sims Reeves had sung "Deeper and deeper still"; with what thrilling expression Mlle. Tietjens had phrased "I know that my Redeemer liveth"; how inimitable Mme. Sainton-Dolby had been in "He was despised"; and what a remarkable voice he had heard in the bass solos of the "Messiah"—that of the famous Weiss, who composed the music of "The Village Blacksmith."

He could go back a good many years, too, could my musical schoolmaster. When in the mood he would tell us how, as a youth, he had been taken to St. Andrew's Hall to hear the great Paganini. With an air of awe he would describe the weird aspect and lean, lank form of the illustrious fiddler, as he stood upon the platform in his closely buttoned swallow-tailed coat, playing amid a silence so intense that his auditors almost feared lest their breathing might break the spell.

"Never before or since," my teacher would say, "have I seen an audience wrought to such a pitch of excitement. It was partly the influence of the individual himself, no doubt; but it was also due to the strangely wonderful beauty of the tone that he obtained from his instrument, and the fascination of a method which completely concealed the nature of the difficulties he surmounted. As I listened I seemed to forget that Paganini was a man. Gradually he assumed the character of a magician, an executant endowed with positively supernatural powers!" And such I imagine was the impression actually produced by this marvelous violinist upon nine out of every ten persons who heard him.

It was in St. Andrew's Hall, also, that I was vouchsafed as a boy the privilege of hearing, on a solitary occasion only, one of the greatest artists the world has ever possessed. I refer to Jenny Lind. The close association which existed between that gifted and noble woman and the city of Norwich is a matter of common knowledge. A bishop of Norwich (Dr. Stanley) it was who persuaded the first of the "Swedish Nightingales" to abandon, on religious grounds, the operatic stage; which premature and much-regretted event occurred in 1849. But the famous singer frequently visited Norwich, and more than once she appeared at concerts given on behalf of the funds of the Jenny Lind Infirmary for Children, an institution founded by her and still flourishing in the old city.

At one of these concerts, some time during the middle "sixties," I heard Jenny Lind sing. The voice, I remember perfectly, was as exquisitely clear and fresh as a young girl's; its sweet tones haunted me long afterward. Of the wondrous art of the great singer I was too young to judge; but I shall never forget what she sang, or the rare wealth of religious sentiment with which she invested the prayer of *Agathe* in the favorite *scena* from "Der Freischütz." Upon the stage, of course, the heroine of Weber's opera always kneels while uttering her touching appeal for her lover's safe return, and Jenny Lind also knelt while singing the same passage upon the platform of St. Andrew's Hall on the occasion I am alluding to.[1]

In later years Mme. Jenny Lind-Goldschmidt used to be a conspicuous figure at the concerts of the London Bach Choir, whereof her husband, Mr. Otto Goldschmidt, was the first conductor. She would modestly take her place in the front row of the sopranos, with the most musical of the Queen's daughters, the Princess Christian of Schleswig-Holstein, for her near companion. Moreover, she took an active part in the training of the female voices, and to her skilful instruction was in a large measure due the facility and brilliancy with which they executed the difficult passages in Bach's B minor Mass (performed for the first time in England April 26, 1876). The great singer died at Malvern, November 2, 1887, and seven years later I was present at the unveiling of the tablet, with medallion portrait, which now does honor to her memory in the south transept of Westminster Abbey. She is so far the only musical artist, other than a composer, whose lineaments have been exposed upon the walls of that ancient fane.

[1] My boyish imagination can hardly have led me astray in this matter. Besides, it was precisely the kind of impulse that the emotional exaltation of this deeply religious woman would have prompted her to yield to, regardless of the every-day conventionalities of the concert-room.

"If Birmingham had its Mendelssohn, Norwich had its Spohr." This pardonable boast, familiar enough to my boyish ears, had reference to the visit paid by Louis Spohr to Norwich in 1839 (when he conducted his oratorio "Calvary" and played a couple of his violin works), and also to the fact that he had expressly composed his oratorio "The Fall of Babylon" for the festival of 1842.[1] Some thirteen years later an effort was made to persuade the Cassel composer to provide another novelty, and my father was requested by the Festival Committee to carry on the German correspondence with him. Spohr undertook the task, and promised to complete a new work for the festival of 1857. But at that time his powers were beginning to decline, and he plainly declared himself no longer satisfied with what he wrote; while the accident which at that time broke his arm fairly precluded all question of further progress with the work. Two years later he died.

[1] It is interesting to recall that a section of the Norwich clergy raised a tremendous outcry against the performance in the concert-room of "Calvary," on account of the nature of the libretto. It was declared to be pure sacrilege thus to perform a musical illustration of the events of the Crucifixion. Nevertheless, the oratorio was duly given under Spohr's direction, and was received with great enthusiasm. In London, in 1847, the same opposition arose when a series of Spohr's works was announced by the Sacred Harmonic Society. This time it proved successful, for at the last moment "Calvary" was omitted and "The Fall of Babylon" given in its place. Thirty-five years later, when Gounod's "Redemption" was produced at Birmingham, the British public was not quite so squeamish.

JENNY LIND ABOUT 1866

From a photograph by C. E. Fry & Son, London

SIR JULIUS BENEDICT

From a photograph by Adolphe Beau, London

Musical Life in London

ONE of the proudest moments that I can recall in my early Norwich life was my being presented to Mr. (afterward Sir) Julius Benedict, who officiated as conductor of the festivals from 1842 until 1878, when he was succeeded by the present conductor, Mr. Alberto Randegger. By the light of subsequent experience, I learned to realize that Benedict was one of the worst conductors who ever held a baton. His head was invariably buried in his score; his arms were ever uplifted, as though seeking a higher level than the shoulder-joints naturally permitted. He rarely gave a cue until it was too late to be of practical value; and he entirely lacked the magnetic power and the sense of ensemble that should be the primary gifts of a good conductor. But at the time I am speaking of these deficiencies were noted only by the few. The vast majority of East Anglian amateurs, including my youthful self, were satisfied to look upon Sir Julius not only as a great conductor, but as a musician whose coöperation brought honor and glory to the festival. Was he not the favorite pupil and friend of Weber? Had he not, when a young man of twenty-three, seen and shaken hands with the immortal Beethoven?

I have been introduced to Verdi and Gounod; I have known and spoken with Wagner; but, great as those privileges undoubtedly were, I do not think they aroused in me the same feelings of mingled pride and awe that I experienced when, as a boy, I was first addressed by a man who had stood face to face with Beethoven. In his biography of Weber, Sir Julius Benedict describes in glowing language how he met the great composer at his publishers' in Vienna, and expresses the great joy and surprise that he felt when Beethoven "actually condescended" to speak with him. He adds:

> I see him yet before me, and who could ever forget those striking features? The lofty, vaulted forehead with thick gray and white hair encircling it in the most picturesque disorder, that square lion's nose, that broad chin, that noble and soft mouth. Over the cheeks, seamed with scars from the smallpox, was spread a high color. From under the bushy, closely compressed eyebrows flashed a pair of piercing eyes; his thick-set Cyclopean figure told of a powerful frame. He approached me with his inseparable tablet in his hand, and in his usual brusque manner addressed me: "You are Weber's pupil?" I gave an affirmative nod. "Why does n't he come to see me? Tell him to come to Baden with Haslinger," pointing to Steiner's partner. Asking for his tablet, I wrote in it, "May I come too?" He smiled, replying, "Ja, kleiner naseweis" (Yes, you saucy little fellow).

And then follows an account of the visit, too lengthy for quotation here.

It was at the suggestion of Malibran that Benedict left Paris and went to England in 1835. He quickly made his mark as an operatic composer, and successfully competed with Michael Balfe and

Vincent Wallace in the race for fame. Like them, he wrote and produced many operas; like them, he left only one that really promises to survive. Indeed, Benedict's "Lily of Killarney" is the sole English opera of the so-called "ballad" type that still shares popularity with "The Bohemian Girl" and "Maritana." Although such a mediocre conductor, he was an admirable accompanist. He had studied under Hummel at Weimar before going to Weber, and was a quite capable pianist. His reputation in this capacity was not a little enhanced by his association with Jenny Lind on her memorable tour in the United States (1850–52). At any rate, after his return to London his services "at the piano" were in request at every kind of musical function, and he was practically the sole accompanist employed at the Monday Popular Concerts during the first twenty years of their existence.

When I first made Benedict's acquaintance he was not far short of seventy. Still a hale old man and a wonderfully hard worker, his eyes were nevertheless beginning to give him trouble, and, when conducting, the distance between his head and the score was growing shorter and shorter. He was much upset by the financial failure of the Norwich festival of 1869 and the comparatively poor results achieved in 1872 and 1875. The latter was the first of these meetings at which I performed the functions of a musical critic, as the representative of my uncle's newspaper, the "Norwich Argus." When it was over, Sir Julius asked me to come and see him, in order to talk over a series of articles proposing some radical modifications in the festival management. These I wrote, and they duly appeared in the "Argus," and certain of the suggestions were carried out with good effect at the festival of 1878. But, as it turned out, that was the last of the Norwich festivals that Benedict was to direct. He shortly afterward underwent an operation for cataract, and then—married again! To add to his troubles, he incurred severe losses in a provincial operatic speculation with the then impresario of Covent Garden, the late Frederic Gye. He gradually relinquished all public work, and died in June, 1885, at the ripe age of eighty-one.

Among the great *prime donne* who sang in Norwich during the "sixties" and "seventies," none was more deservedly popular than Theresa Tietjens. Those of my American readers who saw her when she appeared with Mr. Mapleson's troupe at the Academy of Music, New York, in 1876, cannot fail to have a vivid recollection of her genius both as a singer and an actress. Then, however, she was just approaching the tragical climax of her brilliant career. When I first heard her, at one of the general rehearsals for the festival of 1866 (some eight years after her début in England), her voice was not only fresh, powerful, and penetrating, but it possessed in a greater degree than then that sympathetic charm—that curiously dramatic "human" quality—which was perhaps its most notable attribute.

From a photograph by Elliott & Fry, London

TIETJENS
AS LUCREZIA BORGIA

Her style was marked by the same rare individuality. Her phrasing offered a curious blending of vigor and grace; and she had a trick of employing the *portamento* when approaching a high note, which in any other singer might have been thought almost ugly, but in Tietjens seemed both natural and artistic. At the same time, her attack was superb. Never have I heard the opening phrase of the "Inflammatus" in Rossini's "Stabat Mater" delivered with such magnificent energy and such absolute purity of tone. To hear Tietjens in those days sing "Let the bright Seraphim" (especially to the trumpet obbligato of Tom Harper) was a treat never to be forgotten.

Theresa Tietjens was one of the few leading sopranos of her time (Adelina Patti was also one; Emma Albani, another) who could be regarded as equally distinguished interpreters of oratorio and opera. If Lemmens-Sherrington, being a born Englishwoman, could claim to be the legitimate successor of Clara Novello, the position of the dramatic "star" of oratorio was no less truly shared by Rudersdorff and Tietjens, until the former took up her residence in the United States (1872), leaving her friend and rival to reign supreme. Hearing Tietjens as I did in oratorio, then, some years before I knew her in opera, I was enabled to judge even more accurately of the wonderful effect that resulted from the combination of her histrionic and vocal powers. On the stage she was a tragédienne in the highest sense of the term. The opportunity of arriving at that conclusion was afforded me by the artist herself when I was in my sixteenth year. And the memory of her glorious impersonation, on that occasion, of *Valentine* ("Les Huguenots") has never faded, notwithstanding the profound impression subsequently created by her embodiments of *Lucrezia Borgia, Norma, Medea, Donna Anna, Semiramide, Countess Almaviva, Ortrud* (one of her later efforts), and, perhaps greatest of all, *Leonora* in "Fidelio."

I witnessed two of her performances as *Lucrezia Borgia* which deserve special mention. The first of these (May 4, 1872) took place at Drury Lane, and was remarkable not only for the exceptional beauty and grandeur of Tietjens's assumption, but because on that night Italo Campanini made his début in London as *Gennaro,* and was forthwith hailed (somewhat prematurely, however) as the successor of Mario and Giuglini. The cast further included Faure as the *Duke* and the ever-delightful Zelia Trebelli as *Maffio Orsini,* while Sir Michael Costa was the conductor. That was a night of triumphs.

The other representation (Her Majesty's Theatre, May 19, 1877) is fraught with sad memories and undying admiration for a courageous woman and a true artist. It had been known for some time that Theresa Tietjens was suffering from cancer; and, after much hesitation, the doctors decided to perform an operation before the end of May. "Lucrezia" was announced for the 19th, and among the prima donna's friends it was pretty well understood that this would be her last appearance before the operation was performed.

When the day arrived Tietjens was far too ill to be really fit to sing. It was distinctly against her medical advisers' wish that she insisted upon keeping faith with her manager and the public—a practice that she had persistently adhered to throughout her career. How she contrived to get through the opera I shall never understand. It can only be compared to some splendid example of martyrdom. She fainted after each of the acts, but immediately on recovering consciousness decided to proceed with the performance. Never so much as a look or gesture betrayed to her audience the mortal anguish she was suffering. Only the initiated knew how much of reality there was in the terrible scream of agony uttered by *Lucrezia* in the final scene—when she perceives that her son is dead. As it rang through the house the audience shuddered. Yet the brave artist would not shirk her fall at the end. What it cost her could be guessed, however, from the fact that after the curtain had been twice raised in response to rapturous plaudits, she still lay motionless upon the ground. She had once more become insensible.

In the following week the operation was performed, but the case was hopeless, and on October 3, 1877, Theresa Tietjens breathed her last. She was laid to rest at Kensal Green Cemetery, in the presence of a vast crowd, amid tokens of public grief such as no foreign artist before her had ever been vouchsafed on English soil.

CHAPTER II

Youthful work and experiences in London—My brother Max—French refugees of 1871—Alboni—Joseph Joachim—James Davison and the "Pops"—Manuel Garcia, teacher and friend—The great master's method—His sister Malibran.

MY real musical life in London began in 1874. Down to that year my parents had never contemplated my entering upon a musical or even a journalistic career. When they left Norwich in 1866 and went to reside in the metropolis, I remained behind in the care of my grandparents and did not rejoin them until nearly three years later. Meanwhile my younger brother, Max, had shown considerable aptitude for the violin, and was taking lessons from Louis Ries, the well-known "second violin" of the Monday "Pops." Afterward he studied under the late J. T. Carrodus, and joined the orchestra of the Royal Italian Opera, Covent Garden, of which Carrodus was for many years the *chef d'attaque.*[1] I used to play Max's accom-

[1] Subsequently my brother went to America to become a member of the well-known Mendelssohn Quintet Club. For three seasons he was principal second violin of the Boston Symphony Orchestra, under Gericke and Henschel. In 1888 he accompanied Dr. F. H. Cowen to Melbourne as leader of the Centennial Exhibition Orchestra, and resided in that city until 1891. His health beginning to fail, he returned to Europe and for a time resumed his place in the principal London orchestras. He died at Cairo in 1894.

From an original painting by Ethel Wright

HERMANN KLEIN

paniments in the family circle; and it was solely the fraternal spirit of emulation, impelling me to try to shine side by side with my younger brother, that led me to keep up my study of music.

The terrors of the Franco-Prussian war (1870–1871) drove to London large numbers of refugees, many of them celebrities connected with the leading musical and dramatic institutions of Paris. Not a few of these were compelled to "bring grist to the mill" by appearing upon the stage and in the concert-rooms of the British capital. It was a golden opportunity for hearing and seeing some of the finest artists of the day; and, thanks mainly to the friendly intercourse existing between my parents and certain magnates of the managerial world, I was enabled to enjoy in an exceptional degree the privileges of this "chance of a lifetime." Not least of these managers was the famous John Mitchell, of Old Bond Street, the mainstay of the opera, who first introduced the "French Plays" in London, and taught English audiences to understand and appreciate the consummate art of their neighbors across the Channel.

Then it was that I went to Covent Garden and heard for the first time Adelina Patti, Pauline Lucca, Scalchi, Tamberlik, Mario, Bettini, Faure, Cotogni, Tagliafico; or, at Her Majesty's, Christine Nilsson, Tietjens, Trebelli, Marimon, Ilma di Murska, Mongini, Gardoni, Capoul, Wachtel, Agnesi, Rota, Santley, Foli, Carl Formes. Then it was that in the concert-room I listened to the still marvelous voices of Alboni, Carlotta Patti, and Sims Reeves; heard delightedly the glorious playing of such violinists as Sivori, Vieuxtemps, Wieniawski, Neruda, and Joachim; and revelled in the never-to-be-forgotten art of Clara Schumann and Alfredo Piatti. Looking back after thirty years, and with every wish to avoid the objectionable manner of the *laudator temporis acti,* it seems to me that that was a veritable "age of giants," a period of artistic constellations which, as far as London at least is concerned, has never since been approached.

Among the most interesting of the French refugees of 1871 were the members of the Comédie Française. They gave a memorable series of representations at one of the London theatres, selecting for it most of the gems of their matchless répertoire, with casts that included such artists as Got, Delauny, Mounet-Sully, Worms, Febvre, the Coquelins, Mmes. Sarah Bernhardt, Blanche Pierson, Bartet, Barretta, Reichemberg, and Samary. If I am not mistaken, it was during this season that Sarah Bernhardt made her London début. I saw her for the first time in her exquisite embodiment of *Doña Sol* in Victor Hugo's "Hernani." My father, who saw her in "Andromaque" and "Phèdre," told me that he considered her little, if aught, inferior to the celebrated Rachel, whose triumphs he had often witnessed in Paris during the "forties."

Sarah Bernhardt at this period of her career revealed the fire of genius more completely as an exponent of classical tragedy than in modern rôles. In the latter she had then to contend with two very distinguished rivals, Mme. Fargueil and Mlle. Aimée Desclée, both of whom had already played in London under John Mitchell's management. I remember how delightful Fargueil was at the St. James's Theatre in the plays of Alexandre Dumas *fils;* while the *Camille* and the *Frou-Frou* of Aimée Desclée (the latter her original creation) have never been surpassed. In later years, however, Sarah Bernhardt proved that she had grasped the exquisite art of these gifted women as surely as she had inherited the mantle of Rachel. And for this reason I am inclined to regard her as the greatest "all-round" actress that the world has ever known.

Marietta Alboni, Contessa di Pepoli, the most famous contralto of the nineteenth century, was another of the unwilling exiles who found a home in London in 1871. I then heard her sing on two occasions. The first time was in the "Messe Solennelle" of her beloved teacher and friend, Rossini, which the master had rescored for full orchestra some four years previous,—in fact, only a few months before he died.[1] Thirteen years had

[1] At Rossini's funeral in Paris (November 21, 1868) the principal musical feature was the singing of the duet "Quis est homo," from his "Stabat Mater," by Adelina Patti and Alboni. M. Gustave Choquet remarks (Grove's Dictionary, Vol. III): "To hear that beautiful music rendered by two such voices, and in the presence of such artists, over the grave of the composer, was

elapsed since Alboni was last heard in London, and some time since she had retired from the stage altogether. Even then she was only in her forty-ninth year, and, despite her unusual stoutness, her tones retained well-nigh all their pristine charm of quality and organ-like richness of volume. What a magnificent voice it was! How marvelous—for a pure contralto—its evenness and range! Mr. Julian Marshall, in his article on Alboni in Grove's Dictionary, describes her compass as "fully two octaves, from G to G." To be correct, he should have added quite another half-octave to the head register and nearly as much below; for Alboni sang with perfect ease to the upper C, and could descend when she pleased to the middle space of the bass clef—altogether a scale extending not far short of *three* octaves! The purity and fluency of her style were indescribable. She was one of the last great exemplars of the old Italian school.

The second time I heard Alboni was at a concert given in a private house in Welbeck Street, Cavendish Square, by Alessandro Romili, a young Italian who, prior to the war, had acted as accompanist in Paris to the well-known singer and teacher Delle Sedie. I recollect how perfectly she sang some French pieces and a new romanza ("Il primo amore," I think it was called) expressly

to feel in the truest sense the genius of Rossini, and the part which he has played in the music of the nineteenth century." The artists referred to were a group of some eighteen famous singers who, on the same occasion, took part with the pupils of the Conservatoire in the "Prayer" from "Moïse."

From a photograph by Disderi, now in the collection of Evert Jansen Wendell

ALBONI

composed for her by Romili. But what dwells most vividly in my memory in connection with this concert is her extreme kindness to my brother Max, who was down in the same programme for a violin solo. The great artist insisted on sitting among the audience to listen to the little English fiddler (then about thirteen); and he had just started his solo when one of his strings broke. He gave one glance of consternation round the room and then incontinently burst into tears. The audience looked half amused; but Alboni rose from her seat, walked to my brother, and, kissing him upon the forehead, said, loudly enough for every one to hear, "N'importe, mon petit ami; ne pleure pas! Cet accident-là aurait pu arriver à Sivori lui-même!"[1] Whereupon the boy dried his tears, mended his string, and went through his solo with entire success.

In the spring of the following year (1872) Max obtained a letter of introduction to Joseph Joachim. An appointment was made, and one morning we found ourselves in the presence of the "king of violinists" at the house of his late brother, Henry Joachim, with whom he always resided when staying in London. I do not know which of us was the more nervous, Max or myself (I was there as his accompanist); but I do know that he utterly failed to do himself justice. After he had played a page or two of one of Rode's con-

[1] "Never mind, my little friend; don't cry! That accident could have happened to Sivori himself!"

certos, Herr Joachim stopped him and asked whether he intended making "fiddling" his profession. "Yes," meekly replied my brother. "Well, in that case," continued the great man, in not unkindly tones, "I don't think you need play to me any more for the present. You have still a great deal to do, apart from learning how to hold your violin properly, and how to keep your elbow to your side when you draw your bow across the strings. But you have talent. When you have studied hard for another year or two, I shall be glad to hear you play again." After which, he came to see us out at the front door, and we left the house in a not altogether enviable frame of mind. Of myself he barely took any notice; but six years later we were destined to meet under more favorable circumstances, and to begin a friendship which, I am proud to say, has endured without break down to the present time.

It was during this particular decade that the unique powers of Joseph Joachim reached their prime. I had now become a regular attendant at the "Pops," and it was often my privilege to sit there beside my lamented friend James W. Davison, the critic of the "Times" and proprietor of the "Musical World"; the man who helped Arthur Chappell to establish those famous concerts, and who for twenty years or more wrote the analytical programmes which constituted one of their most important educational features. One Saturday afternoon I was sitting by Davison's side as a glorious treat was nearing its close. Joachim had with marvelous fire led one of the "Rasoumowsky" quartets; he had played the Bach "Chaconne" as he alone in the world could play it; and now he was taking part in Schumann's noble pianoforte quintet, with Mme. Schumann, Louis Ries, Ludwig Straus, and Piatti for his companions.

Just before the finale, the old critic turned to me and said in his abrupt, characteristic way: "My boy, mind you mark this day with a red letter! I have known Joachim ever since he made his début here as a lad of thirteen, under Mendelssohn, at the Philharmonic in '44 [about thirty years previous], but never have I heard him play as he has played this afternoon. From first to last he has been like one inspired." The writer of these recollections took up the record for the five and twenty years that were to follow. Still the grand old violinist came regularly to London, after his former associates one by one had dropped "out of the running";[1] and still he continued to play

[1] Mr. Ries is the sole surviving member of the original Monday "Pop" Quartet. Of the artists named above Dr. Joachim is happily still living; but he no longer appears at these concerts. Mme. Schumann died in 1896, Mr. Ludwig Straus in 1899, and Signor Piatti in 1901. When Mr. Ries retired in 1897, I received from him the following letter: "DEAR MR. KLEIN: I gave myself the pleasure of calling upon you to-day, but was not fortunate enough to find you at home, and therefore write these few lines, telling you—what perhaps you may have heard already—that I have this season resigned my post at the Popular Concerts, after holding it for thirty-nine years! So I say 'Lebewohl' to you as a public man, and thank you for all the kindness you have

season after season, with all the supreme art of yore. Yet never again at any given moment did the absolute inspiration of that afternoon seem to return to him in its full glory. Davison was right. It marked the very apex of Joachim's career.

In the spring of 1874 there occurred an event which was destined to exercise an important influence upon my career. Manuel Garcia, the great teacher of singing, came to live under my parents' roof. We occupied a large house at the corner of Bentinck Street and Welbeck Street, Cavendish Square,—then, as now, the recognized fashionable quarter for London professional people,—and Signor Garcia[1] took the entire ground floor for his "studio" and dwelling apartments.

I should like to describe the brother of Malibran and Pauline Viardot as he was at that time. He had just entered upon his seventieth year, but in appearance and bearing he did not seem much past fifty. He had a light, buoyant step, always walked quickly, and had a keen, observant eye, which, when he spoke, would light up with all the fire and animation of youth. His dark complexion and his habit of rapid gesticulation bespoke his Southern

shown me. I shall now be amongst the audience at the "Pops," where I hope to have the pleasure of meeting you sometimes. With kind regards, Yours sincerely, Louis Ries. September 30, 1897."

[1] In virtue of Garcia's Spanish birth and descent, the prefix "Señor" is frequently used. But in London, where he settled down in 1850, he is always spoken of as "Signor" Garcia, and is so described in the archives of the Royal Academy of Music and other institutions to which he was attached as a professor.

origin; and although equally at home in Spanish, Italian, French, and English, he always betrayed a decided preference for conversing in the French language. His modesty was remarkable. He could rarely be induced to talk about himself; but in his opinions he was firm almost to obstinacy, and a prejudice once formed was as difficult to remove as a liking. In argument he was a close reasoner, and would be either a doughty opponent or a warm advocate. The middle line never attracted him. But at all times he was a true, stanch, and loyal friend.

Fortunately, Signor Garcia took a considerable fancy to me. He was fond of discussing politics, but, having little time to read the papers, would generally ask me for the latest news. He openly expressed his disgust with the policy of the Liberal Government of that day, and found in myself a sympathetic supporter of his views. About music I was afraid for a long while to talk with him. One day, however, he heard me singing in a distant part of the house, and told my mother that I had a very agreeable light tenor voice. She at once asked him if he would be good enough to give me some instruction. He readily consented, and, within an hour, to my intense delight, I found myself taking my first lesson from Manuel Garcia.

The master was then in his prime. For forty years his pupils, from Jenny Lind down, had included some of the best singers that Paris and London provided, while among the many aspirants for vocal fame who came to study with him at our house in Bentinck Street were several whose names yet enjoy a universal reputation. During the eight or ten years that he lived with us, I studied with him for nearly four, and heard him give many scores of lessons beside those which I received. To see and hear Garcia teach was ever a source of unqualified pleasure. Even when annoyed by a pupil's lack of ordinary intelligence, he seldom became abrupt or impatient; and he never worried or confused the student with technicalities not actually essential to the accurate understanding of his method. His voice had virtually gone, but he would liberally employ its *beaux restes* to impart the idea for the proper emission of a note or the phrasing of a passage. As often as not, the sounds that he produced would be positively ugly; but they never failed to convey the desired suggestion, and, though his own voice might tremble with sheer weight of years, he never, to my knowledge, brought out a pupil whose tones were marred by the slightest shade of *vibrato*.

Nor was he at any time guilty of the sin of "forcing" a voice. I say so with all possible emphasis, because that untrue assertion has been made on various occasions, and it should be contradicted as a libel upon a teacher whose first rule was ever to repress the breathing power and bring it into proper proportion with the resisting force of the throat and larynx. The contrary proceeding would have been altogether inconsistent with the system of the *old* Italian school, whereof Garcia is the last really great teacher.

No less stupid, but rather more cruel, has been the recent onslaught—emanating principally from Paris—upon the act of vocal mechanism known as the *coup de la glotte,* a term created by Garcia as the result of his observations on the interior of the larynx with the aid of the laryngoscope, of which instrument he was the inventor. This term, first employed in his wonderful "Traité complet de l'Art du Chant,"[1] was merely meant to describe the movement or "stroke" of the glottis in the act of attacking a vocal sound—a movement as natural as it is indispensable to the clean, definite striking of a note by the human voice. Possibly the practice of the act in question has been worked to excess by would-be imitators of Garcia's method; but certainly it was never so taught by him, and I have never come across one of his pupils who had suffered through its normal employment. Later on, however, I shall have to refer to this subject again, in order to quote in their proper place some words used by the master to refute a particularly flagrant attack upon the *coup de la glotte.*

I was barely twenty-two when I ceased taking lessons from Signor Garcia. Our relations by that time were those of very close friends. We used to chat freely upon musical as well as other topics, and I loved to "draw him out" upon the respective

[1] Published in Paris, 1847, and afterward translated into Italian, German, and English.

merits of the great Italian singers of bygone years. I think his chief object of admiration was the celebrated Pasta, who lived the most brilliant portion of her career in Paris during his own residence there.[1] He would often speak of the ravishing beauty of her voice, the perfection of her *fiorituri*, and the grandeur of her dramatic conceptions. Yet in his inmost heart, I fancy, his famous sister, Malibran, reigned supreme. She was his junior by three years, but at the period here referred to had achieved triumphs unsurpassed by any singer of her time, and yet she had been dead and buried some forty years! He would describe her as the most natural genius he had ever encountered, and also the most precocious. A great deal that has been related concerning her is purely imaginary; but one perfectly true story is that of an incident which happened at Naples one night when, a little girl of five, she was playing the part of the child in Paer's masterpiece, "Agnese."

In this opera there occurs a scene where a hus-

[1] Giuditta Pasta was one of the greatest Rossinian sopranos of her time, besides being a superb emotional actress. She possessed a voice of immense range and power, and a remarkably impressive stage presence. She was born in 1798, made her début in 1815, and died in 1865.

Curiously enough, it was when acting as a substitute for Pasta that Garcia's elder sister, Malibran, in 1824, made her first appearance on any stage at the King's Theatre, London, as *Rosina* in "Il Barbiere." She was then sixteen. In the following year the whole Garcia family went to America, where they met with immense success, producing no less than eleven new operas during their first year in New York.

CHRISTINE NILSSON

From a photograph by Sarony. N. Y.

SCALCHI

From a photograph by Sarony, N. Y.

band and wife, who have quarreled, are reunited through the agency of their little daughter. The tiny Malibran had attended all the rehearsals, and so extraordinary was her memory that she knew the whole opera by heart. On the night of the performance, the prima donna, in the episode above mentioned, either forgot her part or hesitated a moment, when, lo! the little girl by her side instantly took up the melody and sang out with such vigor and resonance that the entire house heard her. The prima donna was about to interfere when the audience shouted, "Brava! Don't stop her. Let the child go on!" And go on the child did, until she had sung through the entire scene, amid an exhibition of true Italian enthusiasm.

How strange it seems when one reflects that the venerable *maestro* who narrated to me this incident, which he witnessed as a boy of eight, is still alive and enjoying good health, and in full possession of his faculties and his wonderful spirits! He resides with Mme. Garcia (his second wife) and their two daughters at Cricklewood, one of the northwestern suburbs of London. What happened yesterday he does not always precisely remember; but the events of nearly a century ago he never forgets. On March 17, 1904, all being well, Manuel Garcia will be ninety-nine years of age!

CHAPTER III

Start of journalistic career—A musical critic at twenty—"Lohengrin" in London—Carl Rosa—His memorable season at the Princess's—Revival of English Opera—Early days of "interviewing"—Sir Michael Costa—August Manns and cheap orchestral music—Jean de Reszke's barytone début.

NEVER having seriously contemplated becoming a public singer, it was no great disappointment when I found, after a couple of years' study, that my voice gave no signs of developing to proportions requisite for a stage career. *Aut Cæsar, aut nullus!* I would either be an operatic tenor or I would be content to be simply a good amateur. The concert-room had no charms for me. Nevertheless, while continuing my lessons regularly with Signor Garcia, I had also to consider the best means for earning a livelihood; and, as I have previously hinted, the opportunity presented itself in a highly congenial direction—that of musical journalism. The work was calculated to aid rather than impede my studies. It lay in a field which, at the time I speak of, was far less overrun than now, and it afforded me an entrée to every kind of musical performance, which in itself was a liberal education for a young man with my instincts and training.

I commenced active work as a journalist, then, in 1875, as London correspondent of my uncle's paper, the "Norwich Argus." In 1877 I undertook the direction of a publication called the "Operatic and Dramatic Album," the duties of which brought me into personal contact with some of the foremost personages in the lyric and theatrical worlds. A year later I was appointed musical and dramatic critic of the "Citizen," which post (during 1879 and part of 1880) I filled while acting as musical critic upon the staff of that fine old weekly paper—long since defunct—the "Examiner." Such, briefly told, is the history of my first five years' connection with London journalism.

Two memorable events occurred in 1875. One was the first production in London of Wagner's "Lohengrin"; the other, the first appearance there of the Carl Rosa Opera Company. The former was regarded almost in the light of an experiment. Never before had an opera by Wagner been performed at Covent Garden. In 1870 his "Fliegende Holländer" had been given at Drury Lane, under the Italian title of "L'Ollandese Dannato" (Luigi Arditi conducting), but without any very marked success. And now here was "Lohengrin," a more advanced example of the composer's method, about to claim the suffrages of a public still notoriously unprepared for the comprehension or enjoyment of what was generally described as the "music of the future." Yet, thanks to the growing numbers of the German community, the event aroused intense excitement, and the opera-house was packed to overflowing. I think it was the worst performance of "Lohengrin" ever seen in an important theatre. Albani (then in her third season) made a sympathetic *Elsa;* Nicolini presented a heroic-looking *Lohengrin* and sang wonderfully well, considering how completely out of his element he was in Wagnerian opera; and Cotogni did creditably as *Telramund.* But the remainder of the cast were beneath notice, while the chorus sang dreadfully out of tune, and the orchestra, under Vianesi, did its best to drown the singers throughout.

Yet, in spite of these drawbacks, the beauty of the music exercised its inevitably powerful sway, and the opera was received with a warmth that grew and grew till it culminated in a tremendous climax of enthusiasm. The "tooth-and-nail" opponents of Wagner, who flourished exceedingly in London at this time, were simply dumfounded. In all probability, "Lohengrin" was as new to them as it was to Covent Garden habitués, and they did not know whether to be more astonished at the subtle fascination of the music or at the ease with which its charm and significance had been grasped by an "unripe" public. In vain did James Davison print Cassandra-like utterances in the "Times"; equally in vain did my dear and valued friend Joseph Bennett limit himself to lukewarm admiration in the columns of the "Telegraph." The success of "Lohengrin" in London was complete. So great was the demand to hear

CARL ROSA

From a photograph by Alexander Bassano, N. Y.

PAREPA-ROSA

From a photograph by Rockwood, N.Y.

the opera that within a comparatively brief space Mr. Mapleson had mounted it at Her Majesty's with a cast including Christine Nilsson, Tietjens, Campanini, and Galassi. On the whole, that was perhaps the more satisfactory production of the two, albeit I fancy Sir Michael Costa penetrated very little further into the meaning and spirit of Wagner's score than did his worthy countryman, Signor Vianesi. His chief interest used to centre in the proceedings of the swan, of which he invariably spoke contemptuously as "Dat goose!"

When Carl Rosa first brought his troupe to the Princess's Theatre, London, in September, 1875, English opera was in a bad way. I am not prepared to assert that it is in a much better way at the present moment. Beyond doubt, however, its fortunes, through the instrumentality of this lamented impresario, underwent a revival that was of the utmost importance, not merely in its influence upon the popularity of opera in the vernacular, but in its effect, as a purely educational factor, upon the subsequent course of operatic enterprise both in England and America. How this latter process came about I shall show later on. Meanwhile let it be said that Carl Rosa was the man who first sounded the knell of "ballad-opera" as a staple form of amusement, and lifted the taste of the British public from its then commonplace level to a plane more closely approaching that of the cultivated audiences of Germany, Austria, and France.

No one could have been better fitted for the task. Rosa was a little over thirty, energetic and industrious to a fault, an accomplished musician,[1] an excellent conductor, and an experienced operatic manager. His first wife, the gifted Mme. Parepa-Rosa (whom he met and married in New York in 1867), was the leading artist of the opera company, which for several years achieved such great success under their joint direction in the United States. They had returned to London in 1873 with the intention of producing "Lohengrin" in English at Drury Lane, but that project was abandoned in consequence of the death of Mme. Parepa. The prima donna had been an intimate friend of my cousin Mrs. J. M. Johnson, and it was at the latter's house on Maida Hill that I first became acquainted with Carl Rosa. I met him there one afternoon while his memorable season at the Princess's was in progress. He had just finished a long rehearsal and still had to conduct the evening performance; but I remember being much struck by his rare spirits and the irrepressible energy with which he threw himself into an argument upon the subject of English musical taste.

"You are surprised," he said, "because they are crowding the house for 'Figaro' and the 'Water-Carrier,' and you fancy it must be Santley that is the draw and not the operas. But don't deceive yourselves. This London public is now ripe for

[1] Carl Rosa came to England first as a solo violinist, and made his début under August Manns at the Crystal Palace in 1866.

English opera of a better sort than Pyne and Harrison provided. It longs for something more than ballad-operas and a 'star' or two. It wants good works and, above all, a good ensemble. See how it appreciates the 'Figaro' ensemble![1] Well, next season I shall produce more unfamiliar operas and a still stronger company. Then gradually I shall introduce Wagner in English, beginning with 'The Flying Dutchman,' and perhaps even test whether London can stand a brand-new opera by a native composer."

He was as good as his word. In the following year, at the Lyceum, Carl Rosa brought out four novelties, including Frederic H. Cowen's "Pauline" (a version of "The Lady of Lyons") and Wagner's "Flying Dutchman." The latter, with Santley in the title-rôle, made a tremendous hit. Coming on top of the success of "Lohengrin" and "Tannhäuser" (the latter had been produced in Italian at Covent Garden just four months previous), it helped to complete the foundation for the love and understanding of Wagner's music which now extend throughout the United King-

[1] The fine performance of Mozart's "Marriage of Figaro" with which Carl Rosa opened his memorable campaign at the Princess's Theatre, London, on September 11, 1875, has always been referred to with pride as the best ever given in the English language. Certainly I, for one, never heard a finer. The cast included Santley as *Figaro,* Campobello (an Italianized Scotchman) as the *Count,* Aynsley Cook as *Bartolo,* Charles Lyall as *Antonio,* Ostava Torriani (a Hamburg artist) as the *Countess,* Josephine Yorke (an American contralto) as *Cherubino,* and Rose Hersee as *Susanna.*

dom, embracing the entire range of the master's works.

Carl Rosa was one of the most restless and indefatigable of industrious men. His plan was to mount all his new productions in the provinces, so as to bring them to the metropolis smoothed and polished by frequent repetition. No sooner had one season ended than he began preparing for the next. In 1877 he did not visit London, and in the October of that year he wrote me from Aberdeen:

I have been very busy bringing out "The Merry Wives of Windsor" (Nicolai), which you will be happy to hear was a very great success. I am glad to learn that you are getting connected with the London press, and will be happy to give you information about my future doings when the time comes; but any announcements at present would, I think, be premature.

He was curiously diffident in the matter of advertisement, and his habit of avoiding rather than seeking publicity offers a striking contrast to the methods of the impresario of to-day. When I knew he was coming to the Adelphi Theatre for a spring season in 1878, I wrote to him asking for portraits of himself and Miss Georgina Burns (who had just made her début as *Anne Page* in "The Merry Wives," and subsequently became one of the most popular sopranos on the English stage) for publication in the "Operatic and Dramatic Album." I received the following reply:

Dr. FREDERICK H. COWEN

From a photograph by Elliot & Fry, London

LUIGI ARDITI

From a photograph by Elliott & Fry, London

ROYAL AMPHITHEATRE, LIVERPOOL,
January 8, 1878.

DEAR KLEIN:

Miss Burns has no biography. She is quite a novice. Of her success I have no doubt, but under the circumstances I think you had better not publish her picture, as I quite understand that you should only give those of well-known artists.

I will send you a biography of myself which appeared in the "Illustrated London News," and which you can easily alter to suit your taste. But do you think *le jeu vaut la chandelle?* Do you think portraits of conductors and managers are sufficiently attractive to the general public? *I think not.*

Sincerely yours,
CARL ROSA.

Those were not the days of "interviewers" or "snapshots," and I frequently experienced difficulty in persuading musical and dramatic celebrities to furnish me with the requisite material for writing notices of their careers. The portraits, of course, could be obtained easily enough, but the actresses and prima donnas always used to be dreadfully afraid lest I should want to publish their exact age. Miss Nelly Farren, for instance, positively refused to permit a word to be written about her, and her portrait went into the "Album" without a line of biographical detail. Another well-known actress, Miss Ada Cavendish, sent me her photo and autograph, but wrote: "I must say you set me a rather difficult task when you ask me for a biographical sketch of my career. Is it absolutely necessary that you should insert one? I really think that the public will take very little interest in my early troubles in the profession. If, therefore, you can do without it, please do so." On the other hand, I sometimes got more information than I really needed, or else I received corrections and thanks after inadvertent errors had appeared in type. Among letters of this kind was one from the eminent conductor, Sir Michael Costa, who was perhaps the severest martinet that ever wielded a baton, but who never forgot that he was a gentleman and could be, when he chose, the very "pink of politeness." As a rule, he did not pay much attention to critics, youthful or otherwise; so, in spite of the inaccuracies, I felt rather flattered when I received from Sir Michael this extremely courteous note:

59 Eccleston Square, S. W.

Dear Sir:

I have received the biography that you have taken the trouble to publish and kindly sent to me, for which I am much obliged. Only two observations you will allow me to make: first, that I composed "Eli" and "Naaman" for the Birmingham Musical Festivals of 1855 and 1864, not for the Sacred Harmonic Society; and, secondly, that my rank in Grand Lodge [of English Freemasons] is Past Grand Warden, not Grand Organist.

I do not hesitate to make the above remarks, knowing

how correct and exact you are, or are desirous to be, in whatever you publish. With best wishes, I remain,

Sincerely yours,

M. COSTA.

Of Sir Michael Costa it is certainly not too much to say that he was in his time the greatest choral conductor that England possessed. He was a born "leader of men," and if I had not formed this impression on my early visits to Exeter Hall, when he was directing the performances of the old Sacred Harmonic Society, I should assuredly have done so at my first Handel Festival in 1874, when he took command of the army of four thousand singers and instrumentalists who obeyed his ample beat with such marvelous rhythmic swing and precision. From the institution of the festival in 1857, Costa alone had trained and directed this army; and so universal was the idea that he alone was capable of keeping it under control, that when the announcement of his serious illness came, just before the festival of 1883, there was an expression of dismay on all sides. The musician who filled the breach happily proved to be in the end as good as his predecessor. Indeed, August Manns, the esteemed and talented conductor of the Crystal Palace Concerts, did much to improve the quality of his vast choir and to raise its level of efficiency and intelligence. Still, he would be the first to admit that the honor and glory of the most striking executive achievement known to music stands principally, if not exclusively, to the credit of Michael Costa, the man who created the machine and left it in perfect working order.

August Manns—still an active veteran, though now in his seventy-ninth year—has the qualities of a purely orchestral conductor in a far higher degree than they were ever possessed by Costa. His work at the Crystal Palace from 1855 to 1900, alike in its educational aspect and its conspicuously beneficial encouragement of native art, will endure, a lasting monument of industry, catholicity of taste, and consistent loftiness of purpose. At Sydenham it was that Arthur Sullivan was first proffered a helping hand by the performance of his "Tempest" music on his return from Leipsic (April, 1862). Thither did Sir George Grove—sometime secretary of the Crystal Palace Company and writer of the luminous analytical notes that so materially enhanced the enjoyment of the famous Saturday Concerts—convey the precious Schubert manuscripts which he had rescued from dust and oblivion in Vienna. There, under the ægis of August Manns, was solved for the first time in England the problem of cheap "classical" orchestral concerts that should attract the masses and initiate them into the delight of listening to good music. There I heard my first symphony (it was Beethoven's "Pastoral"); and there, Saturday after Saturday, I heard the most celebrated soloists that visited our British shores—from Rubinstein and Clara Schumann to Paderewski, from

Joachim to Sarasate, from Piatti to Hausmann and Hugo Becker. To attend these concerts regularly was a musical education in itself.

In central London, during the "seventies," the best medium for hearing good orchestral music was the Promenade Concerts at Covent Garden. These were held in August and September, under the management of Messrs. A. and S. Gatti. My old friend Signor Luigi Arditi was the conductor for the first few seasons, and he was succeeded in turn by Sir Arthur Sullivan and Mr. F. H. Cowen; while later on came a popular Welsh bandmaster, Mr. Gwyllym Crowe. Much that was interesting and instructive the shilling habitué could hear at these "Promenades"; but for me the most notable recollection associated with them is the occasion when Arditi gave the first performance in England of the "Trauermarsch" from "Götterdämmerung." The new tubas had only just arrived, and there was not much time for rehearsing. Nevertheless, it seemed to me that the wonderful excerpt was fairly well played, though I was too breathless with amazement and admiration to be able to form a cool judgment. But I do know that the audience hardly waited for the last note before it burst into frantic applause, and insisted upon having the march played a second time.

During the opera seasons of 1874–75, there appeared at Drury Lane a young Polish singer, who met with emphatic success in leading barytone parts such as the *King* ("Favorita"), *Don Giovanni, De*

Nevers, Valentine, and *Count Almaviva* ("Le Nozze"). He also created a secondary part in Balfe's posthumous opera "Il Talismano," which was produced in June, 1874, with Nilsson, Tietjens, Campanini, and others in the cast. I distinctly recollect him in two characters—*Don Giovanni* and *De Nevers.* It seemed to me that he had a beautiful voice, of almost tenor quality, and both as singer and actor he displayed the highest promise. He appeared then under the name of "De Reschi." Twelve years later he was to return to London and take the town by storm under his own name of Jean de Reszke.

CHAPTER IV

Verdi at the Albert Hall—The Maestro and his old classmate—The Manzoni "Requiem"—Wagner revisits London—The Festival of 1877: its true history—Wagner and Wilhelmj—The Meister and English prejudice—His collapse at rehearsal—Hans Richter—Wagner "in the chair."

IN May, 1876, I saw Verdi conduct his Manzoni "Requiem" at the Royal Albert Hall. This was generally supposed to be his third visit to London, the previous occasions being when he came over in 1847 for the production of the opera "I Masnadieri," which he wrote expressly for Her Majesty's Theatre; and again in 1862 (the Exhibition year), when his "Inno delle Nazioni" was performed at the same theatre. But, according to his intimate friend, Mr. Randegger, the maestro also ran over from Paris one summer, without letting any one into the secret, for the purpose of hearing for himself what the world-famous Handel Festival was like. Mr. Randegger has told me that his surprise was indescribable when he came across Verdi at the Crystal Palace with a score of "Israel in Egypt" tucked under his arm. He insisted, however, that his presence should be concealed; and he seems to have returned to Paris as mysteriously as he came.

At the period of the "Requiem" visit there happened to be residing in London an elderly Italian musician named Deliguoro, upon whom fortune had not smiled very kindly, and who frequently enjoyed the hospitality of my parents' house. An admirable contrapuntist, stuffed full of musical learning, he had the technique of composition at his fingers' ends; but of individual or fresh ideas his brain was utterly devoid. Like most disappointed geniuses, he was unable to perceive his own lack of originality. Once he played me a melody in mazurka rhythm—a commonplace enough Neapolitan tune—which he fondly regarded as an inspiration; and I shall never forget the old gentleman's horror when, a day or two afterward, he caught me strumming his piece by ear upon the piano. I had to swear by all his own particular saints that I would never even hum his tune again. "Some one would be sure to steal it." He was utterly oblivious to the fact that he had virtually stolen it himself.

The announcement of Verdi's coming was a great event for Deliguoro, inasmuch as the master and he had been fellow-students together at Milan, under Lavigna (1831–33). This was just after the preposterous refusal of the authorities at the Milan Conservatoire to admit Verdi as a pupil at that institution because they thought he did not display sufficient promise of talent. Deliguoro's delight at the prospect of meeting his old friend knew no bounds. He had not seen him for quite thirty

WAGNER

From a photograph by Elliott & Fry, London

VERDI

From a photograph by Guigoni & Bossi, Milan

years. "Giuseppe and I were like brothers. We ate, drank, and worked together the whole of the time. His harmony exercises always had more mistakes than mine, and he could never master the art of writing a really good fugue. I wonder whether he has dared to put one into his 'Requiem'! We shall see; for I am going to write and ask him for a ticket to hear it." In due course tickets arrived for the rehearsal and the concert, and Deliguoro showed them to me with the utmost pride.

Most of the distinguished musical folk in London were present at the "grand rehearsal"; and yet the vast auditorium, capable of holding 10,000 persons comfortably, looked comparatively deserted. I sat with Deliguoro not far from the orchestra. He was so excited that I had the utmost difficulty in restraining him from climbing over the barrier and taking Verdi in his arms there and then. Nor were my own feelings altogether calm as I gazed for the first time upon the man who had composed "La Traviata," "Rigoletto," and "Aida." He was then sixty-three years of age, and his closely cut beard was fast turning gray; but he was as active and robust as a youth, his eyes were keen and bright, and his clear, penetrating voice when he addressed the choir (in French or Italian, I forget which) could be heard all over the hall.

At the end of the fugal chorus "Sanctus Dominus," which my neighbor declared to be more scholarly than anything he had anticipated, Verdi came around to speak to his friends among the select audience, and ere long I could see that he was staring in an uncertain way at Deliguoro. Then all of a sudden he appeared to make up his mind, and took a "bee-line" over the stall chairs to the spot where we were standing. "Tu sei Deliguoro, non è ver?" exclaimed the maestro. "Si, si, son Deliguoro," replied his old friend, his eyes brimming over with tears.[1] And then followed a close embrace that I thought would never end. It would be hard to say which of the two former classmates evinced the fuller measure of joy.

But in the midst of the excitement I was not forgotten. Deliguoro presented me to Verdi as "the son of the best friends he had in London, and a youthful but modest musical critic." I added that I had been indebted to Signor Deliguoro for much good teaching and advice in the study of the art. "And you could not do better," said Verdi in French, as he shook me by the hand. "Deliguoro is not only a colossus of counterpoint, but he has a great heart *(c'est un grand cœur)*, and I feel personally grateful to any one who is kind to him." Nor did the great man, who was the soul of generosity, forget his own duty in the matter; for, prior to leaving London, he sent a substantial money gift to the less fortunate friend of his youth, who was destined to survive only a year or two longer.

Surely none who heard that magnificent performance of the Manzoni "Requiem" can have ever

[1] "You are Deliguoro, are you not?" "Yes, yes, I am Deliguoro."

forgotten the combined effect of the beautiful music, the superb singing of the Albert Hall choir (trained by Barnby), the wonderful voices of the soloists, and, pervading all, the subtle magnetic influence induced by the presence and personal guidance of the composer. The solo artists included three members of the original quartet, namely: Mme. Stolz, Mme. Waldmann, and Signor Masini. All possessed noble organs; and the famous tenor, who has never been heard in opera in England, was then quite at his best. But the undoubted gem of the whole performance was the "Agnus Dei," with its octave unison phrases for the two women's voices, sung by Stolz and Waldmann with a delicacy and charm of simply ethereal loveliness. Nor shall I forget the pains taken by Verdi at rehearsal to obtain from his chorus and orchestra of eight hundred a pianissimo in fitting proportion to the exquisite tone of these singers.

A YEAR later Richard Wagner came to London to take part in the series of Wagner Festival Concerts at the Royal Albert Hall, which had been arranged with a view to paying off the debt on the new theatre at Bayreuth.[1] The events of this visit

[1] It will be remembered that there was a deficit of something like 140,000 marks ($35,000) after the opening season of 1876, when "Der Ring des Nibelungen" was performed for the first time in its entirety. London, however, did little toward liquidating this debt. It was ultimately paid off with the gross receipts of some cycles of "The Ring" at Munich, for which the performers all gave their services gratuitously.

are briefly narrated in "Grove" by Mr. Edward Dannreuther, at whose house in Bayswater Wagner stayed—from April 30 to June 4. Evidently, however, Mr. Dannreuther had no desire to dwell in detail upon the incidents of this "London episode." He was even a trifle ashamed that his name should have been associated with it in Glasenapp's biography of Wagner "and elsewhere"; and he expressly states "that he had *nothing whatever* to do with the planning of the 'festival,' nor with the business arrangements." All he did was to "attend to the completion of the orchestra with regard to the 'extra' wind-instruments, and, at Wagner's request, to conduct the preliminary rehearsals."

No doubt such was the case. But thus to disclaim all connection with the enterprise has always sounded to me rather like a slur upon the good intentions of those whose devotion to Wagner's cause had led to the inception and organization of this affair. That Wagner himself was annoyed at certain things which occurred, and that he went away on the whole extremely disappointed, may be safely assumed, if only from what was subsequently said by his native champions of the press in Bavaria "and elsewhere." A great many of those statements, however, were either untrue or grossly exaggerated. The whole truth has never been related, and as I happened to have been "behind the scenes," more or less, throughout the Wagner Festival of 1877, it may be interesting to my readers if I now endeavor, as concisely as possible, to tell the story.

To make matters clear, I must premise that the adversaries and supporters of Wagnerian art in London were then ranged in three distinct camps. There were (1) those who refused to accept his music under any conditions; (2) those who would accept all he had written down to "Tannhäuser" and "Lohengrin"; and (3) those who worshiped both at the temple and from afar, accepting and rejoicing in everything. The first of these sections was gradually dying out, or was being absorbed by the second, as the beauty of the operas heard in London within the previous two years slowly but surely forced its way into the heart and understanding of the people. The prejudice against the later works still prevailed, however, and to such an extent that no London impresario yet dreamed of mounting "Tristan," or "Die Walküre," or "Die Meistersinger," despite the success those works were then meeting with in many Continental cities. All one could say was that musicians were beginning to display an interest in the preludes and excerpts occasionally performed in the concert-room; while, as a matter of course, the London Wagner Society was constantly growing in numbers and strength, and working a steady "propaganda" on behalf of the cause.

Among the most popular artists appearing in England at that time was the eminent violinist, August Wilhelmj, who was one of Wagner's most ardent disciples and the leader of the first Bayreuth orchestra. He was pretty accurately acquainted with the state of affairs, and he it was who originally conceived the idea of inviting Wagner to conduct a series of concerts upon a festival scale in the British capital. He broached the subject during the autumn of 1876, and at first, I believe, Wagner was utterly unwilling to consider the proposition. Twice already had the *Meister* been in England—once in the summer of 1839,[1] and again in 1855, when for a single season he took the baton laid down by Costa as conductor of the Philharmonic Society. His recollections of this second visit cannot have been wholly pleasant; but Wilhelmj showed him how completely the aspect of things had changed, and argued that there was now an immense curiosity to see him as well as hear more of his music. Besides, six concerts at the Albert Hall would assuredly result in a net profit of as many thousand pounds. The temptation was too strong to be resisted; Wagner ultimately decided to go.

Wilhelmj, delighted at having secured the master's promise, at once set about finding a respon-

[1] He then stayed only eight days, and lodged, together with his wife, at a boarding-house (since pulled down) in Compton Street, Soho. This short visit Wagner made en route for Paris, but he also stopped at Boulogne, where he made the acquaintance of Meyerbeer and obtained from him the introductions which gave rise to Heine's oft-quoted remark: "Do you know what makes me suspicious of this young man? It is that Meyerbeer recommends him."

BRAHMS

From a photograph by L. Grillich, Vienna

WILHELMJ

From a photograph by Sarony, N. Y.

sible manager who would undertake the arrangements and advance the necessary capital for the preliminary outlay. Herein lay the initial mistake. Instead of employing some well-known concert agent, the violinist placed the whole business in the hands of a very respectable but inexperienced firm, whose place of business was at the Hengler Circus building in Argyll Street. I will not deny that this firm worked hard and did their best. But unfortunately both they and Herr Wilhelmj were far too lavish in their expenditure. They engaged Materna and the pick of the Bayreuth artists at big prices. The orchestra, with Wilhelmj as leader, was nearly two hundred strong. The disbursements for advertising, printing, programmes, etc., were enormous, and everything was done in the costliest fashion. All this might have been justified had the attendance at the festival reached the expected level. But unluckily the prices charged for seats were prohibitive, and the public refused to come in anything like the necessary numbers.

On the night after Wagner's arrival in London a dinner was given in his honor by his managers at their show-rooms in Argyll Street. Only recognized friends of the "cause" were invited, and I had the honor of being among the number. Toasts were given and responded to, and Wagner made one of the characteristic little speeches for which he was famous. Late in the evening I was introduced to him. He asked me to sit beside him a few minutes, and began by demanding in German my age.

"Nearly twenty-one," I replied.

"Why, you were not born when I was last here. I suppose you know, though, that your critics did not display any great affection for me then. Do you think they are better inclined toward me now?"

I answered that I fancied he would perceive an improved attitude all round.

"I hope so," said Wagner. "I know that some of my best and truest friends live in London, and, sooner or later, their influence must begin to tell."

I ventured to remark that I thought his music in the long run would suffice to accomplish the desired conversion. He turned his keen glance toward me for a moment, and paused, as though wishing to read me through. The inspection appeared to be satisfactory; for a smile suffused his features as he replied:

"Yes; but here they still call it 'music of the future,' and in this land of oratorio who knows how long they will take to get rid of their prejudices, unless the agitators keep stirring them up? Well, we shall see what happens next week."

Then he turned to speak to Wilhelmj, and the brief chat was at an end. I sat still, however, a minute or two longer, and watched with intense interest the play of facial expression, the eloquent curves of the mouth, the humorous light in the eyes, the quiet, subtle laugh, while he addressed in turn the various friends gathered around him. That evening Wagner was thoroughly happy. He felt himself in a congenial atmosphere, content with the present, and hopeful—nay, sanguine—of the morrow. I was glad to have seen him in that beatific mood, and not a little proud to have spoken with him. What a pity that he was not to bid a final farewell to England in an equally satisfied frame of mind!

The final rehearsal for the opening concert of the festival took place at the Albert Hall on May 5. Wagner had himself chosen the programmes. He was to conduct each first part, consisting of selections from all his operas, from "Rienzi" to "Tristan"; while Hans Richter, who now made his first appearance in England, was to direct the excerpts from "Der Ring des Nibelungen" that formed each second part. Most of the preliminary work had been done under Mr. Dannreuther, in whom Wagner reposed great confidence. All that remained was to give the finishing touches and for the composer-conductor to accustom himself to the vast auditorium and the huge crescent-shaped phalanx of orchestral players spread before him.

From the outset, as it seemed to me, he failed to place himself *en rapport* with either. The abnormal conditions appeared completely to upset him. In a word, he succumbed there and then to a severe attack of Albert Hall stage fright—an illness familiar to nearly every artist on stepping for the first time upon the platform of that gigantic amphitheatre.[1] However, after a glance of astonishment

[1] Another bad sufferer that day was Frau Materna. I was speaking to her in the artists' room just before she went on to

round the empty hall, and a few whispered words to Wilhelmj, and yet a few more to Hans Richter (who was posted beside the conductor's desk), the great man raised his baton and gave the signal for the start. The inaugural piece was the "Kaisermarsch," and it was well chosen for the purpose. Its pompous and sonorous strains, proceeding with stately rhythmical movement throughout, were perfectly calculated to show off the imposing volume of the big orchestra in such a building as that. It gave no trouble, and the effect was superb. But, unluckily, instead of imbuing Wagner with a little confidence, this preludial essay left him more palpably nervous than before.

The second piece on the list was the overture to the "Fliegende Holländer." Here, I confess, I looked for something exceptional. I had always understood that Wagner was a fine conductor, at least of works with which he was in true sympathy, and I expected his reading of the "Dutchman" overture to be in the nature of a revelation. Imagine, then, my disappointment and sorrow when it resulted in a complete breakdown! Twice—nay, thrice—did he make a fresh start, while Mr. Dannreuther and Mr. Deichmann (the faithful leader of the second violins) took it by turns to translate his

rehearse, and she was positively trembling with excitement and fear "lest she should be unable to make herself heard in such a huge place." I begged her to sing quite in her usual manner, and, above all things, not to "force" her voice. She afterward thanked me and said that she had been simply amazed at the ease with which she could sing in the hall.

CLARA LOUISE KELLOGG

From a photograph by Sarony, N. Y,

MANUEL GARCIA

From a photograph by W. & A. H. Fry, Brighton

complaints and instructions to the orchestra. But it was of no avail. He utterly failed either to indicate or to obtain what he wanted, and at last, in sheer despair, he threw down his stick and requested Richter to do the work for him. Well do I remember the sharp round of applause with which the band greeted the Viennese conductor as he mounted the rostrum. It was thoughtless—unkind, if you will; for it must have smote with unpleasant sound upon the ears of the sensitive composer. But the overture went without a hitch. It was played as I had never heard it played before.

After this Wagner decided that he would conduct only one or two pieces at each concert, leaving all the rest to Richter. But would the public be satisfied? They were paying to see Wagner as well as to hear his music. The matter was discussed, and it was suggested, as a compromise, that when he was not conducting he should sit upon the platform in an arm-chair facing the audience. This course was actually adopted. At each of the six concerts comprising the festival scheme, after he had conducted the opening piece and acknowledged a magnificent reception, he sat down in his arm-chair and gazed at the assemblage before him with a sphinx-like expression of countenance that I shall never forget. He must have felt as though he were being exhibited, like some strange, interesting animal, for all the world to stare at; and his reflections doubtless were as unenviable as his situation.

Obviously it would have been unfair to estimate

Wagner's ability as a conductor by what he did at these concerts. Yet I fear some of his critics were not wholly considerate in that respect, for the comments uttered in several quarters showed plainly that no allowances had been made. I quite agree with Mr. Dannreuther, therefore, when he says that "at the Albert Hall, Wagner did not do himself justice. His strength was already on the wane. The rehearsals fatigued him, and he was frequently faint in the evening. His memory played him tricks, and his beat was nervous."

To make matters worse, it was quickly perceived that the festival was going to prove a financial failure. Nothing could have been more discouraging than the sight of numerous unoccupied boxes and stalls, and in the cheaper parts a "beggarly array of empty benches." It was determined, just in time, that a couple of extra concerts should be given at reduced prices, the artists and executants accepting half-salary, while all the "plums" of the festival were crowded into the two programmes. This move retrieved the fortunes of the venture. A heavy loss was converted into a profit of £700, which sum was duly handed over to Wagner for his Bayreuth fund. But it was a miserable result in comparison with the expected thousands, and, notwithstanding the polite letters of thanks which he afterward wrote to his English friends, I have more than a vague suspicion that he always looked back upon this eventful visit with mingled feelings of annoyance and regret.

CHAPTER V

Cambridge degrees for Brahms and Joachim—Performance of the "Exercises"—"Carmen" produced at Her Majesty's—Début of Minnie Hauk—A versatile and accomplished prima donna—*Carmen* visits Seville—Anton Rubinstein—Pablo Sarasate—Etelka Gerster—Gayarre—Lassalle—Edouard de Reszke—A rare galaxy of talent—The Richter Concerts.

IN course of the almost daily companionship which, between 1874 and 1880, it was my privilege to enjoy with Signor Garcia, we used, now and then, to attend together some important musical function. Two of these occasions dwell in my memory with peculiar vividness.

Early in 1877, the University of Cambridge decided to confer the degree of "Mus. Doc.," *honoris causâ,* upon two of the world's greatest musicians, Johannes Brahms and Joseph Joachim. The distinguished violinist readily accepted this invitation, together with the customary conditions therein involved,—namely, to attend in person to receive the degree, and to furnish some new composition as an "exercise" to be performed at the university on the day of the ceremony. To Brahms the intended compliment involved a good deal more. It meant a long journey to a country that he had never visited, and, as he afterward bluntly admitted, had never had the smallest desire to visit. He looked upon England as probably the least musical of European countries, and set no store whatever upon honorary degrees, even when bestowed by such an ancient university as Cambridge.[1] He therefore declined the invitation to be present, but expressed his willingness to receive the degree if it could be conferred *in absentiâ;* and he offered as his doctor's "exercise" the new symphony in C minor, No. 1, which had been performed for the first time in the previous November at Karlsruhe. After some consideration the offer was accepted, and March 8, 1877, was the day fixed for the ceremony to take place at Cambridge.

The especial significance of this event, apart from its immediate interest, lies in the important bearing that it had upon the wider understanding and appreciation of Brahms's music in Great Britain. Down to this time Johannes Brahms had been known to the general mass of amateurs as a writer of chamber music; and by all but the cultivated few his compositions were voted abstruse and dull, if undeniably clever. Indeed, even his own countrymen for the most part had failed as yet to grasp the true tenor and might of his genius. Writing in that same year, one of his biographers, Herr A. Maczewski, said of Brahms that the "individual character of his ideas and the intellectual

[1] Brahms was nevertheless genuinely pleased when, ten years later, the Emperor William appointed him a Knight of the Order "pour le mérite" for Arts and Sciences.

SIR MICHAEL COSTA

From a photograph by Grillet & Cie., Naples

HANS RICHTER

From a photograph by The London Stereoscopic Company

qualities of his nature certainly stand in the way of his overcoming opposition and gaining the sympathies of the large mass of the musical public. . . . With him beauty seems to hold a place subordinate to expression, and a certain harshness is in consequence occasionally met with in his harmony which must hinder the popularity of his works" (Grove's Dictionary, Vol. I, p. 270).

If the "Deutsches Requiem" opened the eyes of German music-lovers, it was assuredly the symphony in C minor that awakened English ears to a just and worthy estimate of the gifts of the Hamburg composer. The impression created at Cambridge was to spread within a few years over the entire kingdom. "What a masterpiece for a first symphony!" exclaimed Garcia, as we listened to the rehearsal by the Cambridge University Musical Society under Villiers Stanford. What a masterpiece indeed! And what patience for such a musician to have waited before writing it until he was forty-three years old and could inscribe "Op. 68" upon the score of his symphony No. 1! Of course we all smiled when the opening theme of the finale suggested that unmistakable resemblance to the corresponding subject in the last movement of Beethoven's "Ninth," which Brahms always protested he could not perceive. But the trifling similarity mattered naught unless to lend the new work a greater charm; for Brahms was nothing if not original, and the soul of honesty itself. His beautiful "Schicksalslied" was also performed at this concert, and it helped to confirm the deep impression created by the symphony. Alas, that he should not have been there himself!

But the personal tribute paid that day to his beloved friend, Joseph Joachim, was in every way remarkable. Well-known musicians came from distant parts of the country to be present. It was to do honor to the illustrious violinist whom he had known long years that my own venerable master made the journey from the metropolis—to witness the bestowal upon him of a distinction similar to that which had already been conferred upon himself as the inventor of the laryngoscope. And never has the Public Orator of Cambridge University employed terms more felicitous or more eulogistic than he contrived to put into his Latin speech in this instance. Dr. Joachim's "exercise" consisted of his fine overture in memory of the celebrated poet Heinrich von Kleist, which was played under his own direction. He also gave a superb performance of the Beethoven violin concerto, of which work he is, by common consent, admitted to be the greatest of all interpreters.

In the summer of the following year—to be precise, June 22, 1878—Signor Garcia accompanied me to the first performance in England of Bizet's "Carmen." It was not an easy thing at that time to persuade him to go to the Opera. The singing that he heard did not, as a rule, please him, and he was content to dwell undisturbed with the memories of a glorious past. An opera on a Spanish subject, however, was something of an attraction, especially if it touched upon bull-fighting, which would appear to stir the blood of every Spaniard at any and every period of life. Moreover, I fancy he was acquainted with Prosper Mérimée's story, and had heard some accounts of Bizet's music. I reminded him that "Carmen" had been next door to a failure at the Opéra-Comique three years previous. "I know," he replied, "and the poor composer died of a broken heart three months later. That is the way France generally treats rising talent, including her own. I place little value upon the opinion of Paris regarding new works."

The only bit of "Carmen" then known in London was the "Habañera," which had been sung for a year or so with notable success by that gifted artist, Mme. Trebelli. As a matter of fact, though, the music of this air had been in her possession for a long time; hence I am inclined to believe either that it is a genuine Spanish tune which Bizet adapted and arranged, or else that it was written by him some time before the opera. The "Chanson du Toréador," which eventually helped so much to render "Carmen" popular in every country, had not yet been heard in England. Indeed, Bizet was practically an unknown composer, while the fact of his being a Frenchman was, in the opinion of a Spaniard, distinctly against him as an indication of ability to write or imitate Spanish music.[1]

[1] The general feeling on this subject in Spain amounts almost to a national prejudice. To this day "Carmen," although

I recollect that Signor Garcia was in a very critical mood, albeit prepared, with his customary impartiality, to allow the full meed of praise where praise was due.

The opera was well cast and well staged. Mr. Mapleson had seen it at the Brussels Monnaie during the preceding winter, and it was on the strength of the success won there, alike by the work and by the exponent of the title-rôle, that he had determined to transfer both to the boards of Her Majesty's. The *Carmen* in question was no other than Miss Minnie Hauk, the young American prima donna who had sung at Covent Garden one autumn season when quite a girl, but had not been heard again in London until the present year, when she made her rentrée as *Violetta* in "La Traviata." Her *Carmen* was already famous. It was considered as good dramatically as that of Mme. Galli-Marié,[1] and in a vocal sense far superior. Garcia was simply delighted with the artistic finish, the vivacity and charm, of her performance. He thought she had caught with marvelous instinct and truth the peculiarities of the Spanish type, the coquettish manners and the defiant devilry of the wayward

greatly liked and frequently performed, is less intensely popular in Spain than in other countries—certainly less so than the work of purely Spanish composers such as Albeniz and Breton. At the same time, it takes a born Spaniard to recognize the extremely delicate nuances that distinguish the real native article from the clever foreign imitation.

[1] This artist created the character in Paris. She also appeared in it at Her Majesty's, with a French company, during the autumn of 1886.

From a photograph by L. Minzloff, Konigsberg

MINNIE HAUK

AS CARMEN

gipsy. He admired immensely the individuality of an assumption which, if it was subsequently followed upon more or less identical lines by many excellent artists, has been equaled only by three—I mean Pauline Lucca, Emma Calvé, and Zélie de Lussan.

Nor since have I heard a sweeter, gentler, or more persuasive *Michaela* than Alwina Valleria (née Miss Lohmann, of Baltimore), another American soprano who was just beginning to win her way into the affections of the English public. The *Escamillo*—and an altogether ideal one—was that remarkably fine barytone, Del Puente, who in after years settled down in New York as a singer and teacher; while Campanini sang and acted with superb dramatic power as *Don José.* It was a strong cast, therefore, and Sir Michael Costa conducted the opera with exemplary care, even if he failed to bring into full relief the manifold beauties and exquisitely delicate touches of Bizet's score. But Signor Garcia was simply enthusiastic, and he labored as effectively as any individual in the whole theatre to bring about the triumphant reception that greeted "Carmen" that night. The subject and its treatment alike appealed to him; he thought the story intensely dramatic; the degree of real Spanish color in the music quite astonished him. He had not imagined that any Spanish opera after "Don Giovanni" and "Il Barbiere" could please him so much.

I may be excused for thus dwelling at length

upon the première of "Carmen" in England, because from that moment dates the real popularity of the opera in Europe—a popularity, by the way, that has been exceeded by one opera only, Gounod's "Faust." It was further noteworthy in that it first brought into prominence the two American-born singers—Minnie Hauk and Alwina Valleria—who were to be most closely identified with the rapid upward progress of the Carl Rosa opera enterprise from 1880 to 1886.

I made the acquaintance of Minnie Hauk in London during the season just referred to. A year or so later she married a well-known traveler and writer, Baron Ernst von Hesse-Wartegg. It was in 1880 that she joined the Carl Rosa troupe, and appeared at Her Majesty's in "Lohengrin," "Aida," and "Mignon" when these operas were given for the first time in English; also she made an admirable *Katharine* in Goetz's "Taming of the Shrew." In Wagner's opera she was ably supported by Herr Anton Schott; in "Mignon," by that admirable singer, Joseph Maas, the best English stage tenor since Sims Reeves. In fact, these were all representations of the rarest excellence; and they all threw into a strong light the singular versatility of Minnie Hauk, who could bring out the poetry of *Elsa* or the deep passion of *Aida* as completely as she could the diablerie of *Carmen* or the petulant tempers of *Mignon* and *Katharine*.[1]

[1] Mme. de Wartegg is at the present time living in retirement with her husband at Triebschen, near Lucerne. Her villa ad-

ANTON RUBINSTEIN

From a photograph by Sarony, N. Y.

SARASATE

From a photograph by Scheurich, Berlin

Besides being versatile in her art (she could boast a repertory of unusual dimensions), Minnie Hauk was an accomplished musician, a facile linguist, a kindly hostess, and the most interesting of correspondents. More than one agreeable summer holiday did I spend with Mme. de Wartegg and her mother and husband at their Biningen-Schlössli near Basel, in Switzerland. For the weary worker it was an ideal spot in which to repose and recuperate; likewise for the busy prima donna to study in peace and find inspiration for new parts. She wrote me once from Biningen:

I am studying very diligently a new rôle—or, rather, an old one that I have never yet essayed—that is, *Frau Fluth (Mistress Ford)* in "The Merry Wives of Windsor." I have also to freshen up for my coming season in Berlin my recollection of the "Domino Noir," and *Rose Friquet* in "Les Dragons de Villars," besides other operas put aside for several years. How am I to do all this if I cannot manage to stay at home for once in the early summer? Since we have had the Schlössli I have never been here in May or June, and it has been a delight; for I have never seen the meadows so green and beautiful, or heard such wonderful warbling all day long as from the birds in the park here. I am trying to learn from them; and I feel more and more convinced that Wagner, Bizet, and many other composers have been inspired with their "motives" by listening to the birds.

joins the one at which Wagner resided from 1866 until 1872, and where he completed "Die Meistersinger" and wrote nearly the whole of the latter half of the "Nibelungenring."

5

In course of her numerous tours in different parts of the world (including Japan, where she was unluckily "caught" in an earthquake and had a most providential escape from destruction), Mme. Minnie Hauk used to write me regular accounts of her artistic doings and her varied experiences. From these I have only space to quote the following letter, which has a special interest on account of its reference to the scene of her greatest operatic triumph:

SEVILLE, January 25, 1892.

MY DEAR MR. KLEIN:

What a world of antique novelty I have gone through within the last four weeks! I have lived, as it were, in the atmosphere of the Scriptures, and have seen sights most marvelous. We left Tangiers four days ago, and I can hardly realize that I have seen all this antiquated world peopled as of yore—walking, breathing—in fact, living life as it was lived nearly two thousand years ago!

And now what a change—Seville! I am gratified to find the cigarette girls just as gay and bright—with flashing eyes and rose in hair—as I expected. Not as pretty, perhaps; but at every turn one can imagine a *Carmencita* (and what a common name *Carmen* is here, to be sure!). The city is a dead one, so to speak; but at night it livens up, and at the theatres the castagnette-playing, the dancing, and the singing have the true old Spanish ring. There is something very fascinating about the life here, and I only regret I cannot see it in the spring-tide. To-morrow we leave for the Alhambra, stopping on the way at Cordova to see the great Mosque.

I finished my American season of four months (with Mr. Abbey) at Boston, and sang in all fifty-three times in three operas—"Lohengrin," "Carmen," and "Cavalleria Rusticana." We had crowded houses all the time. It was a most interesting season, but rather fatiguing. I think I have deserved my holiday, and shall rest two months before fulfilling my engagements at Nice, etc.

With united best regards,

Ever yours faithfully,

MINNIE HAUK-DE WARTEGG.

In addition to the events already recorded, there belong to the years 1877 and 1879 some experiences which, for me at least, will ever be replete with interest. In the earlier year I heard for the first time Anton Rubinstein and Pablo Sarasate, and witnessed the débuts of Etelka Gerster and Gayarre. With the exception of a brief visit in 1876, Rubinstein had not been in London for seven or eight years. I now heard him at the Philharmonic, at the Crystal Palace (where I saw him conduct—with all the "extra" movements included—his grandiose but interminable "Ocean" symphony), and at some recitals at St. James's Hall. He was then in his forty-eighth year, and had attained the fullest measure of his extraordinary powers.

Universally acknowledged to be the greatest pianist of his time, the public simply worshiped Rubinstein as an artist and gathered in crowds whenever he appeared. His technique bordered upon the miraculous; his interpretative gifts were worthy of a musician who was himself no mean creative genius; his style, the reflex, as it were, of his massive leonine aspect, was at once the most noble and most original of any pianist I have ever listened to. The fire and passion in his soul poured out at his fingers' ends; and yet his touch could be as gentle and caressing as a woman's. In private life his chief amusement was a game of whist. He loved the game and played it well—as I discovered for myself one evening when I visited him at the old Hotel Dieudonné, in St. James's. Quite a number of friends dropped in after dinner, but Rubinstein simply ignored their presence until he had finished his rubber. Then he went round and warmly welcomed them. After a time he sat down to the piano, and never left it till midnight, giving us a treat that will never fade from my memory as long as I live.[1]

An artist of entirely different calibre, yet barely less serious in his aims and certainly not less remarkable for the flawless perfection of his technical gifts, Señor Sarasate had just turned thirty when he made his first appearance before a London audience. Three years later (October 13, 1877) his rendering of Mendelssohn's violin concerto at the Crystal Palace fairly took the town by storm, and he repeated his triumph at the Philharmonic in the following spring. After 1885 he became an almost

[1] Rubinstein visited London again in 1881, when his opera "The Demon" was produced at Covent Garden, and yet once more (for the last time) in 1886, when he gave his famous series of Historical Recitals at St. James's Hall. As an operatic composer he never won success in England, but his chamber music and songs are among the best-known and most popular in the modern repertory.

DEL PUENTE

AS ESCAMILLO

From a photograph by Mora, N. Y.

GAYARRE

AS VASCO DI GAMA

From a photograph by Benque & Co., Paris

annual visitor to England, and he also toured several years with unvarying success in the United States.

It was quite late in the season of 1877 when Etelka Gerster made her début at Her Majesty's as *Amina* in "La Sonnambula." She was one of Mr. Mapleson's surprises. Beyond a very high register, no one expected anything extraordinary from the newcomer. Imagine, therefore, the delight of habitués when they heard for the first time a voice of exquisitely musical quality and bird-like tone, trained to execute the most difficult *fiorituri* and cadenzas with the utmost care, and capable of running up comfortably to the giddy height of an F in *alt*. Moreover, the Hungarian soprano proved to be a good actress and a conscientious artist, so that her success was never for a moment in doubt. In the following season she accompanied Mr. Mapleson to America, and there began a long series of triumphs too familiar to need recalling.

Gayarre was not a great tenor in the highest sense of the term. Nevertheless, he possessed vocal and histrionic attributes of a very distinguished kind, and chance so willed it that he was destined to "bridge over" to a large extent the interval that separated the final retirement of Mario from the advent (as a tenor) of Jean de Reszke. By birth a Spaniard, and hailing from Pampeluna (the town in which Sarasate was born), Giuliano Gayarre had studied and won his early successes in Italy. He was an exponent of the new quasi-nasal school of tenor singers, which already had Tamagno for one of its leading protagonists. To my ears his production, on the night he made his début at Covent Garden (April 7, 1877), sounded strange and not wholly pleasant. Still, the voice traveled well, and he sang the music of *Gennaro* with so much tenderness, so much charm, allied to genuine dramatic feeling and expression, that the crowded house forthwith accorded him a splendid reception.

I declined to join in the general chorus of "Another Mario!" It struck me as little less than sacrilege to compare with the divine voice of that tenor an organ which could occasionally descend, or ascend, to the utterance of tones that quickly earned the name of the "Gayarre bleat." My criticism drew forth several rejoinders, among them the following from the Covent Garden conductor, Signor Vianesi:

> Wait to hear Gayarre two or three times. You will appreciate him as a true artist. If I can correct him of too much dragging (the present Italian style), he will be "Number One"!

In a measure, this prediction proved to be correct. Of the operatic tenors heard in London during the succeeding ten years, Gayarre was easily the most interesting. Campanini and Fancelli had finer voices; while of the French school Nicolini and Capoul were perhaps more attractive. But in certain operas Gayarre stood, for the time being, upon an eminence by himself. As *Fernando* in "La Favorita" (his best part), as *Jean de Leyden* in "Le Prophète," as *Enzo* in Ponchielli's "Gioconda" (his original creation), and as *Gennaro* in "Lucrezia Borgia," he was for a long time positively without a rival. He was an admirable *Lohengrin,* and was the first singer in this part to vary the charm of the love music in the bridal duet by the judicious employment of a particularly lovely *mezza voce.* He was also excellent in Glinka's opera "La Vie pour le Czar," which he introduced to English audiences for the first time at Covent Garden in 1887.

Eighteen hundred and seventy-nine was the busiest musical year that I ever experienced in London. We had opera from January until July, and again from October to December. Carl Rosa set the ball rolling at Her Majesty's, producing "Rienzi" for the first time in England, and "Carmen," with the piquant Selina Dolaro in the title-rôle, for the first time in the vernacular. Early in April, Covent Garden opened under the sole management of Ernest Gye, whose father had died from the effects of a gun accident in the preceding December. Here the peerless Adelina Patti once more headed the *prime donne;* Scalchi, still in her prime, was the principal contralto; Gayarre, Nicolini, and Capoul were the leading tenors; and to such barytones as Graziani, Cotogni, and Maurel was now added that superb singer Jean Lassalle, for whom was produced Massenet's picturesque but unequal opera, "Le Roi de Lahore."

When Mr. Mapleson started at Her Majesty's toward the end of April it was with one of the strongest companies that he had ever brought together. Christine Nilsson—now at the finest period of her career—led off a group of sopranos that included Minnie Hauk, Etelka Gerster, Clara Louise Kellogg,[1] Marie Roze, and, last but not least, Marie Vanzandt, a youthful débutante whose delightful singing as *Zerlina* and *Amina* took the London world completely by surprise. Trebelli, unapproachable as ever in her way, stood at the head of the contraltos; Campanini and Fancelli were the best tenors; and among the barytones and basses were Del Puente, Galassi, Rota, Behrens, and Foli. Some of the artists here named also took part in the autumn season which Mr. Mapleson gave at the same opera-house in the Haymarket—now, by the way, the site of Mr. Beerbohm Tree's theatre and the Carlton Hotel.

Here let me refer, *par parenthèse,* to the English début of Edouard de Reszke. That event properly belongs to 1880, when he appeared for the first time at Covent Garden as *Indra* in "Le Roi de Lahore." He was then about twenty-six, and his noble bass voice had already developed in full

[1] This charming American soprano passed an exceedingly brief portion of her operatic career in England. Her talents, however, were very warmly appreciated, and in her favorite rôles she commanded the heartiest admiration.

ETELKA GERSTER

From a photograph by Sarony, N. Y

EMMA NEVADA

From a photograph by Sarony, N. Y.

splendor the richness of timbre and amplitude of volume for which it is remarkable. He lacked experience, of course; the art of later years was yet to come. Still, the sonority and grandeur of his tones were an unalloyed delight, notably in such parts as *Basilio, St. Bris, Count Rodolfo,* and *Walter* ("William Tell"), and he instantly won hearty favor. He returned regularly for the four succeeding seasons.

In addition to the concerts of the old Philharmonic Society, there were also those of the new Philharmonic, which in 1879, on the resignation of Dr. Wylde, came under the exclusive conductorship of Mr. Wilhelm Ganz, and survived under his direction for several seasons longer. But in the concert world by far the most important event of 1879 was the establishment of the famous Richter Concerts. They were the outcome of the Wagner Festival of two years before, and, as a matter of fact, were announced for this preliminary season as a series of three "Orchestral Festival Concerts." In subsequent years, when it was palpable that Richter had become a power in the land, the more ponderous title was relinquished, and double the number of concerts were given.

The credit for the idea of starting the new undertaking was originally due to Herr Hermann Franke, a capable violinist (pupil of Joachim), who had been residing for some time in London, and who occasionally gave chamber concerts with the aid of Scharwenka, Robert Hausmann, and other artists. Franke had been very useful to his friend Wilhelmj in the organization of the Wagner Festival, and it occurred to him that profit could be reaped from the tremendous impression that Richter's conducting had created at the Albert Hall. The result justified his expectation; two years later, at St. James's Hall, Richter's feat of conducting not only Wagnerian fragments but Beethoven symphonies entirely from memory furnished an absolute novelty and created quite a sensation. Thenceforth, Hans Richter's popularity in England was assured, and his concerts, given once, and sometimes twice, every year, became a regular feature in the economy of London musical life.

CHAPTER VI

Musical critic of the "Sunday Times"—The Duke of Cambridge and his journalistic sons—Queen Victoria's music-loving aunt—F. Paolo Tosti—The Queen's "Master of the Musick"—Her Majesty's musical library—A State Concert at Buckingham Palace—German opera in London—Gounod conducts his "Redemption."

I NOW pass to the period when I became critic of the fine old London weekly known as the "Sunday Times." This welcome rise in my journalistic status came about by a stroke of pure luck. Late in the summer of 1881 the newspaper changed hands, and the new editor, anxious, no doubt, to show himself a man of action, promptly discharged every member of the literary staff. His procedure almost savored of heroism (of the Quixotic sort), for he was totally unsupplied with new men to take the place of those whom he had so needlessly dismissed. How, I should like to know, could he have hoped to find a more trustworthy dramatic critic than Joseph Knight,[1] or a more brilliant yet learned writer on musical subjects than the late Desmond L. Ryan, then also critic of the "Standard"?

[1] Critic for many years of the London "Globe" and "Athenæum," and present editor of "Notes and Queries."

However, the vacancy existed, and when September arrived, and with it the date for the Norwich Festival, the "Sunday Times" had no appointed critic to represent it at the East Anglian gathering. In this dilemma the over-hasty editor wrote to my Norwich uncle, the late Philip Soman, and asked him to recommend some one who could provide an article upon the festival. I was duly requested to essay the task. A few weeks later I was installed as the regular musical critic of the "Sunday Times," which post I held continuously until I resigned it in November, 1901—a period of over twenty years.

At first the responsibilities of my new position weighed somewhat heavily upon me. I had already won my spurs, it is true; though only just twenty-five, I felt that I possessed the necessary knowledge and experience for my work. But it was no light matter to follow a clever (and then still living) writer like Desmond Ryan, who in turn had been preceded by the present *doyen* of English musical critics, Joseph Bennett (before his services were wholly required by the "Daily Telegraph"). Ere long, however, I was to receive definite assurance that the performance of my labors was commanding satisfaction.

It is not the public that decides in these cases. The readers of a paper are usually the last persons in the world that a British editor would consult concerning the merits or deficiencies of any writer upon his staff. As long as the critic writes

ALBANI

AS DESDEMONA

From a photograph by Sarony Publishing Company, N. Y.

PATEY

From a photograph by W. & D. Downey, London

decent English, avoids libel actions, and is not guilty of exposing a lack of technical knowledge of his subject, he has little to fear from his employer. Strong or weak, fearless or indifferent, honest or venal, he will be permitted to go on publishing his "copy" from one year's end to the other, until some such upheaval occurs as that which had landed me in my present position. The artist, the teacher, the cultivated amateur, the instructed colleague—in a word, those who do not care openly to find fault, even when they dare—are alone capable of judging whether or not the critic has done his work well. And they are precisely the people whose opinion upon the question is rarely, if ever, asked.

The "Sunday Times" again changed hands, for the second time in a twelvemonth; and, instead of being dismissed, I was requested to continue my duties with "undiminished energy and zeal." I was told that my work had won favorable notice in "exalted" quarters, and that if I cared to relinquish the anonymous first person plural in favor of the singular, and sign articles with my own initials, I was at liberty to do so. I gladly adopted this course. Journalistic anonymity is advisable in dealing with politics and the general run of newspaper topics. But where art is concerned, I prefer to conform to the old French principle that the opinions of the paper should be put forth as those of an individual.

It is no secret that the purchasers of the "Sunday Times'' in this instance were the three sons of the Duke of Cambridge—Captain (now Rear-Admiral) FitzGeorge, Colonel Augustus FitzGeorge, and Colonel George FitzGeorge. They all took a deep interest in the then varying fortunes of the paper, and Colonel George FitzGeorge personally undertook the editorship, in addition to the even more onerous duties of dramatic critic.[1] Frequently the three brothers would come down to the office on a Saturday evening and remain until the paper was ready to go to press. The Colonel had the true instincts of a journalist, and would write a bright, chatty article every week.

The Duke of Cambridge himself, too, was evidently interested. I met his Royal Highness more than once at his son's house. Well do I recollect a certain New Year's eve, and the zest with which he joined in ''Auld Lang Syne'' after he had been sitting by the piano for nearly an hour listening to my songs. In his genuine love of music he fully shares a characteristic that distinguishes the whole of the royal family. Until a few years ago the Duke was a regular attendant at the opera. He preferred the stalls to the royal box, albeit, if the Princess of Wales (Queen Alexandra now) were

[1] In this branch, however, the Colonel soon found the work too heavy, and asked me to assist him, as far as I could do so without interfering with my musical duties. These contributions I signed with the *nom de guerre* of ''Avant-scène,'' and for nearly three years (until the appointment of my friend Malcolm Salaman, a son of the composer) I was quite as closely identified with the theatrical as with the musical work of the paper.

present, he would never fail to pay her Royal Highness a visit and enjoy a chat between the acts. One night, at a performance of "Don Giovanni," I had the pleasure of sitting next the duke. His remarks upon the artists were full of sensible criticism. He found fault where censure was really deserved, and expressed a firm conviction that the "Mozart singers" of that day, with the exception of Patti and one or two others, were not to be compared to those whom he had heard in his boyhood.

At this time the venerable Duchess of Cambridge, his Royal Highness's mother, was still alive and residing at St. James's Palace, where our beloved Queen Victoria would visit her regularly on the rare occasions of her coming to London. Music was the soothing balm of the aged Duchess's declining days; and it was furnished almost exclusively by my friend, the well-known song-writer, F. Paolo Tosti. Every afternoon, toward tea-time, with the regularity of clockwork, Tosti would go to St. James's Palace and entertain the Duchess with that exquisite warbling[1] of his own charming songs, for which he was then enjoying such a remarkable vogue. I had already known him, but his intimacy with the FitzGeorges naturally tended to strengthen the bonds of friendship between us. I remember his telling me how sedulously the

[1] I can find no better word to express the unique combination of perfect diction, of true Italian warmth and color, with the peculiarly poignant tones of the *voix de compositeur*, that characterized Tosti's singing twenty years ago.

musical columns of a certain paper were studied in the royal palaces every Sunday; and from some words graciously uttered to me by Princess Christian many years afterward, I have reason to know that Tosti's statement was not mere flattery.

Among my early contributions to the "Sunday Times" was an account of a State Concert at Buckingham Palace. It excited considerable curiosity, inasmuch as critics, I need scarcely say, are not admitted to these functions; indeed, I believe that the occasion I refer to was the last as well as the first upon which a description of a State Concert has ever been written and published by a musical journalist. It was generally surmised at the time that I had obtained the privilege of entrée through the influence of my editor. That was not so. I owed it entirely to the kindness of the Queen's late "Master of the Musick," Sir William George Cusins, who consented to arrange for my presence, on condition that I would not reveal his share in the transaction so long as he remained a court official. And he has now been dead some nine years.

Cusins never realized it, but he was distinctly one of fortune's favorites. The fickle goddess smiled upon him from the day he won the King's Scholarship at the Royal Academy—I think he actually won it twice, by the way. Throughout his career he regarded himself as an underestimated genius.[1] And yet, as the pupil of Sterndale

[1] This was, perhaps, because he felt a certain amount of disappointment in his aspirations as a composer. He wrote a good

BUCKINGHAM PALACE.

FRIDAY EVENING, 15th JULY, 1887.

ROYAL JUBILEE CANTATA, "*Grant The Queen a long life,*" . *W. G. Cusins.*
The Solos by Mad^e ALBANI & Mr. LLOYD.
THE WORDS OVER LEAF.

OVERTURE, "*Der Fliegende Holländer,*" . . . . *Wagner.*

ARIE, (*a*) "*Deh vieni alla finestra,*" (*b*) "*Fin ch'han dal vino,*" . . (*Il Don Giovanni*) *Mozart.*
Mon^r MAUREL.

SONG, "*The Echo Song,*" . . . . *Eckert.*
Mlle SIGRID ARNOLDSON.

DUO, "*Si, la stanchezza m'opprime,*" . . . . . . (*Il Trovatore*) *Verdi.*
Mad^e TREBELLI & Mr. LLOYD.

ROMANZA, "*O Paradiso!*" . . . . (*L'Africaine*) *Meyerbeer.*
Mon^r FIGNER.

ARIA, "*Ah! fors'è lui,*" . . . . (*La Traviata*) *Verdi.*
Mad^e ALBANI.

HABAÑERA, "*Carmen,*" . . . . *Bizet.*
Mad^e TREBELLI.

FINALE, "*O sommo Carlo,*" . . . . (*Ernani*) *Verdi.*
Mesd^es ARNOLDSON & TREBELLI, Messrs. FIGNER & MAUREL, with Chorus.

GOD SAVE THE QUEEN.

Conductor, . . . Mr. W. G. CUSINS.

FACSIMILE OF A STATE CONCERT PROGRAMME

Bennett and Sainton, he won success both as a pianist and a violinist; he was at an early age appointed organist to the Queen's private chapel; he was for sixteen years (1867 to 1883) conductor of the Philharmonic Society; he was honored in various ways by the leading foreign musical societies; and in 1892 he was added to the select list of musical knights. The post of "Master of the Musick" to the sovereign, to which he was appointed in 1870, carried with it many privileges, while its duties included those of conductor of the Queen's private band, as well as of director of the State Concerts. One might have justly thought that Sir William Cusins was the most contented musician in the land. That he was not mattered little; his dissatisfaction was carefully concealed from all but his best friends, and a temper that could rage at white heat was, as a rule, effectually concealed beneath a calm, dignified exterior and the manners of a refined gentleman.

One day he asked me whether I would care to see the musical library of Queen Victoria at Buckingham Palace. I accepted with the utmost pleasure, and spent a couple of delightful hours

deal; his compositions comprising an oratorio, "Gideon," a "Te Deum," a symphony, two overtures, concertos for piano and violin, several chamber works, and songs; besides a "Royal Wedding Serenata" written for the wedding of the Prince and Princess of Wales in 1863, and a "Royal Jubilee Cantata" written for the jubilee of Queen Victoria in 1887. Yet, probably the last thing that English amateurs would have thought of doing was to regard Cusins as a composer.

with him looking through the treasures of that interesting collection. He showed me, among other valuable manuscripts, one of the original scores of the "Messiah," on which he had shortly before published a remarkably clever brochure, throwing considerable light upon the details of Handel's instrumentation. "I am now engaged," he told me, "in compiling a catalogue of this wonderful collection. Her Majesty has granted me permission, and I hope in good time to be able to let the world know what a mass of precious manuscripts and scores and musical works of all kinds there are in the Queen's library." Whether or not that project was carried out before his death I am unable to say. If not, perhaps his successor, Sir Walter Parratt, will undertake to complete it.

After our visit to the library, Cusins took me through the handsome reception-rooms of the palace. It was then that I conceived the idea of asking permission to accompany him once to a State Concert. At first he replied that it would be impossible, but after a moment's reflection said, "Well, I fancy I might manage it if you don't mind coming as a member of the chorus." I answered that I should be only too happy. "Then I will send you a 'command' to attend rehearsal at nine o'clock on the morning of the next concert, and all you have to do is to be sure that at night you wear a white waistcoat. I wear court dress, and the band have their own uniform of black with gold buttons; but the chorus are distinguished by nothing more elaborate than a white waistcoat with ordinary evening dress." So everything was arranged, and before we parted I readily gave the requisite promise of secrecy.

Though magnificent to the eye, and a sight gorgeous and dazzling beyond my powers of description, nevertheless I found that State Concert at Buckingham Palace one of the slowest and most dispiriting functions that it was ever my lot to witness. From my place in the orchestral gallery I commanded a perfect view of the entire assemblage. The Queen was, of course, not present.[1] Her Majesty was represented by the Prince of Wales, who, with the Princess of Wales and the other members of the royal family, occupied seats —not in front, as formerly had been the custom, but upon a high dais at the extreme end of the vast ball-room. At the back of the royal group sat or stood a semicircle of high officers of state and ladies and gentlemen of the household. The general company were ranged upon either side of the room, facing each other, in rows five or six deep; and between them was a gangway or passage broad enough to keep the royal view of the performers entirely free from obstruction.

The concert began at 11 P.M. with the singing of the national anthem. At that moment, as all present rose to their feet, the *coup d'œil* was su-

[1] Queen Victoria never attended either a State Concert or a State Ball at Buckingham Palace after the death of the Prince Consort in 1861.

perb in the extreme. The women, in court dress with nodding plumes and sparkling tiaras, their corsages positively coruscating with jewels and gems of every description; the men, in their various court, naval, and military uniforms, their breasts covered with the ribands and stars of countless orders; the beautiful tapestries and hangings, the sumptuous decoration of walls and ceiling, and the brilliantly lighted chandeliers—all combined to present a profusion and wealth of color, a superb effect of delicate grandeur, such as no court in Europe could surpass. But beyond that, what?—the dullest sort of musical show that can be imagined. True, the artists were some of the best available; but the selection of pieces was necessarily of the miscellaneous or *ad captandum* order, and followed the preference at that time for any but English music. Above all, by the rules of court etiquette applause was strictly forbidden. Number succeeded number without the least token of appreciation; each, in turn, ending amid a silence that could not have been more profound had the locale been a church or the audience a gathering of the deaf and dumb.

Applause being the "salt," not only of the artist's existence, but of any musical performance, it naturally follows that its elimination from a State Concert leaves the whole thing tasteless and insipid from the artist's point of view. Only at the close of the programme did vitality and spontaneity characterize the proceedings. For then the "royal-

REICHER-KINDERMANN

AS BRÜNNHILDE

From a photograph by W. Höffert, Dresden

ANTON SEIDL

1882

From a photograph by W. Höffert, Dresden

ties" descended from the dais, and, with stately tread and bows right and left, walked the entire length of the apartment toward the expectant orchestra. Then the singers, who had already descended from the platform, received from gracious lips the words of praise and thanks that assured them they had done well. It was, for them, by far the sweetest morsel of the entertainment. The compliments over, the royal personages retired, and the company dispersed, some to the supper-room; others to some ball or late reception elsewhere. For my own part, I waited patiently and discreetly in the background until I caught the eye of the "Master of the Musick." He beckoned me to him, took me by the arm, and, without a word, led me along a labyrinth of corridors and passages; I thought it was to let me quietly out by a side door, and was preparing to say "Good-night," when suddenly, to my astonishment, I found myself in a spacious and comfortable room in which, at a large round table, just ready to begin supper, were seated the principal artists who had taken part in the concert! "So much," thought I, "for the chance of keeping secret who brought me here!" But Cusins was both sensible and discreet, and his manner possessed that air of importance and authority which would have carried conviction before a whole posse of court officials. "Ladies and gentlemen," he said in his most impressive tones, "permit me to beg that you will make room for our friend Mr. Klein. I have been requested [it might have been by the Queen herself] to see that he does not leave the palace until he has enjoyed a good supper in your company." And I did enjoy it thoroughly. That convivial gathering was for me by far the pleasantest feature of the State Concert.

Eighteen hundred and eighty-two was London's great Wagner year. Hitherto we had been slowly paving the way only. Now, with almost startling suddenness, the metropolis found itself the scene of two weighty enterprises which were destined to give an even stronger fillip to the spread of the Bayreuth master's art than his own visit in 1877.

To be candid, the double dose, taken well-nigh simultaneously, proved rather too heavy for the receptive capacity of the general public. But the German community again rallied in brave numbers to this musical call from the Fatherland, and, alike with money and plaudits, proffered substantial support to the cause.

Early in the year a troupe had been formed by Herr Angelo Neumann for the purpose of performing "Der Ring des Nibelungen" in the leading cities of Germany, Austria, Holland, England, and Italy. The months of May and June were chosen for the London visit, and Her Majesty's Theatre was engaged. In all, four cycles of the tetralogy were given. Of these I attended two, and then for the first time felt that I was beginning to obtain an insight into the real scope and meaning of this gigantic work. The casts included not a few of the famous artists who had taken part in the initial representation of the "Ring" at Bayreuth in 1876,—among them Niemann, Unger, the Vogls, Hill, Schlosser, and Lilli Lehmann (who sang *Woglinde, Helmwige,* and the "Bird" music); with that admirable artist, Reicher-Kindermann, as *Brünnhilde.* The conductor was the lamented Anton Seidl, who then made his first appearance in London. He at once won the high approval of connoisseurs by the skill which he displayed—with by no means first-rate material—in bringing out with clearness, refinement, and intellectuality the beauties of Wagner's colossal score. It was through no fault of Seidl's that the representations were at many points open to criticism; nor, we may be equally sure, was he responsible for the number of extensive "cuts" which disfigured the last two of the four music-dramas.

The unexpected announcement of "German Opera at Drury Lane" during the same months owed its origin, in the first place, to the extraordinary success previously earned by the celebrated Meiningen troupe at that house; and, in the second, to the renewed activity of Hermann Franke, who, elated by the good fortune that had attended the Richter concerts, had prevailed upon Herr Pollini to arrange with Augustus Harris for a series of performances at Drury Lane, by the entire troupe of the Hamburg Opera House, and with the very popular Viennese *chef d'orchestre,* Hans Richter, as principal conductor. It turned out, from every point of view, a remarkable achievement. The rare excellence of these performances—doubly valuable in that they presented under perfect conditions difficult operas mostly new or unfamiliar to English audiences—has never been forgotten by any who witnessed them. They created a new standard, a new mental perspective, not only for the rising generation of opera-goers, but for those critics whose insular experiences had been confined exclusively to the lyric art of the Italian and French schools. Henceforward, we were to understand what was signified by Wagnerian declamation and diction superimposed upon a correct vocal method, as distinguished from mere shouting and a persistent sacrifice either of the word to the tone or of the tone to the word.

These inestimable traditions were exemplified with marvelous fidelity and force by the Hamburg artists, who, be it noted, comprised at that time several whose rare merit was subsequently to earn for them world-wide reputations. Imagine the advantage of hearing "Tristan und Isolde" and "Die Meistersinger" for the first time with such a noble singer and actress as Rosa Sucher as *Isolde* and *Eva;* with such a glorious *Tristan* and *Walther* as Winkelmann; with the famous Marianne Brandt as *Brangaene;* with that fine barytone, Gura, as *König Marke* and *Hans Sachs!* Those artists were then in their prime, and sang their music as few German singers have sung it since—as, indeed, it could have been sung only by artists trained in the

KLAFSKY

AS ISOLDE

From a photograph by E. Bieber, Hamburg

ROSA SUCHER

From a photograph by E. Bieber, Hamburg

purest of vocal schools. We also had splendid revivals of Beethoven's "Fidelio," with the delightful Thérèse Malten as *Leonora;* of Weber's "Der Freischütz" and "Euryanthe"; and, naturally, of the "Fliegende Holländer," "Tannhäuser," and "Lohengrin." How these operas were conducted by Hans Richter I need hardly say. Enough that the ensemble was superb and the mise en scène, generally speaking, beyond reproach. The esthetic effect of the entire season was in the highest degree beneficial. It also proved to be entirely free from financial loss, a fact which no doubt induced the similar undertaking at Covent Garden two years later, when Richter was again conductor. But the success in that instance was not nearly so marked. The time when German opera should take abiding root in the affections of the London public was yet to come.

In the autumn of 1882 Gounod came to England to conduct the first performance of his fine sacred work, "The Redemption." He was no stranger to London. One of the refugees of 1870, he had made a stay there of considerable duration, and among other pieces brought out his cantata "Gallia," which he conducted at the opening of the Royal Albert Hall in 1871. Even previous to this, however, he had sketched his design for the work which he labeled "Opus vitæ meæ," and there is ample evidence that he spent, from first to last, upward of a dozen years upon the score of "The Redemption." Having arranged with

Messrs. Novello & Co. for its publication (at the highest price ever paid at that time for an oratorio), Gounod arrived late in September to superintend the final rehearsals for its production at the Birmingham Festival. This was the last of the Midland gatherings over which Sir Michael Costa presided, and I owed to him the honor of a personal introduction to the composer of "Faust," who was then sixty-four years of age.

Gounod was one of the most fascinating men I have ever spoken with. His manner had a charm that was irresistible, and his kindly eyes, soft and melting as a woman's, would light up with a smile, now tender, now humorous, that fixed itself ineffaceably upon the memory. He could speak English fairly well, but preferred his own language, in which he was a brilliant conversationalist; and he could use to advantage a fund of keen, ready wit. He was influenced at that time by a recrudescence of that religious mysticism which had so strongly characterized his youthful career; but his tone, though earnest and thoughtful when he was dwelling upon his art, could brighten up with the lightness and gaiety of a true Parisian. He was rather upset, on the morning of the London band rehearsal at St. George's Hall, by the numerous mistakes in the parts, which led to frequent stoppages. The trouble reached a climax in the "March to Calvary," where, after about the ninth or tenth stop, Gounod turned to Costa and remarked:

"Seulement ici puis-je pardonner tous ces arrêts, quoiqu'ils gâtent ma musique."

"Pourquoi cela?" inquired Sir Michael.

"Parce que," replied Gounod, "à ce point il y a douze stations, et à chaque station il faut naturellement un arrêt."

After all the typographical and other errors had been rectified, the march was tried through again and went so magnificently as to arouse the master's undisguised admiration, which deepened with astonishment when Costa informed him that the instrumentalists had never seen a note of the music until that morning. Gounod said to me later, "They are wonderful readers, these English players. There is scarcely a mistake that is due to inaccurate deciphering of the notes. And what makes it even more remarkable is that my work is so full of awkward chromatic progressions." I ventured to observe that since he was last in London our orchestras had been turning their attention somewhat extensively to Wagner.

Gounod retorted quickly, "Yes, I know that. But you will not tell me that Wagner's four semitones in 'Tristan' or his slurred runs *(notes coulées)* in 'Tannhäuser' require more delicate care than my 'framework of the augmented fifth.'"[1] I thought I detected a slight touch of scorn in his voice, and made no attempt to argue the point.

[1] An allusion to the peculiar harmonic structure which the composer had avowedly employed as the predominant feature of the accompanying chords in the "Redemption."

At that same rehearsal Gounod did an unusual amount of singing. The solo vocalists comprised what the new critic of the "Times," Dr. Francis Hueffer, was then fond of describing as the "representative English quartet"—Albani, Patey, Edward Lloyd, and Santley; nor have I forgotten how exquisitely William H. Cummings (now principal of the Guildhall School of Music, London) delivered the touching phrase allotted to the *Penitent Thief*. But, as a matter of fact, Gounod, with his sympathetic *voix de compositeur,* was singing more or less all through the rehearsal, wisely exercising his rare faculty for impressing his exact ideas upon the interpreters of his music. And what beautiful music it was! What a tremendous effect it created at Birmingham! So deeply was Gounod impressed by his triumph there, that, long before the "Redemption" had been produced in Paris, he set about writing his second great sacred work, "Mors et Vita," for the Birmingham Festival of 1885. He was paid an even larger price for this than for its predecessor (I believe the exact sum was £4000 —$20,000), and he fully intended to come over to conduct it. In the meanwhile, however, an action had been brought against him in the English courts by Mrs. Weldon, and, inasmuch as he was mulcted in heavy damages, the composer deemed that "discretion is the better part of valor," and stayed at home in Paris. He never ventured across the Channel again; but I saw him in his native city three years later, as will be related in due time.

SANTLEY

From a photograph by The London Stereoscopic Company

EDWARD LLOYD

From a photograph by Falk, N. Y.

CHAPTER VII

Augustus Harris: actor, *metteur en scène*, dramatic author, theatrical manager, operatic impresario — A great stage-manager and his military aide—Harris and Carl Rosa—English opera flourishes at Drury Lane—Arthur Goring Thomas —Alexander C. Mackenzie—"Esmeralda." "Colomba," and "Nadeshda."

ENTER Augustus Harris! For some time already has the figure of the well-known impresario been looming large upon the operatic horizon of these pages, and it is not only just but expedient that he should now make his actual entry. Accurately speaking, I am aware that his formal managerial connection with opera dates only from 1887. He himself, however, would probably have dated it from his cradle. "My father was stage-manager at Covent Garden," he would say; "and if any infant ever stage-managed his father, I was that infant. Almost as soon as I could run alone he used to take me with him to the theatre. I remember quite well, as a little boy, standing in the wings as he walked about the stage, while the great prima donnas came and petted and kissed me." This was in the "sixties," when Augustus Harris, Sr., was staging the heavy Meyerbeer revivals, and when that brilliant star, Adelina Patti, had not long been shining in the operatic firmament. It is only literally true, therefore, to say that the youthful Augustus, or "Gus," as all his friends were wont to call him, was reared in the very atmosphere of the *coulisses.*

He was educated both in France and in Germany, and, as a matter of course, he went constantly to the theatres in both countries. After his return to England at the age of seventeen, one of his first essays as an actor was to play the part of the boy in "Pink Dominoes," under (Sir) Charles Wyndham's management, at the Criterion. His earliest acquaintance with the duties of an operatic stage-manager was when he accompanied the Mapleson troupe round the British provinces in that capacity. The experience was invaluable; but his chief ambition was to become lessee of Drury Lane Theatre; and, with the assistance of his father-in-law, he was enabled to fulfil that desire when he had barely attained legal age. His first pantomime and his first "autumn drama" were both successful, and ere a year had passed he could boast that he was paying his way at a theatre which had "spelled ruin" for more than one astute manager.

With the dramatic productions of Augustus Harris I am not concerned. I have simply stated the above facts in order to show the association of the musical and theatrical elements in his nature at the earliest period of his career. It must have been late in 1878 or early in 1879 when I was introduced to this remarkable man one night at the Green Room Club. The youthful Drury Lane manager was full of life and high spirits, and I found it very amusing to listen to his vivacious chatter. We had not been talking two minutes before the subject turned on opera—for even then, as in after years, it was his favorite topic. Why, he wanted to know, should London be worse off than the small German cities, where the theatres were subsidized and opera was being performed nearly the whole year round? Why was the English press powerless in this matter? Or was the press merely indifferent, like the people whose opinions and wishes it was supposed to voice? I told him I thought that neither the cities nor the people were indifferent, but that the love of opera had not yet become ingrained in the hearts of the nation; while, as to the question of state support, I was doubtful whether as good results would be derived from it as from individual enterprise working upon independent lines and combining artistic with commercial consideration to the fullest practicable extent. And then followed a very pretty argument, which lasted well into the "small hours."

Augustus Harris was even then a being of extraordinary temperament; brimming over with energy and new ideas, fond of innovations, impatient of the smallest delay in carrying out a project; the strangest imaginable mixture of conceit and modesty, rashness and discretion, extravagance and common sense. He had the gift of imagination in an uncommon degree, and from the outset he seemed to have the faculty of surrounding himself with clever "heads of departments," with useful assistants and with loyal friends. He was neither a first-rate raconteur, nor even a fluent speaker, but he loved to "rattle on" upon a subject that interested him, and he would invariably lead the laugh over his own jokes. In disposition he was honest, frank, and kindly in the extreme, and he was generous to a fault. Such, briefly, was the character of the man who was subsequently to be responsible for the renaissance of opera in England. And such, with slight developments and few changes, it remained until the close of his life. Toward the end he grew more ready to listen to the voice of gossip, and to trust his own judgment less than that of his immediate entourage. Nevertheless, so correct were his perceptions in most things, that he made less than ten per cent. of the errors credited to him by his critics.

If Harris inherited his father's genius as a *metteur en scène*, he brought to it something more. He possessed much higher powers of organization. He had a wholesome capacity for disregarding stupid and worn-out traditions. He learned a great deal from the German stage-managers, and especially from the Meiningen troupe which he brought to Drury Lane. The moving and the grouping of the street crowds in the Meiningen production of "Julius Cæsar" were simply marvelous, and Augustus Harris was wise enough to make the most of that object-lesson. He applied it to every branch of his work—pantomime, melodrama, comic opera, and, last but not least, grand opera. Where he felt that special technical advice and aid were necessary, he was satisfied with none save the best. During the preparation of one of his autumn dramas (I think it was "Human Nature") I went to Drury Lane while a rehearsal was in progress, and sat down in the stalls to watch the training of an army of supers in an imaginary fight with some African natives. In due course this was followed by a home-coming and a triumphal march through Trafalgar Square, with the hero (dear old Henry Neville) at the head of his victorious company. The whole business was splendidly done.

Actively assisting the manager in these operations was a gentleman in a frock coat and tall hat, of undeniably military appearance, who impressed me both by his quiet, masterful manner and the imperturbable patience with which he directed manœuvres to be repeated over and over again until they were satisfactorily executed. After the rehearsal was concluded I went upon the stage. Augustus Harris was talking to his military adviser. He beckoned me to approach. "Klein, I want to introduce you to my friend Major Kitchener, who has been kind enough to come and help me with this 'soldiering' work. What do you think of it? Did you ever see such fighting and marching on the stage before?" I certainly never had, and I offered my congratulations. They were accepted, with a murmur of thanks and a shake of the hand, by the man who was afterward to be the hero of Omdurman and the victor in the great South African war. He had gladly consented to place his knowledge and experience at the disposal of the popular theatrical manager.

The art-union of Augustus Harris and Carl Rosa was an outcome of an affinity—of a peculiar magnetism which brought together men who had ideas in common and could definitely work them out to their mutual gain and for the benefit of the world at large. Alas! their partnership was all too brief. What it would have achieved had it endured another ten or fifteen years, I will not attempt to guess, though undoubtedly it would have set opera upon a far more solid and exalted pedestal than it occupies in England at the present moment. Still, as it was, it accomplished much. The Carl Rosa seasons at Drury Lane marked a distinct forward stride in the progress of opera in the vernacular, particularly in the evidence that they afforded of the existence of a school of young British composers imbued with genuine talent and evincing an unsuspected mastery of the modern forms now essential to appreciation and success. More than this, the association of the two managers helped to develop the artistic side of the younger man, and to mature the aspirations which eventually were realized in the brilliant opera revival of 1887.

It was at Easter, 1883, that Carl Rosa inaugurated his first season at Drury Lane. He must have felt it a great relief to be able to depend upon his new partner for the administration of all matters relating to the stage management and *mise en scène*—departments which he had hitherto kept entirely under his own personal control. Since 1880 he had been assisted in the work of conducting by Mr. Randegger, who was now relinquishing much of his time as a teacher for, what was to him, the more pleasurable occupation of wielding the baton. Every branch of the undertaking was carefully supervised. The band and chorus were specially augmented, and the company was an excellent one.

Under these favorable circumstances, two new operas by English composers were brought to a hearing, namely, Arthur Goring Thomas's "Esmeralda" and Alexander C. Mackenzie's "Colomba." It was purely an experiment, and Carl Rosa himself had little faith in its success. I remember his saying: "I look upon this as a duty that I owe to native art, and not as a business speculation. Mind, both these operas are interesting and beautiful, or I should not have accepted them. But they are by British composers—by men whose names are hardly known to the public. How, then, can I dare hope they will succeed?" And yet they did succeed—"Esmeralda" by virtue of graceful, emotional strains allied to a moving and ever-effective drama; "Colomba" on the strength of musical merits that overcome, temporarily at least, the incubus of a clumsy and ponderous libretto.

"Esmeralda," indeed, made quite a hit from the

first. "Who is Goring Thomas?" people began to ask. Musicians knew him as a Royal Academy student who had finished his education in Paris, and had become so intensely imbued with the mannerisms of Gounod and Massenet that he was practically incapable of putting music to any but French lyrics.[1] His cantata "The Sun-Worshipers," produced at the Norwich Festival of 1881, was so unoriginal that, despite its evident talent, it had barely escaped ridicule. "Esmeralda" showed an immense advance, and in later years its charm was potent enough to attract the favorable notice of Jean de Reszke, Lassalle, and Melba, who appeared in a revised version of the opera in French at Covent Garden and also in New York. The original English cast, however, was not to be despised: Georgina Burns as *Esmeralda*, Clara Perry (now Mrs. Ben Davies) as *Fleur de Lys*, Barton McGuckin as *Phœbus,* James Ludwig as *Claude Frollo,* Ben Davies (making his début in opera) as *Gringoire*, and Leslie Crotty as *Quasimodo*—a first-rate ensemble. The libretto was by Messrs. Alberto Randegger and Theo. Marzials, the former of whom conducted the performance, and later superintended the production of the opera at Cologne.

The contrast between "Esmeralda" and "Colomba" was very striking; the methods of the two

[1] He told me this himself for a fact. It took him years to learn how to handle English poetry, and he never thoroughly mastered the knack of doing so.

From a photograph by the London Stereoscopic Company

ALWINA VALLERIA

composers were "wide as the poles asunder." That of A. C. Mackenzie's was as unmistakably Teutonic as Goring Thomas's was purely Gallic. The subjects both had been taken from French sources; and, sombre though it might be, there was no reason why Prosper Mérimée's "Colomba" should not have furnished material for an opera-book quite as effective as his "Carmen." But, whereas the authors of "Esmeralda" continually introduced bright relief in their opera, Dr. Francis Hueffer in "Colomba" sought to emphasize only the darker episodes of the Corsican vendetta, while carrying his craze for accurate "local color" to an extreme that bordered upon the absurd. At that time there was no gainsaying the dictum of the critic of the "Times"—particularly when he trudged about the stage at rehearsal, umbrella in hand, now communicating his ideas to the performers, now "laying down the law" across the footlights to the poor composer, who sat in his place in the orchestra patiently awaiting the pleasure of his autocratic collaborator. Yet, thanks simply to the beauty of the music (the orchestration was especially fine), "Colomba" made its mark with the more cultivated section of the public, and opened the eyes of the critics to the rare talent of the Scottish musician who, five years later, was to succeed Sir George Macfarren as principal of the Royal Academy of Music. The title-rôle was admirably created by Alwina Valleria; Barton McGuckin played the hero, *Orso;* and that capital basso, Franco Novara, whose real name was Nash, was also in the cast.

The success of these operas made a deep impression upon Carl Rosa and Augustus Harris. They began to see that there was a future in store for the rising English school. The two composers were each commissioned to write another opera; and meanwhile, in 1884, a work more genuinely English than either "Esmeralda" or "Colomba" —namely, "The Canterbury Pilgrims" of Villiers Stanford—was brought out at Drury Lane with marked success. The name of Mackenzie also derived wide prominence that year through the triumph of his fine oratorio, "The Rose of Sharon," at the Norwich Festival,[1] which resulted in his being requested to write a work ("The Story of Sayid") for the Leeds Festival of 1886. With so much to do, no wonder Goring Thomas was ready before him with a new opera. The composer of "Esmeralda" had been fortunate enough to discover a new librettist in Mr. Julian Sturgis, an American littérateur unknown to fame in England, who had submitted a promising scenario upon a Russian subject. The title of the new opera was "Nadeshda." Goring Thomas devoted the best part of 1884 to writing the music, and it was an-

[1] Always to be remembered as the occasion of the début in England of Miss Emma Nevada, who, in order to identify herself completely with her part, appeared at the concert as the *Rose of Sharon*, wearing a pink costume, with pink hat and gloves, and with her copy of the oratorio bound in the same soft tint—in fact, everything *couleur de rose!*

nounced for production at Drury Lane in April, 1885. Unusual secrecy was observed with regard to the work,—almost as much, in fact, as in the case of a new Savoy opera,—but I persuaded the composer to lend me an advance copy of the book, and published a notice of the story in the "Sunday Times." This evoked the following letter from the ever-nervous Carl Rosa:

10 Warwick Crescent, Maida Hill, W.
24th March, 1885.

Dear Klein:

I saw the "Nadeshda" plot to-day, and must confess it is admirably written. But where did you get the material from—from an artist, eh? I have only this morning sent words of the tenor song now to be sung to the printer's, and did not want to get copies in the hands of the press before the book was complete.

Sincerely yours,

Carl Rosa.

"Nadeshda" made an instantaneous success. It was pronounced immeasurably stronger than "Esmeralda," the music showing a wonderful advance alike in originality and dramatic grip. Handsomely staged by Augustus Harris, splendidly sung by Alwina Valleria, Josephine Yorke, Barton McGuckin, and Leslie Crotty, it achieved the hit of the season and evoked eulogies that must have delighted the soul of the modest composer. During the following autumn and winter, "Nadeshda" was brought out in several Continental cities, and, knowing how little Goring Thomas sought advertisement on these occasions, I used to take pleasure in letting him know what was going on. Occasionally he would come to me for information; as when he sent me this letter:

RATTON, WILLINGDON, SUSSEX,
January 9, 1886.

MY DEAR KLEIN:

I heard accidentally this morning from Mme. Viardot[1] that "Nadeshda" is going to be given in Berlin. Can you tell me when? Her late pupil, Mlle. Leisinger, is to sing the soprano part, and wrote to her to ask where she could get a score. I have not heard anything about it, and should be very glad if you could give me any news. Please send your reply to 52 Wimpole Street, as I am coming up on Saturday.

With best wishes for the New Year, believe me,

Yours truly,

A. GORING THOMAS.

Mackenzie was less lucky in his second attempt. Again he had the misfortune to be hampered by one of Dr. Hueffer's elephantine librettos. Hence "The Troubadour," with its ghastly climax, wherein the erring heroine is compelled by her husband to drink a goblet filled with the blood of the fascinating *Guillem de Cabestanh,* proved too much for even those who admired the melodic charm and dramatic power of the music. This was the novelty

[1] Pauline Viardot-Garcia, the famous singer and teacher, then residing in Paris, a great friend of the young English composer.

A. GORING THOMAS

From a photograph by Window & Grove, London

SIR ALEX. C. MACKENZIE

From a photograph by Elliott & Fry, London

for 1886. Not much more successful was Mr. Frederic Corder's "Nordisa" in the following year; but the ball by now had been fairly set rolling, and the public, both in London and the provinces, had awakened to the fact that there were native composers equal to the task of writing operas to which the world would listen. By what chain of untoward circumstances the progress of this native movement was impeded, if not stopped altogether, will be made clear later. But let me say here that the "unkindest cut of all" was the premature and tragic death [1] of the gifted Arthur Goring Thomas, one of the most lovable men, one of the most inspired lyrical writers, and one of the most earnest, painstaking musicians that England ever produced.

[1] In the autumn of 1891 he sustained a severe fall, from the effects of which he never altogether recovered. On the evening of March 20, 1892, he committed suicide by throwing himself under a train at the West Hampstead station of the Metropolitan Railway.

CHAPTER VIII

Decay of old Italian opera—Rise of the young Italian school—Masterly mismanagement and financial collapse at Covent Garden—Pauline Lucca—A notable dinner-party—Marcella Sembrich's surprise—Antonin Dvořák relates the story of his romantic career—Camille Saint-Saëns—The French master and English oratorio.

THE history of Italian opera in London during the middle "eighties" is a history of "decline and fall." As the fortunes of English and German opera improved, so did the glorious "palmy days" of the older school recede deeper and deeper into the shadows of the past. There is no need to dwell at length upon this process of deterioration; the causes thereof are well known and understood. I shall note rather the events which ever and anon revived the flickering embers and kept them burning until finally the requisite fuel arrived from a new and unsuspected source.

Interest was keenly excited by the production at Her Majesty's, in July, 1880, of Boïto's "Mefistofele." The work had been much talked of since its revival, in revised form, at Bologna in 1875, and Mr. Mapleson took creditable pains to mount it in such fashion that there should be few loopholes for criticism. Truth to tell, it was an exceedingly good representation all round. Christine Nilsson's embodiment of the dual rôle of *Margherita* and *Helen of Troy* had much of poetry and charm; Trebelli was as fascinating and artistic as ever in the contralto parts; Campanini made an excellent *Faust;* and Nannetti lent rare sardonic color and alertness to the part of *Mefistofele.* Sir Michael Costa was still vigorous enough to conduct Boïto's opera in his old resolute, vigilant manner; and very delighted he was over its success, which lent quite a special distinction to the season.

At this time there was little thought of a "young Italian school." Nevertheless, Verdi had been silent since "Aida";[1] and the success of Boïto was bound to draw attention to the claims of Ponchielli. The Cremonese musician had been writing and bringing out operas for a quarter of a century, two of which at least—"I Lituani" and "La Gioconda"—had met with emphatic favor in Italy. Mr. Ernest Gye now determined to try "La Gioconda" at Covent Garden; and he produced it there in May, 1883, before a crowded and demonstrative house. A fine cast was engaged—Gayarre as *Enzo,* Cotogni as *Barnaba,* Edouard de Reszke as *Alvise,* Scalchi as *La Cieca,* and an American soprano, Marie Durand, who had already won fame in Italy, as the heroine, *La Gioconda.* The opera was warmly received, and for a few representations drew good houses. It never became as lastingly popular, however, as either "Aida" or "Mefistofele," in

[1] Originally brought out at Cairo in December, 1871.

the former of which, by the way, Josephine de Reszke, the elder sister of Jean and Edouard, had sung at Covent Garden during the season of 1881.

Meanwhile, the strength of Mr. Mapleson's combination at Her Majesty's, already seriously affected by the death of Tietjens, received a fatal blow through the secession of Christine Nilsson, who retired from the operatic stage in 1881. This gifted artist, the second and last of the great "Swedish Nightingales," was one of the most remarkable singers of her time. Her voice, a pure soprano of very lovely quality, possessed a singularly pathetic timbre, a curious commingling of sweetness and power, to which she allied a charm of expression that was absolutely haunting. Moreover, she was a born actress, and her characteristic spontaneity was of a kind that enabled her to stamp such characters as *Mignon, Ophelia, Marguerite, Alice,* and *Elsa* with the most marked and refreshing individuality. Christine Nilsson had been about eight years before the public when I first heard her in 1872 at Drury Lane in "Robert le Diable"; and her impersonation of *Alice*—the favorite rôle of her renowned countrywoman Jenny Lind—shone resplendent amid a constellation of stars that included Mongini as *Roberto,* Gardoni as *Rambaldo,* Foli as *Bertramo,* and Ilma di Murska as *Isabella.* She had then just returned from a prolonged concert-tour in America, and her marriage at Westminster Abbey with M. Auguste Rouzeaud was one of the promi-

BOÏTO

From a photograph by A. Ferrario, Milan

PAULINE LUCCA

From a photograph by Rockwood, N. Y.

nent events of the season of 1872. Sixteen years later she bade her final farewell to British audiences at a concert given at the Royal Albert Hall.

The financial collapse of the "Royal Italian Opera" occurred after the season of 1884. I do not pretend to lay bare the secrets of the masterly mismanagement that led to the failure of the company which then held the sub-lease of Covent Garden. The late Earl of Lathom—most gracious and amiable of Lord Chamberlains—was not, perhaps, a sufficiently strong man to preside over such an enterprise. Neither Ernest nor Herbert Gye (co-directors of the company) had inherited the administrative talents of his father; and it is generally supposed that Ernest, who had been for some years the husband of Mme. Albani, was considerably influenced in his management of the concern by the advice of his wife, one of the principal *prime donne* of the establishment. Apart from this, the only real explanation is that society had begun to lose interest in the opera as a social function, and chose to be conspicuous by its absence on all but the "Patti nights." For the career of the celebrated diva was now at its zenith, her wondrous voice in its prime, and her incomparable vocalization had become absolutely perfect. Not even society could afford to remain away when the magic name of Adelina Patti was "in the bill."

Yet there were other great artists in the troupe beside those whose names have been mentioned in the last page or two. A host in herself was the accomplished and captivating Pauline Lucca, who, after an absence of ten years, returned to Covent Garden in 1882 to gratify opera-goers once more with her unrivaled impersonations of *Selika* in "L'Africaine," *Cherubino* in "Le Nozze," *Zerlina* in "Fra Diavolo," *Leonora* in "La Favorita," and other characters. Despite her twenty-three years upon the stage, this brilliant artist was now also at her best; her voice had lost none of its freshness, and the piquant grace of her style and the marked originality of her conceptions were even more striking than before. Her *Selika*[1] I can best describe in a single word as a "dream"—a supreme achievement to be mentioned in the same breath with the *Rosina* of Adelina Patti and the *Marguerite* of Christine Nilsson. Supported by Mierzwinsky as *Vasco da Gama*, Lassalle as *Nelusko*, Bagagiolo as *Pedro*, and Valleria as *Inez*, Pauline Lucca's performance in "L'Africaine" is to be folded in the lavender of one's memory. She was also heard here then for the first time in "Carmen"; and her impersonation of Bizet's heroine, while differing in many essentials from Minnie Hauk's, was distinguished by all the attributes of voluptuous charm, subtle power, and dramatic intensity that the character demands.

I owe to Pauline Lucca, or Baroness Wallhoffen, as she then was in private life, a recollection of one

[1] Pauline Lucca studied the rôle of *Selika* under Meyerbeer, and sang it on the first production of "L'Africaine" in England in 1865, two years after her first appearance at Covent Garden.

of the most enjoyable evenings I have ever spent. During the summer of 1884 she graciously expressed a wish to give a dinner in my honor. In mid-season, however, the hard-worked critic has little time to spare, so it was first arranged that the dinner should come off on a Sunday. Afterward it was found necessary to postpone the date until the following Wednesday. Unfortunately, a performance of "Tristan" was announced for that day, and, as I felt in duty bound to attend it, I wrote the baroness a letter expressing my regret that I should be compelled either to ask for a further postponement, or else deny myself the pleasure of coming to her dinner. In reply I received the following characteristic note:

[Translated from the German.]

June 25, 1884.

I beg you, worthy friend, not to be angry—it is impossible for me to choose another day. You can go on, anyhow, to the opera for two hours afterward. You know "Tristan und Isolde" is long; thus you will not be neglecting your duty, for which I should never forgive myself were I the cause. We will sit down punctually to table. With hearty greetings from house to house,

Yours truly,

PAULINE WALLHOFFEN.

It was impossible to resist so polite and persuasive an invitation. I went to the dinner, and made up my mind not to miss the last act of "Tristan." But I had not exactly reckoned upon the nature of the attractions from which I should have to tear myself away. In point of fact, it was a remarkable gathering. Beside the prima donna and her husband, the party comprised Mme. Marcella Sembrich and Herr Stengel (to whom then she had not been long married), Signor and Mme. Bevignani, M. Mierzwinsky, M. Edouard de Reszke, and others. The meal was extremely merry, and it lasted a couple of hours. When we had joined the ladies I made signs indicative of an early departure; but my hostess simply laughed and said: "Now we have got you here, we mean to keep you. No 'Tristan' to-night! I have requested a fair young violinist to play expressly for you, and the Chevalier Emil Bach[1] has been good enough to come round for the purpose of accompanying her."

This rather chilled me. To listen to "fair young violinists" was no particular novelty, and I began to feel that I should prefer "Tristan." But I could say nothing, and waited with as much grace as I could command. In due time the "young violinist" was announced. The door opened, and, who should enter, fiddle in hand, with a solemn bow, but Mme. Sembrich, laughing mischievously

[1] Then quite a newcomer in London. He settled down there as a pianist and teacher, and composed the operas "Irmengarda" and "The Lady of Longford," both of which Sir Augustus Harris mounted at Covent Garden. Mr. Bach died quite suddenly in 1902.

Copyright by A. Dupont, N. Y.

MARCELLA SEMBRICH

and ready to begin her solo. I then remembered that the vivacious little Galician lady, who had been delighting London for the past four seasons, was an accomplished violinist as well as a brilliant singer. She played us piece after piece, and under the spell of her art I fear duty was too quickly forgotten. My hostess was right. There was no "Tristan" for me that night.

In this year (1884) I made the acquaintance of Antonin Dvořák, who came to London for the purpose of conducting a performance of his "Stabat Mater." The work had made a great sensation when given in the previous year by the London Musical Society under Barnby. It was again performed at the Worcester Festival of 1884, under the composer's direction; and he came over yet a third time to conduct his cantata "The Spectre's Bride," which he wrote expressly for the Birmingham Festival of 1885. During this last visit, Dvořák came to my house in London with the object of giving me some particulars of his early life, which duly appeared in the "Sunday Times." His name at that period was scarcely to be found in a single musical dictionary, and though the omission has since been rectified, the dates and details are so often incorrect that it may be worth while for me to give here the story of Dvořák's romantic career, told as nearly as possible in his own words:

"I was born in 1841 at Mühlhausen (in Bohemian, Nelahozeves), about four miles from Kralup. My parents were poor. My father was a butcher and intended me for his trade. At the age of thirteen I was taking lessons in singing and the violin from our village schoolmaster, Josef Spitz, and sang in the choir on Sundays. At fourteen, perceiving that I had musical talent, my father sent me to live with my uncle at a place called Zlonic (near Schau), where I was taken in hand by the organist, Anton Liehmann, and in 1856 I began to study the piano.

"In Bohemia every child must learn music and, if possible, sing in church. I think this law explains the development of so much natural talent for music in my country. It is not only the gipsies and their music that are the responsible factors. There are the beautiful national 'chorales,' which the people so dearly love. They sing them as they work in the fields, and the spirit of music enters their souls. Of course they love to dance—are they not Slavs? Why, after church they revel in music and dancing, sometimes until early morning! In fact, it is the favorite amusement of the race. Admission to these dance-meetings is always free, but a collection is made afterward for the musicians. I used to be among the fiddlers and received my share, which I always gave to my father.

"When my father came to live at Zlonic in 1856–1857, he taught me his trade, and I learned how to buy sheep and kill them. But I liked my musical studies better, especially now that I could begin to read a little and dip into the scores of such masses as Haydn's in D minor, Mozart's in C major, and Cherubini's in D minor. The feeling developed; I wanted to try to write something; but the different keys for the clarinets, the bass trumpet, the horns, and the trombone worried me greatly. Still, I was too proud to ask for these to be explained. At last I managed to write a polka, and showed it to my teacher. He found only one mistake—in the trumpet part, which should have been in F major. I carried my piece home in triumph, and it was tried by the band. But, alas! the whole thing to my ears sounded totally wrong.

"Then I began to work at counterpoint and the organ, teaching myself most of the time. I got hold of a big book on counterpoint, full of 'figured bass,' the meaning of which was not explained; but as soon as I understood I used to read whole masses from the 'figured bass.' At last some of my father's friends, believing that I possessed real talent, persuaded him to send me to Prague. I stayed with some relations, and was allowed eight gulden (about 13s.) per month during part of the two years (1857 to 1859) that I spent in the capital. I entered a college which still exists for the instruction of organists and musical directors, and became a pupil of Josef Pitsch. On his death I studied under his successor, a very clever musician named Krejci, who was choirmaster at a large church and took me there to sing with his best pupils.

"My studies now ended. Of instrumentation, it is true, I understood very little. As for Mozart and Beethoven, I only just knew they had existed.

But I had to earn a living somehow. And how was it to be done? Well, I thought, I can play the violin decently, I must try to get a place in a band. So I went to a Kapellmeister, who had a band of eighteen or twenty, and asked him whether he would take me. He engaged me to play the viola at twenty-two gulden (£1. 15s.) a month, and I was delighted. I also joined a sextet that used to perform regularly at a lunatic asylum, and there I was engaged to play the organ for the Sunday services. We used to play at various cafés, giving potpourris and overtures of every description; and I remember that the overture to "Maritana" was frequently in our programme. This was in 1860.

"One Sunday I went to hear 'Der Freischütz' at the German Theatre. The Bohemian National Theatre was not yet in existence. Bohemian artists then had to sing in German, but, as a concession, were allowed to sing an opera in their own language every Sunday afternoon. The 'Freischütz' made an enormous impression on me; but I could not afford the necessary ten kreutzers (1s. 8d.) very often. I used to contrive, however, to hear good concerts occasionally by slipping into the orchestra and hiding behind the drums. In this way I saw Spohr in 1859, when he conducted a grand concert to celebrate the fiftieth anniversary of the Prague Conservatoire; and then it was that I heard Beethoven's 'choral' symphony for the first time.

"In 1861 I wrote my first two serious compositions, the string quintet in G and the quartet in A minor. I persuaded some friends to play the quintet, and they were rather pleased with it. It reminded them of Haydn, Mozart, and early Beethoven. Thereupon I showed it to my teacher, Krejci, and was very proud when he expressed himself contented. Next year the new National Theatre was built, and I was engaged to play in the orchestra. The first operas given were Bellini's 'Capuletti ed i Montecchi' and 'Norma,' Rossini's 'Otello,' and Cherubini's 'Water-Carrier.' In 1863 I went to Hamburg to play in the band at the exhibition. At home in Prague we all lived in the same house, and my companions used to laugh at me for working so hard at composing—one especially who is now a Kapellmeister and conducts my operas. But I persevered, and had the good fortune to make the acquaintance of a valuable musical friend in Karl Bendl, who used to lend me his scores. Among other works, I studied the quartets of Onslow and Beethoven's septet, and so gradually developed fresh ideas.

"Most of my compositions of that epoch are long since torn up or burned; and I wrote quantities of stuff after I had thrown up my theatre engagement and taken to teaching in order to have more time to compose. I had now (1871) a great ambition to write an opera. I found a libretto entitled 'König und Köhler' (King and Collier) and set to work upon it. In due time I submitted the score to the manager of the National Theatre, who ordered it to be tried at rehearsal. I confess it was very Wagnerian. I had heard 'Die Meistersinger,' and the new influence was very strong upon me. My music was horribly difficult. At the piano rehearsals the singers could make little of it; with the chorus it was still worse—infinitely more difficult, they said, than Wagner. Ultimately everybody laughed at me, and my opera was refused.[1] Four years later I completely rewrote the score, more in the national style, and made it easy to sing and play. It was then produced with great success, and helped my reputation materially.

"In 1874 I was appointed organist of St. Adalbert's Church, at the enormous salary of one hundred and sixty gulden (£13) per annum, for which I had to get up at half-past five o'clock every morning. The payment worked out at about two kreutzers (eight cents) per mass. Meanwhile, too, I had indulged in the luxury of taking to myself a wife, a very musical Prague lady, who for many years sang contralto in one of the churches.

"At last, in 1875, I was granted the 'artist' stipend of four hundred gulden (for one year only) from the Kultusministerium at Vienna. To obtain this I had sent in as 'exercises' my opera and my symphony in F, Op. 25. The second year I sent in my 'Stabat Mater' and my grand opera

[1] Dvořák was not ashamed to acknowledge that he was at this time very much influenced in his harmony and instrumentation by Wagner. He saw him conduct, and used to follow the master as he walked the streets of Prague. He admired him immensely.

'Wanda,' which was played a few months later with immense success. Yet from these works no stipend resulted [!]. I tried again by adding my pianoforte concerto, the piano variations in A flat, and the string quartet in D minor, and this time was favored with an allowance of five hundred gulden. Next year, through the influence of Johannes Brahms, Edward Hanslick, and Herbeck, the sum was raised to six hundred gulden.

"I now wrote to Brahms and asked him if he would kindly use his influence with some publishers to bring out my compositions. He replied that he would be happy to do so, and a little later on I received a satisfactory communication from Simrock, of Berlin, who afterward told me I was the first person on whose behalf Brahms had yet interested himself. Simrock paid me nothing for my 'Marischen' duets, but he asked me to compose the 'Slavische Tänze,' and gave me three hundred marks (£15) for them. That was the first money I ever received for a composition."

And here Dvořák's narrative ceased. I need add naught to it concerning the years that came after, for their history is as an "open book" both to the Old and to the New World, where the gifted Bohemian has been a leading light and a familiar figure. One of the most original and remarkable creative musicians of our era, he is also one of those whom success has not spoiled. But if the pen of this great and modest genius be less active, less prolific, than of yore, it is only necessary to glance at the story of those strenuous early days to understand why Antonin Dvořák is a little tired, and not unwilling to continue the *otium cum dignitate,* or at least to work lightly and at his ease, during the remaining years of his existence.

Another famous contemporary composer whom I am proud to count among my best friends is Camille Saint-Saëns. I was introduced to him by Signor Garcia, whom he used to visit at Bentinck Street whenever he came to London. At that period he was regarded by English amateurs (ignorant as yet of the very existence of César Franck and his disciples) as the leader of the advanced French school. Orthodox musicians considered him eccentric; more modern thinkers admired his mixture of Teutonic severity with the ultra-saccharine melodiousness of Gounod. Both parties agreed to recognize in the then organist of the Paris Madeleine (a post held by Saint-Saëns from 1858 until 1877) a musician of prodigious talent, endowed with a versatility that enabled him to shine in every branch of his art, and possessed of a mastery of technique that could adapt itself to whatsoever style he might for the moment choose to exploit. He was as brilliant a pianist as he was an organist,—his habit of playing the one instrument never spoiled his exquisite touch for the other,—and his gift of improvisation was marvelous.

Saint-Saëns made his début in London, in 1871, at the Musical Union; but I did not hear him until 1879, when he played his own pianoforte concerto

SAINT-SAËNS

From a photograph by Elliott & Fry, London

DVORÁK

From a photograph by Sarony, N. Y.

in G minor at the Philharmonic. He was then anxiously canvassing the chances of mounting his new opera, "Samson et Dalila," which had been produced at Weimar in 1877, under the auspices of his friend Franz Liszt, but had not yet been granted a hearing in the composer's own country.[1] He quickly learned, however, that our puritanical laws precluded all likelihood of his biblical opera finding its way to the English stage. During the next few years we became very close friends. I always called upon him when I went to Paris, and he rarely missed coming to see me when he was in London.

One of these visits happened at a very sad moment. I was out when M. Saint-Saëns called at Bentinck Street, and he found the members of my family in a state of terrible agitation. One of my younger brothers had been playing with a pistol and had accidentally shot himself through the head. He had expired only a few minutes before. The youngest boy, Manuel,[2] who had witnessed the

[1] "Samson et Dalila" was not actually heard in France until 1890, when it was brought out at Rouen with the late Elena Sanz as *Dalila.* This clever artist also took part in the first concert representation of the work in England during the Promenade Concert season at Covent Garden in 1893. "Samson" has never yet been performed upon the stage in England.

[2] Some ten years later Manuel went to reside in New York, where our brothers Alfred and Charles had already earned prominent positions—the first as an actor, the second as a dramatist. Deciding to adopt a musical career, Manuel seriously took up the study of composition, and in due time published several songs and pianoforte pieces which met with favor. His first substantial

mishap, endeavored to explain what had occurred to M. Saint-Saëns. He caught the words "mon frère" and "mort," and immediately jumped to the conclusion that it was I who was dead. He burst into tears, and was so much affected that some time elapsed before he could be made to understand that I was not the victim. Later in the day we met, and the warm-hearted Frenchman gave me an embrace that showed plainly his gladness at once more seeing me in the flesh.

Finding that England was a much likelier ground for oratorio than opera, he arranged through Messrs. Novello for the performance of his attractive setting of Psalm xix, "The Heavens declare," which was duly performed (and very badly into the bargain) by the Sacred Harmonic Society at St. James's Hall in 1885. Two years later a much better rendering of the psalm was given at the Norwich Festival under Mr. Randegger. Meanwhile Saint-Saëns had expressed to me his desire to write an oratorio upon the subject of Moses, and asked me whether I would furnish him with the necessary biblical text. I readily consented, and, after arranging the plan with him, set to work upon my task. In a few weeks I sent the text to Paris. He was not entirely satisfied, and returned it for alterations. These evidently answered the purpose,

success, however, was the musical piece "Mr. Pickwick," which he wrote in collaboration with Charles and conducted during its run at the Herald Square Theatre, New York, in the winter of 1903.

for, toward the end of 1886, he wrote me: "I find that now it is all right. The monotony which made me uneasy exists no longer." After this I heard nothing until he came to London in the following June. He then gave some recitals, and accomplished his memorable feat of performing his own four pianoforte concertos at one sitting,[1] which, as it took place on the anniversary of Waterloo, was generally supposed to be intended as a revenge for the defeat of the French in that immortal battle. During the holidays I called upon the wayward master when passing through Paris, but he was out of town. Still without news of "Moses," I wrote him a long account of the success of his psalm at Norwich, and that I was hoping to arrange for the production of the new oratorio there. I received in reply the following letter:

[Translated from the French.]

PARIS, October 18, 1887.

MY DEAR FRIEND:

Nothing could be more agreeable than the news you give me of my Psalm. I cannot console myself for not having gone to hear it; I was detained in Paris by some business at the opera. When you were in Paris I was compelled to leave hurriedly for Boulogne. I sent you a telegram from Creil asking you to come and dine with me the following day; but, whether through a mistake in the address, or some other cause, the telegram never reached you.

[1] St. James's Hall, June 18, 1887; Mr. W. Ganz, conductor.

Should the oratorio be arranged for Norwich, I shall be very glad. I shall, as you say, have all the necessary time for devoting myself entirely to it, which seems to me indispensable for a work of this magnitude. You will undertake to negotiate with a publisher; I should very much like Novello. . . . "Moïse" will probably be my last work. It must worthily crown my career!

Your faithful and affectionate,

C. SAINT-SAËNS.

But the Fates were not kind to "Moïse." The Norwich authorities were unwilling to pledge themselves so long beforehand to accept a work of unknown proportions. I then opened negotiations with the Leeds committee; but difficulties were also raised in that direction, and in the midst of the delay it came to the ears of Saint-Saëns that Anton Rubinstein was just completing a biblical opera in eight tableaux, entitled "Moses," which would shortly be produced at St. Petersburg or Moscow.[1] This was enough for the French composer. He at once relinquished all idea of writing an oratorio upon the subject. I asked him to return my text, and after a few weeks it came back accompanied by the following brief epistle:

Voici "Moïse," et avec lui mes meilleures amitiés.

C. SAINT-SAËNS.

[1] As a matter of fact, Rubinstein had been engaged for nearly twenty years upon this big work, which, however, was not produced until 1894. It was then mounted at Riga with a company of no fewer than four hundred performers, and upon a scale of the utmost scenic grandeur.

CHAPTER IX

Franz Liszt—His last visit to London—A marvelous survival of a glorious past—Rubinstein's farewell to England: his "historical recitals"—An operatic débâcle—Lago to the rescue—Growth of the Wagner Cult—Hans Richter and Arthur Sullivan—England's greatest musician: his ideas, habits, and attributes—"The Golden Legend" at Leeds Festival—Georg Henschel.

THERE was, for musical dwellers in London, something almost providential in the visit paid by Franz Liszt during the spring of 1886. He had not stood upon British soil for forty-five years. There seemed to be but the remotest likelihood that, at the age of seventy-five, he would ever trouble himself again to travel over land and sea to a country whose attitude toward him and his works had invariably been chilly and unsympathetic. But the persuasions of his pupil and protagonist, Walter Bache, who worked so long and lovingly to obtain recognition and appreciation for his master's works, at last proved effectual. On the evening of April 3 he arrived. On the morning of the 20th he departed. Three months later—on the night of July 31—he died at Bayreuth of pneumonia, resulting from a bronchial cold, which he aggravated by attending one of the first performances of

"Tristan und Isolde," given at his old friend Richard Wagner's Bühnenfestspielhaus.

I was one of a party of guests invited to meet the Abbé Liszt on the night of Saturday, April 3, at Westwood House, Sydenham, where he was to be the guest of Mr. Henry Littleton (then head of the firm of Novello & Co.) during his stay in England. I went early, and was just in time to see him welcomed by his host after a fatiguing journey from Paris. He had been met at Dover by Mr. Alfred Littleton, the eldest son and present head of the house, who gave me an interesting account of the trip. There could be no doubt that Liszt was extremely dubious concerning our real feelings toward him. In fact, the position was very much akin to that in which Wagner had stood nine years before, only with this important difference: that Wagner came "professionally," for the purpose of extracting British gold from British pockets, whereas Liszt was here, purely in a private capacity, to attend some performances of his works. He was simply nervous, therefore, lest, being no longer a public artist, he should be shining in the reflected light of his past glories as a virtuoso in an atmosphere that was uncongenial to him as a creative musician.

An hour after his arrival he entered the vast oak-paneled apartment which had just been added as a music-room to Westwood House. It was crowded with all the musical notabilities then in London, every one of them anxious to gaze upon the visage of the man who was then perhaps the most interesting musical figure in the world. Dressed in his semi-priestly garb, the venerable abbé walked slowly down the steps leading to the floor of the room, and smiled graciously upon the groups that saluted him as he passed. He looked somewhat tired, and it was remarked by those who knew him that he had aged considerably during the last few years. But his still bright eye, his still brilliant powers of conversation, his still industrious habits, all precluded the smallest suspicion that the end was so near. His attention that evening was largely monopolized by old friends; still, many new ones were brought to his notice, and I had the pleasure of being introduced with a kind word or two by the loyal and indefatigable Walter Bache, who, with others, took part in a programme of his compositions.

Liszt himself did not then play, though, when spending subsequent evenings at home in the Littleton family circle, he almost always went to the piano of his own accord and enchanted them with some piece or improvisation of his own. Once he surprised them by extemporizing marvelously upon themes from his oratorio "St. Elizabeth," performances of which he attended both at St. James's Hall and the Crystal Palace. The welcome he received everywhere exceeded in warmth and spontaneity the expectations of his most fanatical admirers. Still more did the scenes enacted during his stay astonish this most petted and fêted of septuagenarians, with whom—anywhere outside "cold, unmusical England"—such outbursts of enthusiasm had been the concomitants of a lifetime.

I first heard him play on April 6, when he went to the Royal Academy to hand over to the committee of management the sum of £1100, raised through the efforts of Walter Bache for the foundation of a "Liszt scholarship" at that institution. The shout of joy uttered by the students when he sat down at the piano was something to remember. It was followed by an intense silence. Then the aged but still nimble fingers ran lightly over the keys, and I was listening for the first time in my life to Franz Liszt. To attempt to describe his playing, after the many well-known Weimar pupils and distinguished writers who have tried to accomplish that task, would be mere presumption on my part. Even at seventy-five, Liszt was a pianist whose powers lay beyond the pale to which sober language or calm criticism could reach or be applied. Enough that his greatest charm seemed to me to lie in a perfectly divine touch, and in a tone more remarkable for its exquisitely musical quality than for its volume or dynamic force, aided by a technique still incomparably brilliant and superb.

Two days later Liszt proceeded to Windsor Castle, where he was received with the utmost cordiality by Queen Victoria. He played several pieces to Her Majesty, who told him that she cherished a

From a photograph by Elliott & Fry, London

LISZT

vivid recollection of his playing when he last visited London in 1841. On his return to town in the evening, he attended a reception given in his honor at the Grosvenor Gallery by Walter Bache. This was in some respects the most striking function of the series. The gathering was in every sense a representative one, and the famous abbé, as he went round chatting from group to group, seemed positively radiant with happiness. To repeat his own words, addressed to myself: "You have so overwhelmed me with kindness in this country that I shall be quite sorry when the time comes for me to leave you." The programme comprised his "Angelus" for strings, a chorus for female voices, a pianoforte piece, and some songs; and finally, amid a scene of great excitement, he himself played the finale of Schubert's "Divertissement à la Hongroise" and his own Hungarian rhapsody in A minor. This glorious treat furnished the crowning feature of a memorable evening—doubly memorable because it was the last time but one that Franz Liszt touched his instrument in the presence of a public or quasi-public assemblage.

It was a very strange coincidence that the season which witnessed Liszt's final adieu to England should have likewise been the occasion of Anton Rubinstein's last visit. The one left in April; the other came in May. Within a period of six weeks we heard and saw, for the last time, the two greatest pianists that the world had then known. The leonine Russian gave at St. James's Hall that wonderful series of "Historical Recitals" which has since become historical in every sense—that marvelously comprehensive cycle wherein he illustrated the progress and development of pianoforte music from its earliest epoch down to the penultimate decade of the nineteenth century. It was, alike mentally and physically, an extraordinary *tour de force.* No one save Rubinstein would have attempted the Herculean feat involved in the execution of such programmes. What must the task have been for the executant, if the bare labor of listening was an exhausting process? But Rubinstein was a giant, and the considerations that applied to ordinary pianists did not arise in his case. These recitals yielded the largest sum ever taken at St. James's Hall for a series of seven concerts, the gross receipts amounting to £6000 ($30,000). An extra recital was given, and out of the proceeds Rubinstein divided £300 ($1500) among various charitable institutions.

The fortunes of Italian opera were now at their lowest ebb. The season of 1885 had been almost wholly barren, and that of 1886 was little better. Incapacity and indifference reached their climax with the disgraceful and humiliating scene that occurred at Her Majesty's Theatre on the night of March 6, 1886. Some unknown person, evidently without experience as a manager, had there started a season of Italian opera with a company of incompetent artists. On the fourth night it completely collapsed under circumstances unprecedented in the annals of opera in a great city. I quote my own description[1] of what occurred.

The second act of "Faust" had concluded when the orchestra refused to proceed further unless their salaries were instantly paid. Their claims were partly satisfied, and, after an interval of inordinate length, in the course of which the audience displayed the noisiest impatience, the opera proceeded for another act, with the accompaniment of about half the band. But the crisis had only been deferred. After the curtain had fallen again there was another long "wait," and the disturbances recommenced. At length, in response to deafening calls, the stage-manager came forward and announced that it was impossible to proceed. The stage-carpenters had refused to set the next scene, and the opera could not, therefore, go on. A howl of derision and anger greeted this statement; but the audience, having made up its mind to the worst, was preparing, amid a fearful din, to depart, when the curtain rose once more and a whole army of stage assistants came down to the footlights with outstretched arms and aprons, as though to implore the charity of the house. The gestures were understood, and, with one accord, the remaining occupants of the gallery and upper tiers began flinging a shower of coppers and small silver coins down on to the stage, uttering the while all sorts of satirical and uncomplimentary epithets. However, the occupation was too expensive to last long, and in a minute or two this disgraceful episode came to a termination, ending also a night of horrors that will never be forgotten by those who witnessed it.

[1] "Musical Notes," by Hermann Klein, London, 1886.

After this Her Majesty's remained closed for over a year. Mapleson was too much in debt to dare start upon any fresh speculation; and, indeed, so sore was his plight that his old friend Mme. Patti felt constrained to come forward later in the year and appear in a performance of "Il Barbiere" at Drury Lane for the benefit of the unlucky impresario. Meanwhile Covent Garden was tenantless, and it seemed in the highest degree probable that we should experience the novelty of a London season completely without Italian opera.

The man who prevented that calamity (if calamity it may be termed) was Signor Lago, formerly *régisseur* at Covent Garden under the management of the Gyes, father and son. With the support of the tenor Gayarre and some financial backing, the new impresario contrived to form a capital troupe and to give a short but respectable season of opera. Although he brought out no novelties, he introduced several new artists worth hearing—among them Ella Russell, Giulia Valda, and Francesco D'Andrade, all of whom made their mark. The company also included artists like Albani, Scalchi, Cepeda, Gayarre, Pandolfini, and Maurel, with Bevignani as the conductor. Of course, a solitary undertaking such as this could not suffice to retrieve the fortunes of Italian opera. It served, however, to prove that the genus, if moribund in Great Britain, was not yet utterly extinct, and its repetition in the following year helped still further to reawaken public interest

CAMPANINI

Copyright, 1900, by A. Dupont, N. Y.

JAMES H. MAPLESON

From a photograph by Hall, N. Y.

and engender the confidence which ultimately made possible the real revival. In his way, therefore, Signor Lago did palpable service to the cause of opera in London; but he had neither the Napoleonic spirit nor the administrative ability and courage for carrying his mission through to the true goal.

It is worth pausing for a moment to note how quickly the popularity of Wagner was rising at this period. Only the distant onlooker could perceive how large a place the master was beginning to fill in the hearts of English music-lovers. Failing the opportunity for hearing his complete works upon the stage, they had perforce to be content to hear them, either whole or in part, upon the concert platform. The demand for this kind of thing became remarkable, and it was satisfied by the most conservative as well as the most advanced musical institutions. Imagine two concert performances of "Parsifal" (with very few cuts, moreover) being given in London only a couple of years after the first production of that glorious music-drama at Bayreuth! Yet this was actually done in the autumn of 1884 by the Royal Choral Society, under Joseph Barnby, with Thérèse Malten (the original *Kundry*), Gudehus, and Scaria in the principal parts. And really the exacting work was very creditably interpreted. By the way, Malten and Gudehus were again in London in 1886, when they sang at the Richter Concerts in long excerpts from "Tristan" and "Siegfried," supported by Pauline

Cramer and Georg Henschel. I never cared particularly for the tenor—his voice was always hard and metallic; but Malten's noble organ was never in grander condition, and she sang with a degree of dramatic intensity and emotional warmth that was absolutely thrilling.

The success of Hans Richter in England continued to be extraordinary. Indeed, after a time it began to create something of a feeling of jealousy among those purely British musicians who then held, and, perhaps, not unjustly, that their country had too long been the happy hunting-ground of "distinguished foreigners" generally, and of foreign conductors in particular. The feeling, however, did not find expression openly until after the appointment of Richter to succeed the late Sir Michael Costa as conductor of the Birmingham Festival. This proceeding evoked a display of actual resentment. For my own part, I failed to see that it was called for in the case of a man of such commanding genius; so I plainly stated that I approved the appointment and could not sympathize with those who objected to it. My remarks brought me a shoal of deprecatory letters—among them the following one from Sir Arthur Sullivan:

1 Queen's Mansions, Victoria Street, S. W.,
19th May, 1884.

Dear Mr. Klein:

In looking over the "Sunday Times" I am greatly grieved and disappointed to read your comments on Herr Richter's appointment to the conductorship of the Birmingham Musical Festival.

I think all this musical education for the English is vain and idle, as they are not allowed the opportunity of earning their living in their own country. Foreigners are thrust in everywhere, and the press supports this injustice. If we had no men who could do the work I should say nothing—but we have.

Yours very truly,
ARTHUR SULLIVAN.

Now let me say at once that Sir Arthur Sullivan was incapable of entertaining sentiments of mean and petty jealousy. As conductor of the Leeds Festival,—a post which brought all the honor and labor that he sought in this direction,—he did not desire Birmingham for himself. Neither did he refuse to admit the application to his own art of the essentially British principle of "free trade." His motto was simply, "Charity begins at home"; and, if he felt strongly on the subject, it was because he had seen in the course of his career too much of that "thrusting in of foreigners" which was the curse of English musical life during the greater part of the nineteenth century. As principal of the National Training School for Music,[1] he had had practical experience of the difficulty in finding lucrative employment for young native executants. Hence his conviction that if money were spent upon their education, it was only fair

[1] Opened in 1876 with eighty-two free scholarships and carried on until 1882, when it was absorbed by the larger institution now flourishing under the title of the Royal College of Music. Eugen d'Albert was among the pupils trained at the earlier school.

that they should enjoy preference over musicians of foreign birth and training. Happily, he lived long enough to see this patriotic aspiration in a large measure fulfilled.

I did not reply, either by writing or in print, to Sir Arthur Sullivan's letter, but went to see him on the following Sunday, when we threshed the whole matter out to our mutual satisfaction. That was the first of the many Sunday-afternoon chats that I enjoyed in the library of his comfortable apartment in Victoria Street. He was an inveterate cigarette-smoker, and from the moment I entered until the time I left, a cigarette was scarcely ever out of his mouth. He was a bright, interesting talker, full of genuine Irish mother-wit, yet withal earnest, emphatic, and impressive when he wished. He was devotedly attached to a parrot that was also a good talker, and would amuse him by insisting on spelling Polly with only one "l." At the period to which I am referring he was already a sufferer from the painful malady which eventually carried him off; but his hair had not yet turned gray, he still wore the familiar bushy whiskers shown in his early portraits, and he was robust enough to indulge frequently in his favorite pastime, lawn-tennis.

Sullivan was not naturally what one would term a born worker. He turned to labor not so much for love of it as through sheer necessity. The most successful and popular English musician of his day, a great favorite with royalty, the *enfant gâté*

SIR WILLIAM CUSINS

From a photograph by W. & A. H. Fry, Brighton

SIR ARTHUR SULLIVAN

From a photograph by Chancellor, Dublin

of society, the demands upon his time were so excessive that it was a marvel how he managed to get through his long list of public and private engagements. At this period, much, if not the greater part, of his composing was done between midnight and four or five o'clock in the morning.

"I find it impossible," he would tell me, "to settle down to a score during the daytime. I wait till every one is in bed; then I go to my desk, and perhaps finish the instrumentation of a whole number before I finally lay down my pen. The streets are so quiet, the atmosphere is so peaceful, and I have no fear that I am going to be disturbed every few minutes." The rate at which he could "score" was prodigious; and, notably in the case of his comic operas, he would leave certain mechanical details till nearly the last moment, knowing that by dint of an extra spurt he could always finish in time.

On the other hand, there were scores over which he lingered tenderly and long, as over a true "labor of love." One of these was "The Golden Legend." He showed it to me during one of our Sunday chats, and pointed with pride to what he hoped would be some novel effects in the prologue—the wailing "diminished" chords for the violins, the exulting clang of the bells, the blare of the brass instruments, the poignant cry, "Oh, we cannot!" uttered by the disappointed demons, and, lastly, the contrast when the organ comes in and the monks chant their grand hymn in broad unison. Novel, indeed, did these effects prove in the rendering—strokes of pure originality on the part of a composer who had heretofore ventured slightly, if at all, beyond the limits of treatment laid down in the scores of his beloved masters, Schubert and Mendelssohn.[1] My outspoken admiration won for me the promise of a copy of the full score of "The Golden Legend" as soon as it should be published; and in due time that copy arrived, with the composer's autograph upon the title-page.

This beautiful work was written for and brought out at the Leeds Festival of 1886. There can be no doubt that it immensely enhanced the reputation of the composer, whose genius as a writer of comic operas had been brilliantly exemplified eighteen months before by the production of "The Mikado." The laurels yielded by the Savoy operas were of necessity shared by Sir Arthur with his talented collaborator, Mr. W. S. Gilbert. In regard to the Leeds cantata, the composer certainly owed much to Longfellow's lovely poem and to Mr. Joseph Bennett's adroit adaptation thereof; but, this apart, there was no one to divide with him the glory of a supreme triumph, of an artistic achievement that stood "head and shoulders" above all his previous

[1] Seven years later I saw Sir Arthur Sullivan alone in a pit tier box, at Covent Garden, listening to a performance of "Die Meistersinger." After the second act I went to speak to him, and noticed that he had before him a full score of Wagner's work. Presently he pointed to it and remarked: "You see I am taking a lesson. Well, why not? This is not only Wagner's masterpiece, but the greatest comic opera that was ever written."

efforts. The overwhelming success at Leeds was the more remarkable in that it came at the close of the greatest festival ever held there—following new works of such calibre as Dvořák's oratorio "St. Ludmila," A. C. Mackenzie's cantata "The Story of Sayid," and Villiers Stanford's fine choral ballad "The Revenge," not to speak of a phenomenal performance by the Yorkshire chorus of Bach's great Mass in B minor, never before attempted at a provincial festival. The most tremendous ovation of all, though, was that which greeted the composer of "The Golden Legend" when he laid down his baton at the close of the noble choral epilogue. Such ringing British cheers had not been heard in that magnificent hall since Queen Victoria opened it in the "fifties."

It was on such occasions as this that Sullivan's native modesty stood out most conspicuously. Only with difficulty could he be persuaded to return twice to the platform; he complained that the girls of the choir had pelted him with too many nosegays the first time. When he retired to the artists' room I followed him, and heard his words of gratitude to the singers—Albani, Patey, Lloyd, and Frederic King—who had so loyally carried out his ideas. To Mme. Patey he was even apologetic. He said to the gifted contralto: "I am sorry I did not write you something that was worthier of you;[1] but I was in pain the whole time,

[1] Referring to the air "Virgin who lovest," in the last scene but one of the cantata.

and I am bound to say the music exactly illustrates the torments that I suffered.'' He literally told the truth. The number in question is the only one in the cantata that does not faithfully reflect the spirit of the text.

If Sir Arthur Sullivan had a weakness, it was his notable penchant for the turf. He dearly loved to go to the races, and was a regular attendant at the meetings held at Newmarket, Sandown, and elsewhere. He once owned two or three race-horses—a luxury to which his fairly wealthy position quite entitled him. But I believe I am correct in saying that he never succeeded in winning a stake. Nor did I find him particularly successful as a ''tipster,'' though few men had so many intimate friends among the members of the English Jockey Club. The last time I ever saw him was at one of the suburban race-meetings, three months before he died. As we walked away together he remarked sententiously, "I haven't backed a single winner. My luck is out. But never mind; I have seen the winner of next year's Derby, and when the time comes I mean to back him.'' That, alas! he never lived to do. Which, perhaps, explains why Mr. William C. Whitney won the ''blue riband'' of the English turf with Volodyovski, the horse to which Sir Arthur referred.

His name may occur again in these pages, but I shall have no better opportunity for paying a

LILLIAN HENSCHEL

From a photograph by Falk, N. Y.

GEORG HENSCHEL

From a photograph by the London Stereoscopic & Photographic Company, London

tribute to the memory of the musician whose loss the whole world still deplores. Sullivan was a man of singularly sweet and amiable disposition. There was much more impulsive warmth and emotional depth to his Irish nature than one would have judged from his manner, which impressed most people as being cold and reserved. He had uncommon powers of self-repression, and he used them more than he really needed. As a conductor, this was no doubt to his disadvantage; yet if magnetism were lacking, neither sympathy nor control was, and his slightest sign was instantly obeyed. Only those who saw him work at rehearsal could tell how completely he was master of the situation. At the performance he purposely avoided a demonstrative style; hence was his beat often described as "lethargic" by those who studied his manner instead of the effects that he produced.

And, after all, modesty was the true secret of his hatred of display. Success never engendered an overwhelming confidence in self, and to the very last it pleased him to be assured that he had done something worthy of his name and talent. To prove this I cannot do better than reproduce a letter which he wrote me only a year before his death —premising that the opera mentioned was "The Rose of Persia," and that he had a short time previously resigned his position as conductor of the Leeds Festival:

1 Queen's Mansions, Victoria Street, S. W.,
19 November, 1899.

Dear Klein:

O si sic omnes! I am still young enough to be pleased at reading (in real live print, mind you!) a few kind words written in a kindly spirit such as I have just read in the "Sunday Times."[1]

To-day I am just out of prison, having finished the score of the new opera at 3.15 A.M., and I feel strange at having nothing to do except rehearsing. By the way, if you want to know what the music, pure and simple, is like, you will find a full rehearsal of band and voices going on at St. Andrew's Hall [Wells Street, London] on Wednesday next, from 11 A.M. onwards.

About Leeds—I could tell you much, but cannot write it. As H. K. suggests, I hope they won't take a foreigner as my successor. If they do, it will be a terrible disappointment to *someone.*

Ever yours sincerely,
Arthur Sullivan.

The Leeds conductorship was eventually bestowed upon Sir C. Villiers Stanford. There was never, indeed, much danger of the "hated foreigner" being appointed. Probably the only conductor, not an Englishman by birth, who would have stood a chance was Georg Henschel, and he, so far as I am aware, was not among the candidates for the vacant position.

More than a quarter of a century has passed

[1] This refers to a notice of his setting of Rudyard Kipling's poem "The Absent-minded Beggar."

since Mr. Henschel made his début in England, and his wide circle of friends there must long ago have made up their minds to regard him in the light of a British subject. When he first came I saw a good deal of him, and, curiously enough, his late gifted wife, then Miss Lillian Bailey, lived opposite our house in Bentinck Street, where we could hear by the hour her sweet, penetrating tones as she labored steadfastly at those old florid Italian airs, the study of which furnishes the sole true medium for the acquisition of a fine vocal technique. After he had terminated his connection with the Boston Symphony Concerts, Mr. Henschel permanently settled down in London, and there for many years he shared the principal concert work with the eminent and evergreen barytone, Charles Santley. As singer, as composer, as conductor, as accompanist, and as teacher, Henschel long ago demonstrated his remarkable talent and his even more extraordinary versatility. In a word, he has fairly earned the right to be called the "Admirable Crichton" of his art.

In the autumn of 1886, Mr. Henschel started the enterprise known as the London Symphony Concerts, which he carried on with conspicuous skill for several years. Unfortunately, their pecuniary results offered an inadequate return for the care and energy that were bestowed upon the rendering of a singularly eclectic and interesting series of programmes. Truth to tell, Mr. Henschel never figured in the public mind as a great or even a strong conductor. His readings of the classical masterpieces might be conscientious and artistic, but they lacked individuality, force, and warmth. On the other hand, the vocal recitals which he gave with the aid of his accomplished wife never failed to attract, by virtue of the unique interpretative charm with which the two singers invested their delightful selections.

From a photograph by The London Stereoscopic & Photographic Company, Limited

SIR AUGUSTUS HARRIS

CHAPTER X

Augustus Harris and Italian opera—An ambitious scheme—To France and Spain in search of artists—Engaging the De Reszkes—The great tenor's early career—Madrid and Mancinelli—An amateur bull-fight—Seville—Opening of the Drury Lane season—Jean de Reszke's triumph—A barytone's temper.

EARLY in the spring of 1887, I was lunching one day with Augustus Harris at the old Albion Restaurant, opposite Drury Lane Theatre.[1] As a rule, the busy manager allowed himself, at most, twenty minutes for his midday meal (a year or two later he allowed himself no lunch at all); but on this particular day he lingered over his coffee, called for cigars, and proceeded to deliver himself of what was, to me, a wholly unexpected piece of news. Leaning back against the upright wooden partition which separated the tables in the old-fashioned dining-room, and with a bright, familiar gleam in his penetrating eyes, he said:

[1] The resort, in the days before theatrical clubs existed, of all the best-known actors and managers in London. The walls of the smoking-parlor were hung with portraits of Sarah Siddons, John Philip Kemble, Charles Kemble, Edmund Kean, Macready, and other histrionic celebrities of the century. What became of the pictures I cannot say; but the place, if not yet pulled down, has been used for some years as a kind of warehouse.

"Klein, I have made up my mind to do something big."

This was not very astonishing. Augustus Harris was always doing "something big." His pantomime and autumn dramas were the very biggest things of their kind; and in the summer of the previous year he had mounted a new comic opera by Hervé, entitled "Frivoli," which was at once the costliest spectacle and the most dismal failure of his managerial career. This recollection suggested a rather cruel expression of hope on my part that he did not intend going in for more French opéra-bouffe. He smiled and shook his head:

"No; it is to be the real thing this time. What I am going to do is to give a month of Italian opera on a large scale at Drury Lane, at the height of the London season!"

Still smiling, Harris stared hard at me, to judge the effect of his words. I was genuinely surprised, and told him so. Did he not think he had sufficient responsibilities already without launching his ship upon the treacherous waters of Italian opera, which had wrecked one English impresario after another, and profited none?

"I know. But why should I suffer the same fate? Why should not opera pay, provided it be well done? All this talk about Italian opera being 'moribund' is merely because the management of it has been going from bad to worse, because society is no longer interested and the public has lost confidence. Look at what Carl Rosa has done and is doing for English opera! He has won over the public, and makes money in the provinces, if he can't in London. See what Lago did last year at Covent Garden with what I consider a mediocre company and limited resources! Economy helped him out, it is true; but at least he proved that Italian opera was still gasping! He is going to try again this year; this time, however, I mean to show him that 'opera on the cheap' is not what London actually wants. He may get the old fogies and habitués at Covent Garden; I intend to draw the real aristocracy to Drury Lane."

I saw that he was serious, and I realized that his conclusions, to some extent, were just. Grand opera in its noblest form, of whatever school or language, if adequately presented, could not die in England any more than in other countries of equivalent musical calibre. And England, I may say, is now not half so "unmusical" as it is habitually depicted. Without the aid of a state subvention, opera upon a "grand" scale all the year round might be impossible. But not even for three months in the year would society, or, indeed, any section of the public, be willing to purchase guinea stalls and pay high prices all round for performances of only moderate excellence, supported by two or three "stars" and an otherwise second-rate personnel. I agreed that Lago could not go on long under present conditions, and I told my companion that I thought he might stand a chance if he could contrive to get together a strong company.

"There," said Harris, "is where you can be of service to me, if you care to." I replied that in such a good cause I should be only too delighted to assist him in every possible way. "Then," he continued, "come abroad with me at Easter. I have already prepared the ground in several directions. I have even engaged my conductor—a man quite unknown, but said to be very clever—Luigi Mancinelli. He is now conducting at Madrid, and I want you to go there with me to listen to some artists whom he has recommended." I said that I would do so with the utmost pleasure. Then suddenly an idea occurred to me, and I continued:

"I know of a splendid tenor for you—if you can get him. He sang here years ago as a barytone, but is really a tenor, and I heard him last summer at the Paris Opéra in 'Le Cid.' He has a magnificent voice and is a thorough artist."

"You mean Jean de Reszke," broke in Harris. "I have been told about him, but have not quite decided what to do."

"Don't hesitate. He will make a great hit here now; and his brother Edouard, who has already sung at Covent Garden and has the finest bass voice in the world, of course will have to come too."

"I shall see if I can get them both," said the new impresario, and with that we parted.

In less than a fortnight the two brothers were engaged—Jean at £100 ($500) a night, and Edouard at £320 ($1600) a month—salaries which they were then well content to accept.[1] In such fashion did the preparations for the campaign commence, quietly and without fuss. For the moment everything was kept secret. The pantomime had not yet run its course, and there was still a four weeks' Carl Rosa season to be held at Drury Lane during the month of May. Augustus Harris naturally desired, therefore, that the public should not be informed until his plans were more matured. At Easter we started together for Paris, en route for Spain.

Little did I then dream that the mission upon which we were setting out was to have results of far-reaching magnitude; that it was to affect the whole future of opera in England, and also in an appreciable degree the nature and methods of operatic enterprise in the United States. Still less did I imagine that the words which turned the balance in favor of the engagement of Jean de Reszke were also to mark the turning-point in the singular career of that illustrious artist—to lift him from the sluggish waters of the stream of

[1] It has been asserted that M. Jean de Reszke's services were offered in 1886 to Signor Lago at a very moderate salary, and refused. There is good reason to doubt the accuracy of that statement. It is possible, of course, that some musical agent in London or Paris did offer to try to secure the new tenor for Signor Lago; but if so, it was not done at M. de Reszke's instigation. And in any case the "refusal" would not have come so much from the impresario as from Signor Gayarre, who was at the back of the concern, and would assuredly have objected to the engagement of an artist who might prove a formidable rival to himself.

Parisian operatic life; to pave the way for his brilliant rise to fame in the two great English-speaking lands; and to lay the foundation of a friendship that should enable me materially to aid in kindling those Wagnerian aspirations which have borne such precious and universally cherished fruit.

The position of affairs should now be tolerably clear to the reader. I have traced the influence of Carl Rosa upon Augustus Harris through the dark period that followed upon the collapse of the Gye régime. I have demonstrated the mighty power that was wielded by Wagnerian and German opera in the education both of the managers and the music-loving communities for whom they catered. In London, at least, the hour for the operatic renaissance had arrived, and with it the man. In America, no doubt, the time for reaping the new harvest was also near at hand. Mapleson, who had all but reached the end of his tether at home, could no longer send to America Italian companies worthy of attention. The sole European attraction upon whom an American manager could rely with certainty was Mme. Patti—a name to conjure with any time these forty years—a genius whose light gives no sign even now of growing dim. On the other hand, German opera, thanks to the crusade so bravely led by Dr. Leopold Damrosch, had become firmly established in New York, and the love of Wagner had entered even more deeply into the hearts of the people there than in London. Consequently, the time was ripe for a bolder and more extended movement on both sides of the Atlantic. In due course it came.

But to return to our journey. Augustus Harris made the briefest possible stay in Paris. We arrived in the morning and called upon Choudens, the publisher, to arrange for the exclusive English rights, as far as they could be secured, of certain popular French operas. This done, we took breakfast with M. and Mme. Edouard de Reszke and their family, including, of course, Jean, then a lively bachelor of less than forty. Edouard remembered me at once, and reminded me of our last merry meeting at the dinner given by Pauline Lucca.

The elder brother made a great impression both upon Harris and myself. Already an enormous favorite in Paris, Jean de Reszke seemed to be wholly free from affectation or conceit; in a word, a delightful man and a thorough gentleman. His conversation was marked by ease and freedom, and it offered a fascinating combination of humor and intellectuality. He then spoke very little German and still less English, though as a boy he had studied both languages. French and Italian, of course, he spoke fluently; indeed, in the former tongue his accent was so pure and his diction so correct that, had I not known him to be a Pole, I should readily have taken him for a Parisian.

The arrangements between Jean de Reszke and his new impresario were quickly settled. He would make his appearance on the opening night in "Aida," and follow this up as quickly as possible by singing *Lohengrin* (in Italian) for the first time on any stage. He realized that London had known him as a barytone, and he was anxious to make manifest without delay that he was a genuine tenor. I asked him how the mistake had first arisen.

"It is difficult to say," he replied. "We were always a musical family, and accustomed to attend operatic performances whenever there were any going on in Warsaw. My parents were both very musical, and my mother had a fine soprano voice. I remember once, in Warsaw, her singing the duet from 'Semiramide' with Trebelli. When I was only fifteen I began to take lessons from Ciaffei, an old tenor, who was a professor at the Conservatoire at Warsaw. He decided that I was a barytone, and what part do you think he gave me to study first?—*Leporello!* Notwithstanding this, I always had good high notes. When I made my début at the Fenice at Venice, in 1874, in the 'Favorita,' I finished up the *caballetta* with a ringing A natural. The real test, of course, lies in the capacity for sustaining the *tessitura.* A barytone may be able to bring out a B flat or even a B natural, but no example has yet been known of a barytone who was capable of sustaining the tenor *tessitura* through long and heavy rôles. The thing is a rank impossibility."

I inquired how long he had given himself to effect the necessary change of method.

ZÉLIE DE LUSSAN

From a photograph by Reutlinger, Paris

MARIE ENGLE

From a photograph by Moreno, N. Y.

"Two years, of which I spent part in Paris and part in Poland. That was from 1877 to 1879. I made my reappearance at Madrid as *Roberto,* and was immediately hailed as a real *tenore robusto.* I assure you I found it much more easy and comfortable than singing barytone. My voice at the end of the performance felt a great deal less fatigued. But I still had to work very, very hard to feel myself thoroughly equipped at all points. Then there came an offer to appear here at the Italiens, and I sang my first French rôle when I created *John the Baptist* in 'Hérodiade' four years ago."

He expressed his regret that we could not remain to hear him in "Le Prophète," which he considered his most successful opera in Paris. For my own part, I should have liked it above all things; but Augustus Harris—one of the most restless specimens of concentrated nervous energy that ever lived—had fully determined to proceed forthwith to Madrid, and no amount of persuasion could deter him from leaving Paris that same night. We accordingly bade the brothers "au revoir," and looked forward to meeting them again in London early in June. Thirty-six hours later we were safely installed in the Spanish capital.

Our first business was to find Signor Mancinelli. He lived in a house overlooking some public gardens not far from the royal palace, and on the way thither Harris confided to me for the first time that he was not quite sure whether he ought to have engaged the man we were then going to see, or his brother, Marino Mancinelli, who was the conductor at the Lisbon Opera-house, and, according to some people, the more gifted of the two. On this point I was happily able to reassure my friend. I had not seen both brothers; but, when at Bologna in 1879, I had seen Luigi Mancinelli direct at the Teatro Comunale a remarkably fine performance of Gounod's "Faust" (with a Covent Garden soprano, Mlle. Turolla, as *Margherita*), and I had considered him a *chef d'orchestre* of the first order. Harris was able quickly to confirm this opinion for himself by means of a representation of the selfsame work at the Royal Opera-house.

The season in Madrid was fast approaching its termination. The audiences, however, were still tolerably brilliant, and the two infantas, aunts of the present King of Spain, then a baby in arms, were present nearly every evening. Queen Christina, naturally, did not go to the opera; but by a welcome chance I saw her one day at the hotel where we were staying in the Puerta del Sol. The queen-regent, who was attired in deep mourning, came to the hotel for the purpose of visiting some distinguished Russian personage whose name I have now forgotten; and, as Harris and I bowed low when she passed down the stairs, Her Majesty returned our salute with a gracious smile.

Shortly after our arrival we went to pay our respects to the British ambassador, Sir Clare Ford, who received the Drury Lane manager with marked cordiality. He invited us to a déjeuner in honor of some of the opera artists, among the guests being the late Lord Beaconsfield's popular secretary, Lord Rowton, who had not long been raised to the peerage. We met, among others, Gayarre; Battistini, the barytone; Mme. Kupfer-Berger, a well-known dramatic soprano; and Guerrina Fabbri, the contralto,—all of whom were subsequently engaged for London, with the exception of Gayarre, who was, as a matter of course, to be once more the principal tenor of Lago's season at Covent Garden. In addition to these, a new light tenor, De Lucia, was also secured; and altogether, as far as the men were concerned, there was ample reason to be content with the results of our visit. As regards the *prime donne* I was not equally impressed. Neither the two above named, nor two Italian sopranos recommended by Mancinelli (who then had no experience of English audiences), proved to be suited to the London operatic boards.

One of the many attentions bestowed upon us by the ambassador was to send us tickets for a private bull-fight given by the Duchess de Alba in the great bull-ring at Madrid. I could not confess to an overwhelming desire to witness one of these spectacles, but I was naturally curious; while Augustus Harris was positively anxious to see one, in order, as he explained, to note the necessary points for a realistic production of the last act of "Carmen." This particular bull-fight, it seemed, was an extremely select annual affair, to which the

Duchess invited all her friends, and in which the performers, from the matador down to the humblest banderillero, consisted of the *fine fleur* of the youthful aristocracy of Spain. They made a brave show, did these young fellows, in their handsome costumes. The programmes were printed upon yellow satin, and the select assemblage, though not nearly large enough to fill the huge galleries of the Plaza de Toros, comprised some of the most fashionable families in Madrid.

Among the ladies present was that fine artist Mme. Christine Nilsson, who a few months before had become the Countess Casa de Miranda. She confided to me that she did not really care for bull-fights, and had come solely in order to please the Count—a statement fully to be credited from the manner in which she constantly used her fan to shut out the proceedings in the arena from her view. From the standpoint of sport, however, the affair was a dire failure. The bulls refused to show fight, and the amateur matadors were never exposed to any risk from which their agility as runners could not speedily have removed them.

It was not at this absurd function that Augustus Harris obtained the real suggestions for the projected revival of "Carmen." We went subsequently to one of the regular bull-fights at the same amphitheatre, and at this he made plentiful notes for the procession of the Alcade, the picadors on horseback, and the group of banderilleros, for all of whom he ordered real and costly Spanish costumes. He even arranged for an exact copy of the curious hurdle-like contrivance, drawn by three ponies, which is employed in dragging the bodies of the dead horses and bulls out of the arena. Not satisfied with this, we paid a twenty-four hours' visit to Seville in order to obtain touches of the true *couleur locale.* We went to the great cigar and cigarette factory where *Carmen* is supposed to conduct herself with so much impropriety. We obtained photographs of the Giralda Tower; we sketched the entrance to the Plaza de Toros; and we gathered together every authentic detail that it was possible to procure for uniforms, costumes, and scenery. Thus it was that the *mise en scène* of "Carmen," as mounted by Augustus Harris, proved to be by far the most accurate and picturesque that had ever been vouchsafed to Bizet's opera.

I must not dwell longer upon the events of this interesting Spanish trip; nor is it necessary to describe in further detail the preparations for the Drury Lane Italian season. Enough to say that the troupe finally collected by Augustus Harris was the strongest heard in London for several years. The opening representation of "Aida" on June 13, with brand-new costumes and fresh scenery expressly imported from Italy, fairly took critics and opera-goers by surprise. The triumph of Jean de Reszke was instantaneous and complete. Here, at last, was the great tenor for whom the world had been waiting since the death of Giuglini and the retirement of Mario! Edouard de Reszke was unable to leave Paris in time for this performance, but he arrived later in the month, and worthily supported his brother on their débuts in "Lohengrin." On the whole, despite Mme. Kupfer-Berger's vocal shortcomings as *Aida* and *Elsa,* the rendering of both Verdi's and Wagner's operas aroused the admiration of experts; while the inspiring zeal and magnetism of Luigi Mancinelli were readily recognized.

Soon London began to talk. It was a new thing to find a series of operas placed nightly upon the stage with the highest care and efficiency, and distinguished not only by a rare liberality in the mounting, but by the improving touches of a stage-manager courageous enough to sweep away the more absurd anachronisms that disfigure the traditions of Italian opera, and capable of replacing them with artistic and appropriate ideas of his own. Naturally the audiences did not numerically realize Harris's hopes. His losses, especially during the first fortnight of his four weeks' season, amounted to many thousands of pounds. But any comparison between the work that he was doing and the dull representations at Covent Garden, or the still more slipshod performances at Her Majesty's,[1] was all in favor of the new impresario.

[1] Here Mapleson was making one of his expiring efforts. Its only noteworthy features were a revival of "Fidelio" with Lilli Lehmann, now heard for the first time in one of her great parts; and a solitary appearance of Patti in "La Traviata." But the public refused to respond, and, no more capital being available, the ill-starred campaign quickly ended.

The Prince and Princess of Wales, who had at once become ardent admirers of Jean de Reszke, came several times to hear him. By degrees society followed, *more suo,* the royal example; and, just when the brief campaign was reaching its close, people began to perceive that Italian opera, so called, as given at Drury Lane, was a still vital and attractive art-product.

But the successes of the season were not all for the Polish brothers. Among the procession of old and new friends that traversed the scene were some very notable figures. I recall an exceedingly good performance of "Don Giovanni" with Maurel as the *Don,* Minnie Hauk as *Zerlina,* and Lillian Nordica (little more than a débutante, and not yet the favorite that she was to become later) as *Donna Elvira.* I remember the débuts of Marie Engle as *Adalgisa,* of Sigrid Arnoldson as *Rosina,* of Amelia Groll as *Donna Anna,* of De Lucia as *Alfredo,* of Battistini as *Rigoletto,* and of Navarrini as *Ramfis.* Again, there was Del Puente, sympathetic as ever, in his old parts of *Escamillo* and *Germont père;* while the veteran barytone Pandolfini was still fine as *Amonasro,* which rôle he was the first to sing at Milan and Paris. Glancing at these names, American readers will be able to judge for themselves not only of the extraordinary merit of the new ensemble, but of the extent to which it embraced the practically "untried" talent that was to constitute in after years the best part of the brilliant constellation revolving in their own operatic firmament.

The proudest night of the month for Harris was that on which he revived "Les Huguenots" with a splendid cast, and in such fashion as to make old habitués declare that "the son had beaten the father at his own game." Imagine Jean de Reszke at this time as *Raoul!* Always remarkable for its refinement, distinction, and passionate warmth, his impersonation was just then peculiarly imbued with the spirit of the true Meyerbeer school. Alike in a vocal and a histrionic sense, it was supremely great. His "velvety" tones, fresh, clear, and mellow as a bell, were emitted with an unsparing freedom that would thrill the listener not once, but twenty times, in the course of a single scene. There was no "saving up" for the last act then; it was "laissez aller" throughout, with plenty to spare at the finish. And what tenderness, withal, in that famous grand duet of the fourth act! Not Mario himself had phrased the "Tu m'ami, tu m'ami!" (this was still an Italian performance) with a greater wealth of delicious surprise and pent-up adoration. Little wonder that Nordica nearly lost her head through nervousness and emotion. It was the very first time she sang *Valentine;* she had studied the part in less than a week, and for a young, inexperienced artist,—so youthful, so pretty, so winning that she fascinated others beside *Raoul,*—her achievement was in the highest degree creditable. The fifth act, generally suppressed in England, was on this occasion duly given, but the

Copyright by A. Dupont, N. Y.

MAUREL
AS DON GIOVANNI

noise of the firing and the smoke from the gunpowder proved too much even for Augustus Harris. It was subsequently omitted, as usual.

Thanks to the vagaries of one of the artists, this memorable performance came near to not being given at all. The opera was to have begun at eight o'clock, but it was quite a quarter past before Mancinelli took his place in the orchestra. Then another wait ensued. Thinking there must be something amiss, I went behind the scenes to make inquiries. I was informed that there was trouble with the principal barytone, and that if I went to his room I should find Mr. Harris there. I hurried to the dressing-room, and found that a lively dispute was going on between artist and manager. The latter, as usual in an emergency, was calm, self-possessed, and apparently in the best of tempers; the singer was gesticulating wildly and nearly beside himself with rage. I ventured to ask what was the matter.

"Matter!" shouted the indignant barytone. "Do you see this specimen of an English-made costume? Did you ever gaze upon such a disgraceful fit? How am I supposed to play a fastidious gentleman like *Nevers,* and go upon the stage in a doublet that his valet would have declined to put on? Look at this right sleeve! It fits so abominably that I have had to tear it clean away at the shoulder to make it hang decently!"

Looking closely at the garment, I did indeed perceive that it was torn at the seam under the arm;

but otherwise there was nothing wrong with it. A richer and handsomer doublet no reasonable *Comte de Nevers* could have desired to wear, and I told the gentleman what I thought. He flung himself into a chair, and declared that he positively refused to go on the stage in such a costume.

Matters were now becoming rather serious. In the next room I could hear Jean de Reszke and Edouard getting their respective voices into trim by the execution of aërial flights and descents into the depths below. Moreover, I could hear the audience in the distance stamping and clapping their hands with impatience. I turned to Harris, and asked him whether another *Nevers* was available.

"I have sent for Del Puente," he replied, "but I am not sure that we shall be able to find him." Then, struck by a sudden idea, Harris addressed himself once more to the recalcitrant barytone: "Listen, monsieur. Your complaint about this costume is merely a bit of caprice. It fits you perfectly well; and even though you have torn the sleeve, a pin or two will easily put that right. I now ask you to let this performance commence. If you do not, I shall go before the curtain and tell the audience exactly why it is that they are being kept waiting."

I added a word to the effect that I should not fail to give my colleagues of the press a precise and particular account of what had occurred, unless the artist instantly put an end to a situation that was at once ridiculous and offensive to the public. The effect of this double shaft was electrical. A moment later the irate singer had risen and called for pins, and the incident was closed. Less than half a dozen people knew what had happened, for the secret of the delay was not allowed to leak out. The opera began, without comment, half an hour late, and, thanks to the *Comte de Nevers* and the fifth act, it was not over until nearly one o'clock in the morning.

CHAPTER XI

The Operatic Renaissance—Royalty and society interested—A brilliant Covent Garden season—Début of Melba—The famous "French Trio": their life in London—A vocal duel—Bayreuth in the first "Meistersinger" year—A visit to Ems and its consequences.

SIR ARTHUR SULLIVAN once described an English triennial festival as a kind of musical boa-constrictor which so overfed itself during a given week that it required the whole of the intervening three years to go through the operation of digesting the feast. Some such period of rest for the purpose of assimilation would appear to have been needed by the metropolis after the Gargantuan operatic banquet which it enjoyed during the summer of 1887. At any rate, ten consecutive months elapsed before serious opera was again heard there. Even Carl Rosa kept severely in the provinces, contenting himself with a revival of Balfe's opera, "The Puritan's Daughter," and producing, for the first time in English, Meyerbeer's "L'Etoile du Nord" and Halévy's "La Juive." The annual visit to Drury Lane had now become, indeed, a thing of the past.

But in the meantime Augustus Harris was not idle. Quick to perceive the effect that his brilliant

Copyright by A. Dupont, N. Y.

MELBA

AS MARGUERITE

little season had created, and feeling pretty sure that he had frightened all his rivals out of the field, he set about preparing the ground for still more extended operations in the near future. His heavy loss over the initial experiment did not trouble him. "I shall recoup myself," he said, "with the aid of society. I shall work this time upon a totally different plan. Instead of burdening myself with the whole responsibility, I shall have the support of the leaders of fashion and be guaranteed a big subscription before I start." This sounded both wise and promising; but I asked, "Do you expect the leaders of fashion and their following to come to Drury Lane?" "Certainly not," was Harris's reply. "I have every intention, all being well, of taking Covent Garden at the earliest practicable date, and directing the regular season of the 'Royal Italian Opera' there next summer."

The secret of the manager's ambition was out at last. He had only used his own theatre as the stepping-stone. He had wanted to prove that he was equal to the task; and, with such material as he could now command, the rest seemed comparatively easy. However, there was an enormous amount of work yet to be done. He needed all his friends to help him in the good cause; and I, for one, earnestly begged him to consider me always at his disposal. My duties as a critic had not so far proved an obstacle to the exercise of friendly offices, freely (and, of course, gratuitously) vouchsafed; nor had my interest in the enterprise prevented me from writing about every performance with perfect impartiality. Harris knew this as well as I did, and his thanks, both then and always, were expressed with the utmost heartiness.

But for the accomplishment of the next important step, Augustus Harris owed nearly everything to the enthusiasm and influence of Lady de Grey and Lady Charles Beresford. These popular women, veritable pillars of society, had already watched with something more than superficial interest the progress of the Drury Lane experiment. They were devoted lovers of opera, and intense admirers as well as personal friends of the de Reszkes. What more natural than that they should desire to see the personnel of the Harris establishment transferred to its proper home, shining in a worthy atmosphere amid fitting and congenial surroundings? All the impresario stipulated was that a certain number of boxes should be subscribed for. This was enough for the two ladies. With the aid of Mr. Harry V. Higgins, brother-in-law of Lady de Grey, they immediately began the hunt for subscribers, restricting their canvass, of course, to such members of the "smart set" as would be acceptable to themselves and their friends; and this, of course, was only an added inducement to join it. The requisite number of boxes were speedily taken up, and by a certain date the fair canvassers went to Mr. Harris with their list.

Meanwhile the astute manager must have got wind of the success that was attending the search. At any rate, he suddenly discovered that he had been too modest in his demands. It began to occur to him that Covent Garden Theatre and its contents, including piles of well-worn costumes and stacks of shabby, useless scenery, were now getting into an extremely dilapidated condition, and that in all probability it would cost him an outlay of two or three thousand pounds to renovate the opera-house sufficiently for occupation by a high-class troupe and an aristocratic *abonnement*. He was afraid that unless so many more boxes were subscribed for, he would not dare venture to lease the theatre. Lady de Grey and Lady Charles Beresford obligingly saw the reasonableness of the request, and tried again—to such good purpose that within a few hours nearly all of the boxes on the grand and pit tiers were definitely allotted. This time Harris simply beamed with delight. He saw himself the proud impresario of Covent Garden, with the largest subscription known for years; and that, for the moment, may be said to have constituted the summit of his ambitions.

During the extensive preparations which now ensued, London, as I have already hinted, troubled itself little about opera. Music-lovers found ample food for enjoyment in their "Pops," at which Clara Schumann, Joachim, Neruda, Charles Hallé, Fanny Davies (now the most popular English pianist of her sex), and Piatti were the leading lights. They took pleasure in listening to fresh examples of English talent, such as Cowen's fine "Scandinavian" symphony, his oratorio "Ruth," and his cantata "The Sleeping Beauty"; Stanford's "Irish" symphony; Parry's oratorio "Judith"; J. F. Bridge's cantata "Callirhoë"; Stainer's "Crucifixion"; and Hamish MacCunn's overture "The Land of the Mountain and the Flood." The Philharmonic Society gave a most interesting season, with Frederic Cowen (*vice* Sir Arthur Sullivan) as conductor. Mme. Schumann played at the opening concert; and subsequently two famous masters, Edvard Grieg and Peter Iljitsch Tschaikovsky, made their first appearances in England, the former playing his concerto in A minor, while the latter conducted his serenade for strings and the variations from his third orchestral suite. The wonderful boy pianists, Josef Hofmann and Otto Hegner, made their London débuts; and Hans von Bülow, returning after a six years' absence, executed his "Beethoven Cyclus" at what proved to be his last series of performances in an English concert-room. Von Bülow was a great pianist, but a much greater conductor.

On Monday, May 14, Augustus Harris inaugurated his first Covent Garden season.[1] The as-

[1] I may mention that the impresario owed a great deal, during his entire period of operatic management, to the loyal and devoted services of his "right-hand man" and *alter ego,* Mr. Fred G. Latham, who subsequently, for several years, exercised similar functions in America for Mr. Maurice Grau.

pect of the house offered the strongest possible contrast to the records of the preceding ten years. The Prince and Princess of Wales headed one of those brilliant assemblages that were formerly associated only with "Patti nights," and altogether there was abundant evidence that, with the reawakening of an exalted social interest, the fortunes of the "Royal Italian Opera" were once more in the ascendant. The de Reszkes did not appear at the outset. With wise diplomacy, the impresario kept back for a space his strong trump card, and in the interim showed his new subscribers that he possessed alike the ability and the resources for presenting their favorite operas with attractive ensembles and fresh features of stage treatment. In "Lucrezia," the opening opera, the perennial Trebelli filled her old part of *Maffio Orsini;* in "Carmen" the gipsy was impersonated for the first time by Nordica; a successful début was made as *Michaela* by Marguerite Macintyre, a pupil of Manuel Garcia; in "La Traviata" Ella Russell appeared; in "Faust" Albani and Trebelli; in "Don Giovanni" Sigrid Arnoldson, Fürsch-Madi, and D'Andrade.

Then, on the 24th, was given "Lucia di Lammermoor," for the début at Covent Garden of a new light soprano who had been winning laurels at the Brussels Monnaie. This was Mme. Melba. For months we had been reading wonderful accounts of Mme. Marchesi's Australian pupil, and curiosity concerning her vocal powers had been roused to a high pitch. It was not actually her first appearance before a London audience. She had sung two years before, under her own name of Mrs. Nellie Armstrong, at a concert at Prince's Hall (now the Prince's Restaurant in Piccadilly); but, beyond admiring the quality of her voice, I had not been much impressed by her efforts on that occasion. Augustus Harris also heard her in 1886 at the annual dinner of the Royal General Theatrical Fund, at which he presided. She had been introduced by Mr. Wilhelm Ganz, and sang, of course without fee, the "Ave Maria" of Gounod. But it was not until nearly a year later that Harris was preparing his Drury Lane season, and then, naturally, he gave no thought to "Mrs. Armstrong," who was working hard with Marchesi in Paris.[1]

Mme. Melba's initial success at Covent Garden was not wholly unequivocal. The audience, truly,

[1] In the "Daily News" (London) my esteemed colleague Percy Betts recently gave the following amusing account of the narrow escape that Mme. Melba had of being engaged for English opera during her visit to London in 1886: "Mr. Ganz, very naturally, thought a great deal of her voice, and promised to introduce her to Carl Rosa. Mme. Melba at that time was extremely anxious to go upon the operatic stage in this country rather than in Paris, for she was diffident as to her French accent. It was therefore practically arranged that if he approved of her voice Carl Rosa should engage her for five years, on the sort of sliding scale which he at that time adopted; although the terms were very moderate indeed. An appointment was made for a certain day and hour at Mr. Ganz's house, and Carl Rosa scribbled a note on his shirt sleeve. The busy impresario doubtless forgot that, owing to the exigencies of the laundry, unless a note pencilled

went into raptures and gave her an enthusiastic reception. But in the light of calmer judgment the critics took exception to certain "mannerisms" of style; and I, for one, while noting the extraordinary beauty of her timbre and her exceedingly brilliant vocalization, was fain to declare that her singing was "to an extent deficient in that indescribable something which we call charm"; that "her accents lacked the ring of true pathos"; and that, despite admirable intelligence, "the gift of spontaneous feeling had been more or less denied her." As an actress she still had everything to learn. In point of fact, it was not during this season that Melba began to build up the pyramid of her real London triumphs. The raising of that structure commenced only after another twelvemonth of hard study and practical stage experience.

The impatience with which the return of the de Reszkes was awaited can be better imagined than described. It was emphasized by the fact that they were to be accompanied by their friend and confrère Jean Lassalle, and that the "French Trio," as they were subsequently rather inaptly designated, would make their rentrées together in a gorgeous revival of "L'Africaine." That was a great night. The house was literally crammed

on a shirt cuff is transferred the same night to the diary it is apt to be overlooked altogether. In the result the appointment entirely slipped Carl Rosa's memory, and Mme. Melba, after waiting at Harley Street for an hour or two, very naturally got impatient, and declined further to entertain the matter."

from floor to ceiling, and the Prince and Princess of Wales led the applause that greeted the now famous Polish tenor on making his début upon the stage of Covent Garden in the rôle of *Vasco di Gama.* He sang magnificently, while Lassalle's *Nelusko* was, if possible, more fervid, more picturesque than ever. Nordica was less well suited as *Selika* than as *Marguerite* in "Faust," which part she sang with the three distinguished artists later in the season. Altogether, though, it was a remarkable performance, and fairly set the seal upon Jean de Reszke's renown in England, besides adding materially to Augustus Harris's prestige as a *metteur en scène.*

While they were in London at this time, MM. de Reszke and Lassalle stayed at the Continental Hotel in Regent Street, where they occupied adjoining apartments and took their meals together. I frequently used to join them at lunch or dinner, and a cordial welcome always awaited me. Then we would chat over the events of the preceding night's performance, discuss its merits and deficiencies, and point out improvements that might be introduced in the future. It was not less amazing than interesting to see how these three gifted artists would criticize each other's gestures and attitudes. Sometimes they would move away the table and make room to go through some scene with full stage action—going over it again and again until they had it to their common satisfaction. On these occasions I had to play the part of spectator and deliver my verdict upon the general effect.

TAMAGNO
AS OTELLO

Or else we would talk "art"—talk it steadily by the hour. And what a delight that was, with men whose only aim was to reach the highest goal by the noblest path! How we discussed voice-production and breathing! Not a detail of that wonderful subject was left untouched. Now Jean would show us how a tenor should manage his tones so as to form the perfectly equal scale. Now Lassalle would illustrate the marvelous simplicity of the "one and only" method which he designated "la grande ligne." Finally, Edouard would strip to the waist to give us an example of his extraordinary control of the abdominal muscles, whereby, in expanding the ribs and completely filling the lungs, he seemed to raise the lower half of his figure until, like one barrel sliding inside another, it had concealed itself in the vast cavity of his chest.

Once, I remember, our party of four was joined by Tamagno when the celebrated Italian tenor was playing *Otello* at the Lyceum. We all had supper together after the performance and were in the jolliest of moods. Tamagno had a slight cold on the chest, but protested that it made no difference whatever in the singing quality of his head tones. Catarrh in the nose, he said, was fatal, but a chest cold made not the least difference to him. Upon this, Lassalle offered to wager that he could sing higher with his falsetto than Tamagno with his *voce di petto*. The challenge was accepted, and forthwith the two began a vocal duel the like of which I am certain I shall never hear again. Out came Tamagno's A's and B flats, as quickly responded to with the falsetto equivalents from Lassalle's sturdy throat. Then the Italian went "one better"; and the Frenchman, in order, as he said, to help himself up the scale, mounted his chair and emitted the B natural; whereupon Tamagno also stood upon his chair and brought out not only a high C, but a ringing D flat. Lassalle was now for mounting the table, but, this being "ruled out" as an unfair advantage over a less athletic opponent, he proceeded to get the necessary notes from the eminence of his chair, amid terrific applause from the rest of the company. Tamagno now made a bold dash for a D natural, but did not quite succeed; and as Lassalle fared no better, we pronounced the result a "dead heat." Which, at that somewhat advanced hour of the night, was perhaps rather a blessing for the neighboring occupants of the hotel.

One great piece of fun, in which Edouard and I were wont to indulge for the especial amusement of Jean, was an imitation of the later declamatory style of Wagner. At that time neither brother knew by heart two consecutive bars of any more advanced score than that of "Lohengrin." Edouard, however, shared the wonderful imitative faculty of his elder brother, and had a sufficiently good notion of the character of Wagnerian recitative to be able to caricature it with facility. Accordingly, I would improvise upon the piano a "fearful and wonderful" series of *leitmotiven,* varied by strange dissonances and startling modulations, which Edouard for his part would follow from key to key with marvelous alertness, declaiming the while the most unvocal phrases in an impossible guttural language which might as easily have been mistaken for Chinese as for German. The effect of this absurd improvisation *à deux* was certainly very ludicrous, and from no one did it evoke heartier laughter than from the artist who was ere long to portray in ideal fashion the noblest of Wagner's heroes.

Among the remaining features of the opera season of 1888 to which attention may be drawn, was a revival of Verdi's "Un Ballo in Maschera," Jean de Reszke playing *Riccardo* for the first time, with Scalchi, Sigrid Arnoldson, and Lassalle in other parts. "Guillaume Tell" was given for Lassalle and Edouard de Reszke; and the latter also made a notable hit in Boïto's "Mefistofele," in which, by the way, the parts of *Margherita* and *Helen of Troy* were for once separately undertaken by Marguerite Macintyre and Ella Russell. I may further mention the highly favorable début of Zélie de Lussan in her captivating embodiment of *Carmen;* while Nordica essayed for the first time the rôle of *Aida* with entire success. The results of the season of 1888 were, as a whole, artistically and financially satisfactory. Not only was it unattended by loss, but the attitude of Augustus Harris's new clientèle clearly indicated that that all-important factor, the regular subscription, might hereafter be counted upon as permanent. This in itself was an enormous step toward regaining the path of prosperity. In the direction of stage reform, of greater catholicity of taste, of improved working in every branch of the enterprise, there yet remained much to be accomplished.

Above all, there was need to strengthen the repertory. Covent Garden had too long furnished a surfeit of hackneyed Italian operas; of modern works of the best type it offered too few. The genius of Wagner was represented by a paltry two or three of his earlier operas, and there seemed little, if any, prospect of the number being added to in the immediate future. With this thought in my mind, I approached Augustus Harris during the last days of the season and begged him to give the matter of the repertory his serious attention, particularly with the view to mounting, if possible, more of Wagner's works.

"I shall only be too glad to do that," he said. "I don't exactly see yet how I am to cast the later Wagner operas, but that question can be left open for the present. Meantime, I think I should like to go to Bayreuth this summer. Will you come with me?" I replied that I had already arranged to go with some friends early in August.[1]

"That will be too late for me," said Harris. "I must be back early in August to begin the re-

[1] I had then not long been appointed a professor of singing at the Guildhall School of Music, and my various duties kept me in town until the end of July.

ELLA RUSSELL

From a photograph by Alfred Ellis, London

LASSALLE

From a photograph by Benque & Co., Paris

hearsals for the autumn drama. I will take Mancinelli[1] with me, and let him have a lesson in the Wagnerian business as carried on at 'headquarters.' "

Three weeks later I met impresario and conductor together at Bayreuth on the day that they were to take their departure. Both were full of the wonders they had seen and heard. The works given that year were "Parsifal," "Tristan," and "Die Meistersinger"—the Nuremberg opera for the first time at Bayreuth. I asked Harris which of the three he had decided to do at Covent Garden next season.

"Parsifal," was his unblushing reply; "that is, if Frau Cosima will oblige me with the necessary permission. But I am afraid she won't. Seriously, though, I should like to do the 'Meistersinger,' even if I have to give it in Italian and get the text specially translated. If only Jean de Reszke would sing *Walther!* See poor old Gudehus in the part here, and then imagine for yourself what a perfect *Walther* Jean would make!"

I made no comment, but took a mental note of Harris's wish. It occurred to me that there might be a chance before long of helping him to realize his idea.

[1] The Italian conductor had quickly become a favorite, and the admiration of his undoubted gifts had been enhanced by the production at the Norwich Festival, in 1887, of his oratorio "Isaias," wherein originality and fine musicianship were alike conspicuous.

My experience at Bayreuth that summer was wholly delightful, despite the customary heat and the inevitable dust. The representations were of transcendent excellence, the casts incomparable; for example, "Parsifal" with Alvary, Scheidemantel, Wiegand, and Thérèse Malten; "Tristan und Isolde" with Rosa Sucher and Heinrich Vogl; "Die Meistersinger" with Bettaque, Gudehus, Friedrichs, and Reichmann. The conductors in turn were Hermann Levi, Felix Mottl, and Hans Richter. In a word, those were among the "palmy days" of the Bayreuth Festspiel. After leaving the sleepy old Bavarian town, I went for a fortnight to the Austrian Tyrol. Then, instead of returning direct to London viâ Cologne, I left the Rhine steamer at Coblenz and paid a visit of two or three days to Ems.

My reason for going to Ems was simply this: Jean and Edouard de Reszke were staying there, together with Lassalle, and I had a special object in wishing to see them. I was only just in time, for they had all but completed their "cure," and were intending to be off to Poland or Paris in a day or two. At Ems also was Mme. Nordica, accompanied by her mother; and a very pleasant evening we all spent together on the day of my arrival. Next morning I took breakfast with the famous trio at their hotel—a prelude to what was to prove one of the most interesting incidents of my life. It was raining hard, I remember, and we had plenty of time to linger over our coffee and cigars. Naturally, the conversation turned upon Bayreuth, and I had to give a detailed account of what had taken place there. This was precisely what I wanted. I took care, however, to dwell with particular frequency and emphasis upon one of the works that I had heard, and I referred to its beauties so often that at last Lassalle said:

"I wish you would tell us something more about this 'Meistersinger.' Tell us the story!"

I turned to Jean and Edouard: "But, of course, you both know the plot of the 'Meistersinger.' Would it not weary you to listen while I relate it to our friend here?"

"Indeed no," rejoined the elder brother; "we have only the haziest notion of the story, and I should be really glad to hear it properly narrated."

I thereupon proceeded to describe, with all the eloquence at my command, the manner in which *Sir Walther von Stolzing* sets about his wooing of the fair *Eva*, and how, with the aid of the poet-cobbler, *Hans Sachs*, the gallant knight eventually succeeds in overcoming the prejudices of the well-meaning mastersingers and winning the hand of the goldsmith's daughter. I emphasized every point in the comedy; I dwelt upon its rare commingling of humor and poetic sentiment; I enlarged upon the wondrous art of the composer in treating his exquisite pictures of medieval German life; in short, I so brought my listeners under the spell of the story that at last they had wrought themselves up to a pitch of interest bordering upon excitement. A professional Persian story-teller could not have desired a richer reward for his efforts. I lost no time, but quickly set about driving the wedge home:

"If you can find such pleasure in a simple narrative of this plot, imagine what must be the delight of hearing the opera itself! And that you can accomplish by the simple process of going to Bayreuth before the end of next week!"

I said it without seriously hoping that my advice would be acted upon. But the influence of the moment was more powerful than I had imagined. The three artists forthwith declared their intention of setting out for Bayreuth without delay; and, to make good their words, they immediately sent off a telegram requesting that seats should be reserved for the final series of representations. At the same time, Lassalle, who could not read German, wired to Brussels for a French translation of the libretto, which, I believe, reached him in time. Mme. Nordica, who was on the point of leaving Ems, was duly apprised of their determination and invited to accompany them; which she did. On the following day I again breakfasted with the three friends—this time on the summit of the Marlberg. I was quite prepared to hear that they had altered their minds; but, on the contrary, they were more bent than ever on going. In the afternoon I left Ems for England. Later in the month, I received from Mme. Nordica this letter:

BERLIN, August 21, 1888.

DEAR MR. KLEIN:

I thought you would perhaps like to know how we enjoyed our Bayreuth experience. Well, it was truly most sublime!

My mother and I remained in Ems and went along with the "Monsters." And a very jolly journey we had. I was fortunate enough to get tickets for both operas, and after each act we adjourned to the café, hard by, to talk it over. I think Lassalle enjoyed it least of all. But at the last moment all were very *triste,* because, after all their calculations, M. Lassalle received a telegram from France calling him home to his children. So Jean and Edouard were obliged to "trudge" on to Breslau, while their friend fled back to Paris. Your humble servant plodded on to Berlin, and here end the riotous and mirthful scenes with which we are fully acquainted.

I am having splendid success here.

My mother wishes to be kindly remembered, and so does

Yours very sincerely,

LILLIAN NORDICA.

The effect of the visit to Bayreuth was such that Jean de Reszke and Lassalle decided without further hesitation to study "Die Meistersinger" for the following season. Meanwhile, a proposition had for some time been laid before the "trio" by Mapleson for a visit to the United States in the spring of 1889. This was seriously considered, and for a while it seemed highly probable that the famous artists would make their advent in America under the banner of the old impresario of Her Majesty's. As usual, however, the latter was able to command everything but the necessary capital, and so the project came to nothing. The advanced point reached in the negotiations is clearly indicated by the following letter, which I received early in November:

[Translated from the French.]

PARIS, Wednesday.

MY DEAR FRIEND:

At last Lassalle has returned from Lyons, and I am able to give you an answer on the subject of Mapleson. With Lassalle nothing has been signed. Mapleson has verbally settled the clauses of the contract, but no signatures have been exchanged; and it is even very disagreeable, because Lassalle, as a matter of delicacy, will accept no other engagement while Mapleson shows a sign of life. My brother and I have arranged the bases of our contracts, the salary, the repertory, the number of representations, etc.; but we are waiting in vain for the contracts. Mapleson was to have given us certain guarantees that we asked for, and for our part we also, as a matter of delicacy, are waiting until he decides to come and sign these clauses. There you have the truth: as in London, so at Ems, we talked over with Mapleson the whole of the project for America, discussed figures, and separated good friends; but in words only—in writing not so much as a shadow! This is very annoying for us, for we are refusing quite a quantity of business for this "unsigned" America. I hope that Mapleson will end by arranging the entire affair, for just now he is counting a little too much on our patience. My dear friend, I shall be delighted to see you at the première of "Roméo." A place will be reserved for you. Bayreuth was superb! I cherish the memory of it among my most poetic souvenirs. A thousand friendly greetings and a shake of the hand from your devoted

JEAN DE RESZKE.

But not until I saw him in Paris did I learn from Jean de Reszke's own lips the deep and ineffaceable impression that the Bayreuth representations had left upon him. His decision to essay the rôle of *Walther von Stolzing* had, however, been communicated to Augustus Harris without delay, as also the intimation that Lassalle would play *Hans Sachs.* It is not too much to say that the news filled the enthusiastic manager with genuine pleasure. He at once commissioned the late Giannandrea Mazzucato to prepare an Italian translation of the text, and bade Mancinelli mark the "cuts" essential for reducing the score of "Die Meistersinger" to the Covent Garden limits of that period—a task which the worthy conductor performed with characteristic liberality. These were regrettable but indispensable adjuncts of an otherwise welcome experiment, the ultimate success of which was to lead to results infinitely more important and far-reaching than I could have dreamed when I related that simple story of medieval Nuremberg over the breakfast-table at Ems.

CHAPTER XII

Patti and Jean de Reszke in "Roméo et Juliette"—Historical night at the Paris Opéra—Carl Rosa's death—The controlling influence at Covent Garden—Lightning opera production—"Roméo" in French; "Die Meistersinger" in Italian—First gala night—Queen Victoria and Jean de Reszke.

A HAPPY, if fortuitous, circumstance was that which brought upon the same scene, toward the end of 1888, the two most illustrious lyric artists of their time. The rising star of Jean de Reszke had displaced no more familiar planet; it simply filled a vacant foremost position in the constellation of operatic favorites. For some four years Adelina Patti had ceased to appear regularly in opera in London; but in the concert-room and upon the Continental stage she still enchanted vast audiences, and, in every sphere alike, the brilliant orb of the "queen of song" continued to blaze with undimmed splendor. Now, in my opinion, there would have been ample space for these two famous stars to shine in company at Covent Garden without one detracting in the smallest degree from the brightness of the other. Yet, with all his pluck, Augustus Harris never ventured upon this "great emprise." Whether from motives of economy or for some more obscure reason, I cannot say; but,

From a photograph by Benque & Co., Paris

JEAN DE RESZKE

AS ROMÉO

if the former, he had before him the striking example of the "coalition season" of 1879, when Gye and Mapleson united their wonderful array of forces at Covent Garden and made between them a net profit of £24,000 ($120,000).

Strangely enough, it was Paris that was to do the trick. That highly favored institution, the Académie Nationale de Musique, was to have the honor of including in its bill, "for a few nights only," the distinguished names of Adelina Patti and Jean de Reszke. They were no strangers. They had known each other in the earlier days when the tenor was singing as a barytone, and the diva had given much friendly advice and encouragement to the young Pole, whom she was wont to address by his *petit nom* of "Giovannini."

The occasion that brought them together again was the first performance at the Grand Opéra of Gounod's "Roméo et Juliette." Curious had been the history of this work in the two capitals. It was first produced at Paris at the Théâtre-Lyrique in 1867, the part of *Juliette* being then sung by Mme. Miolan-Carvalho, the original *Marguerite* of Gounod's "Faust." In 1873, when the Théâtre-Lyrique disappeared, "Roméo et Juliette" was transferred to the boards of the Opéra-Comique, and at about the same time it was given at Covent Garden in Italian, with Mario and Patti in the title rôles. Later on the renowned prima donna (then the Marquise de Caux) appeared in the same version with the handsome French tenor, Ernest

Nicolini, who was subsequently to become her second husband. Notwithstanding these interpretative advantages, neither in Paris nor in London did "Roméo et Juliette" take any real hold upon the affections of the public. "Faust" was by far the most popular opera of the day. "Roméo" seemed to be merely tolerated because it was by the same composer and on account of its Shaksperian subject, rather than for any intrinsic merits of its own. I know not which were the unkinder toward it, the French or the English critics. The latter plainly called it a dull, tedious opera. One of the former complained that the "symphonic element dominated it too much"; that the *duo l'alouette* required "more naïve emotion, fewer heart-rending dissonances and violent cries, more art and more nuances"; finally, that the composer had "preferred to make concessions to the doctrine of the music of the future, while discarding the exigencies of taste and ear, and making of it a realistic drama."[1]

Autres temps, autres mœurs! During the "eighties" a distinct change of attitude began to manifest itself in Paris toward "Roméo et Juliette." I recollect a performance at the Opéra-Comique in 1886, with Talazac and Adèle Isaac, that delighted not only myself but a crowded and demonstrative house. At last Gounod, still hale and hearty, arranged for his work to be transferred

[1] "Dictionnaire Lyrique," by Felix Clément and Pierre Larousse.

from a stage that was too small for it to the opera-house where it ought originally to have seen the light. The directors, MM. Ritt and Gailhard, had the discrimination to foresee a valuable addition to their répertoire, and determined to mount it with a superb *mise en scène* and the finest obtainable cast. Gounod himself undertook to conduct the inaugural performance, and, in compliance with the stupid traditions of the Paris Opéra, he consented to furnish the music for a ballet, without which at that time no work, whatever its source, could obtain admission to this law-ridden stage.

I went to Paris expressly to attend this most interesting première, which took place on November 28, 1888. Seats were not only at a high premium but virtually unobtainable, and I owed the possession of mine to the courtesy of Jean de Reszke. Many a time I have looked upon the heavily gilded and slightly sombre interior of the Paris Opera-house, but never when it contained such an audience, such a gathering of famous men, of elegant, jewel-bedecked women, as appeared there on that memorable night. The *grandes dames* of the French aristocracy were present, displaying a sartorial splendor that recalled the halcyon days of the Second Empire, and what that implied I can only leave my fair readers to guess. On taking the conductor's seat, Gounod was overwhelmed with acclamations. His calm, serene countenance wore an encouraging smile, and no one would have dreamed that the veteran composer was as anxious as though it were the first performance of a brand-new opera.

At the outset, indeed, every one was nervous. Many years had elapsed since Mme. Patti had appeared at the Opéra, and, often as she had enacted *Juliette,* this was the first time she had sung the part in French; in the waltz air—long one of her favorite concert-pieces—she did what was for her the rarest imaginable thing: she made a slip that carried her four bars ahead of the accompaniment ("Elle sautait quatre mesures!" as Gounod subsequently put it). Yet, thanks to her extraordinary presence of mind, the great prima donna regained her place so quickly that probably not twenty persons in the audience noticed the error. Moreover, she sang the whole waltz with such grace and *entrain* that an encore was inevitable, and on the repetition her rendering of it was the most brilliant I have ever heard her give. The youthfulness and charm of her assumption were astounding, while her fine acting in the more tragic scenes indicated a startling advance in histrionic force over her effort in the same opera ten years earlier.

The new *Roméo* proved worthy of his association with this perfect *Juliette.* The mere fact that it was Jean de Reszke may be deemed sufficient guarantee of that to-day; it is not easy, however, to convey an idea of the striking revelation which his impersonation offered as, step by step, scene by scene, it unfolded itself for the first time upon the same plane with Patti's exquisite conception. Every attribute that distinguished the one arose, strong and clear-cut, in the other. Never before, at least in their operatic mold, had the hapless Veronese lovers been so faultlessly matched. Where was "monotony," where was "tedium," now? The interest of that delicious sequence of love-duets acquired a fresh intensity, and became "cumulative" in such a degree that the final scene in the tomb formed a veritable climax of musical as well as dramatic grandeur. The genius of Gounod stood in a new light; and his personal triumph on this occasion was a fitting corollary to that of the great artists who were his chief interpreters. Again and again did they appear before the curtain, hand in hand, an illustrious trio,—to be converted into an illustrious quartet after Edouard de Reszke had invested with his own unique organ notes the grateful phrases of *Frère Laurent.* From first to last, it was a historic performance.[1]

[1] The following is the translation of a letter which Gounod addressed to Jean de Reszke in 1892 (the year of the composer's death), on the day after the tenor's appearance in the one-hundredth performance of "Roméo" at the Paris Opéra:

"MY DEAR JEAN:

"You literally surpassed yourself last night. Perhaps that surprises you? It does me, too. Nevertheless, it is true. Never have you carried to such a height that beauty of diction and gesture, that correctness and expressiveness of accent, that control of voice production—in a word, that perfectly balanced proportion which alone makes the great artist by placing him beyond

It was natural that the tremendous success now reported from Paris should draw the attention of Augustus Harris to Gounod's hitherto neglected opera. He immediately secured such performing rights as were surviving in the work, and arranged to give it at Covent Garden during the season of 1889. Therewith came about a decision which was to lead to one of the most important innovations of the new régime. Why revive "Roméo" in Italian? Why not give it in the original French? The establishment in Bow Street might still bear the courtesy title of "The Royal Italian Opera"; but with two thirds of the active repertory French and German, this was surely a misnomer, or would be so but for the pious superstition that London society never cared for opera unless sung in Italian.

Not only did the de Reszkes prefer to sing in French, but many members of the company were now taken from the Paris and Brussels opera-houses. Among them was Mme. Melba, who was to replace Mme. Patti as *Juliette* in the Covent Garden cast. On the whole, therefore, it was found easier to perform "Roméo" to the original text than to any other; and this happy contingency,

the danger of extremes, the perpetual temptation of the incompetent. Thanks and bravo, again and always! May heaven preserve you and leave us your beautiful art as long as possible! Of such as you we have great need. Remember me to dear Edouard, who, like yourself, has the air of having been born in his rôle, and believe me, both of you,

"Cordially yours,

"CH. GOUNOD."

while it enhanced the London success of the opera, also opened Harris's eyes to the weighty fact that operas sounded best—and were most acceptable to his subscribers—in the language to which they were composed. The full demonstration of this truth was not to come, however, until later on.

Meanwhile, a serious blow was inflicted upon the cause of opera in England through the death of Carl Rosa, which occurred in Paris on April 30, 1889. Failing health had for some time materially restricted the scope of his labors; and, in the opinion of his best friends, he committed a signal error when he converted his enterprise into a limited liability company. On the other hand, he did a good stroke of business when he induced Augustus Harris to unite with him and make it a joint undertaking. Thereby, poor fellow, he lengthened the life of the concern, if powerless to prolong his own. I have shown before how admirably these gifted men worked together, and it was a thousand pities that they were not permitted to "run in double harness" a few years longer. The harm wrought by this premature separation was serious in every way—most of all, perhaps, in that it shifted an excessive load of work and responsibility upon the shoulders of the surviving partner. Augustus Harris now became managing director of the Carl Rosa company, as well as lessee and manager of Drury Lane and impresario of the Royal Italian Opera; and, even in an age of huge trusts and giant administrators, that was too much for a single individual to undertake.

It is apropos to note here the imperceptible but steady growth of an influence which was to exercise an important bearing upon the trend and ultimate development of the Covent Garden enterprise. The subscription for the season of 1889 was larger than ever. The Prince of Wales (now King Edward VII) was taking a deep personal interest in the opera, and he and the Princess were among its most regular attendants. Closely in the royal wake followed an ever-augmenting section of the aristocracy, overflowing by this time from grand- and pit-tier boxes into several rows of stalls. Now, the "interests" of these subscribers had to be studied, and the duty of representing them *vis-à vis* with the manager was fulfilled with much tact by Mr. Harry V. Higgins, the brother-in-law of Lady de Grey. Her ladyship never for an instant relaxed the hold which her initial efforts had given her in the control and working of the organization. At first purely artistic and disinterested; then guided by a general consensus of opinion; finally, dictated by her own individual ideas—the wishes of this indefatigable lady have grown to be the commands—nay, the absolute law—of the most independent opera-house in Europe.

I do not purpose writing the "inside history" of this matter. Indeed, it would scarcely concern my present task to touch upon it at all, save for the purpose of rendering the progress of events

From a photograph by Benque & Co., Paris

EDOUARD DE RESZKE
AS FRÈRE LAURENT

clear to the reader. It is enough, then, to say that Lady de Grey (whose husband, Earl de Grey, had been an habitué of the opera for many years) occupied from the outset a position of extraordinary power and influence. A *persona grata* at Marlborough House, the intimate personal friend of Jean and Edouard de Reszke, the recognized leader of the subscribing body, it would have been strange indeed had this tireless supporter of the enterprise failed to become one of the most potent factors in its internal economy.

During the early days of the renaissance much diplomacy was used by all parties. Mr. Higgins would convey suggestions to Mr. Harris, who would thereupon have a chat with Lady de Grey and promise to do his best to meet her wishes. Needless to add that they seldom passed unheeded. As time went on the *modus operandi* gradually altered. When Harris became overwhelmed with his various duties he was glad to rely upon Mr. Higgins for advice, or even to go to Lady de Grey "for instructions." A new prima donna had to be engaged, a new opera to be commissioned, a Continental success to be mounted, a new box-subscriber to be passed and admitted. Ere any of these things could be done it was essential that Lady de Grey should be consulted. So by degrees her word became law; and law it remains to this day. With the artists at Covent Garden Lady de Grey is very popular. With those who fail to obtain engagements she is naturally the reverse;

and I dare say she is often blamed for refusals for which she is not primarily responsible.

Personally I have always found her the amiable lady that the world supposes her to be, despite the knowledge that a hand of iron is hidden beneath the velvet glove. And she certainly has a devoted second in the present managing director of the Royal Opera Syndicate. The chairman, Earl de Grey, naturally represents his wife's views. The secretary, Mr. Neil Forsyth, has a well-earned reputation for urbanity, energy, and tact. On the whole, the machine works smoothly, and from a practical view-point nothing can be urged against a concern that pays its shareholders a regular and substantial dividend. At the same time much might be said regarding the artistic demerits of a system that depends so largely upon individual fancy, impulse, and even caprice. The best results cannot possibly be obtained where the personal equation is allowed to take precedence of loftier considerations. The most we can hope is that an improved standard of public taste will compel the observance of those higher traditions which lend prestige to the leading subsidized opera-houses, and which Augustus Harris adopted and handed down to his successors in a much more flourishing and unsullied condition than the latter probably have ever realized.

The opera season of 1889 demands further attention for at least two productions out of the three which it yielded. It opened, at Covent Garden, with Bizet's "Pêcheurs de Perles," given in Italian with Ella Russell, Talazac, and D'Andrade in the cast; but the work signally failed to please. In June the de Reszkes returned, with Melba and Lassalle, and on the fifteenth a French performance of "Roméo et Juliette" shed lustre for the first time upon the annals of a London opera-house. The full cast was as follows: *Roméo,* M. Jean de Reszke; *Frère Laurent,* M. Edouard de Reszke; *Tybalt,* M. Montariol; *Mercutio,* M. Winogradow; *Capulet,* M. Seguin; *Duc,* M. Castelmary; *Stefano,* Mlle. Jane de Vigne; *Gertrude,* Mme. Lablache; and *Juliette,* Mme. Melba; Signor Mancinelli, conductor. The chorus sang in French, and the mounting of the opera was almost entirely new. "Roméo" attracted crowded audiences throughout the season. I may mention that the rôle of *Juliette* was subsequently filled with no less success by Mme. Emma Eames, who, by the way, had studied it under Gounod when she succeeded Mme. Patti in the part at the Paris Opéra.

Meanwhile preparations were in active progress for the eagerly awaited representation of "Die Meistersinger." These were so far advanced that it took Mancinelli less than a month to get his material into highly creditable shape. To attain perfection another month was, of course, needed; but when, I should like to know, during or since the Harris era, did a difficult and unfamiliar opera ever receive at Covent Garden an adequate allowance of time for thorough rehearsal? A month for a big Wagner work was considered ample, and, truth to tell, the results accomplished in that absurdly small space of time gave such remarkable satisfaction that no struggle was made to obtain a more liberal concession. London was now learning the lesson of lightning opera production which New York was to imitate later on—as, for example, in the recent instance of Paderewski's "Manru."

Both Jean de Reszke and Lassalle had been working hard at their parts all through the winter and spring. Toward the end they received valuable assistance in their studies from the veteran *maestro al piano,* Herr Saar, a well-known figure at Covent Garden for upward of a quarter of a century. This excellent musician—a genuine type of the old German school—was the conductor at Strasburg, and familiar with every note of Wagner's scores. He shared my intense enthusiasm on the subject of Jean de Reszke's "predestination" for the great Wagner rôles, and his joy over the approaching advent of the new *Walther von Stolzing* knew no bounds. I was often present when he came round to the Continental to do a morning's work with the great tenor. His good-humored face would be wreathed in smiles as he sat down to the piano; and when Jean sang the "Probelieder" or the "Preislied," with a charm that gave them a new meaning, the old accompanist would gaze heavenward through his spectacles with a look of ecstasy that was far more eloquent than words. He objected to the cuts; he cordially disliked the Italian text; but he was aware that both were indispensable, and he had the satisfaction of knowing that we all agreed with him.

For, notwithstanding the poetic merit and rhythmical vigor of Mazzucato's adaptation, Jean de Reszke was even now beginning to rebel against the open vowels and soft consonants of the Italian tongue as a medium for the utterance of the crisp, rugged verse, the expressive Teutonic sounds, the biting sibilants and gutturals of Wagner's original text. He felt that his declamation was even losing force in the very act of giving it birth—that it had not yet acquired the intense dramatic quality which had so appealed to him in the enunciation of the Bayreuth singers. All this was to be acquired in good time, though we little imagined then that the fulfilment was to be so complete; for as yet the Polish tenor had not declared to a soul (and probably had not yet conceived the idea) that he would ever sing an opera in the German language. And for the moment musical London was content to be radiantly happy over Jean de Reszke's first appearance on any stage (July 13, 1889) as the hero of Wagner's "Die Meistersinger." It was a great occasion, and the public recognized it as such by crowding the house in every part. Rarely have I known Covent Garden to be pervaded so completely by an atmosphere of excitement and curiosity. Only five years previous the same opera had been given there in German before a comparatively lukewarm assemblage of Wagner partizans. Now every section of the operatic community, united in love and admiration for a great artist as well as for a great composer, was fully represented. That the sticklers for the exact letter grumbled at Mancinelli's prodigious cuts may go without saying; but that could not be helped, and, indeed, their complaints were almost unheard amid the general chorus of gratification and pleasure.

The reader will forgive me if I say that on that memorable night I felt, deep in my heart, a sensation of joyful but modest pride at the thought that I had been in some measure instrumental in bringing about that felicitous achievement. I shall be ever grateful for the words of thanks with which Jean de Reszke and Lassalle responded to my congratulations when I went on the stage to see them after the first act. Both seemed to be in the seventh heaven. Edouard, the future *Hans Sachs,* was present; and to the lips of us all there came more than once the word "Ems!" The Bayreuth experiment had turned out a brilliant success.

Looking back with calm reflection upon the *Hans Sachs* of Lassalle, I must admit that his delineation of the poet-cobbler was too refined, too delicate, too "gentlemanly" to be altogether correct. Yet his noble voice and artistic phrasing imparted an added beauty to his music, and the benevolent,

LUIGI MANCINELLI

Copyright, 1894, by A. Dupont, N. Y.

LADY DE GREY

From a photograph by W. & D. Downey, London

kindly spirit of the character has never been more delightfully portrayed. The very attributes of refinement and distinction that were out of place in *Hans Sachs* enabled Jean de Reszke to realize in ideal fashion the attractive personality of the Franconian knight, especially in the half-timid, half-angry moments when he rebels against the dull bigotry of the Nuremberg mastersingers. The entire embodiment presented features of originality that surprised by their freshness no less than by their truthful adherence to the Wagnerian conception; and, as with his *Lohengrin,* so with his *Walther,* the vocal rendering of the part constituted a veritable revelation. The final rendering of the "Preislied" on that hot July night was something that never before had been approached, and has not since been surpassed.[1]

One of the events of this season was a gala performance at the Opera in honor of the Shah of Persia. Such celebrations subsequently became of frequent occurrence, but this was noteworthy as the first that had taken place at Covent Garden since the visit of the Emperor and Empress of the French many years before. The Queen, of course,

[1] The cast, in addition to MM. Jean de Reszke and Lassalle, included Mme. Albani (*Eva*), Mlle. Bauermeister (*Magdalena*), M. Isnardon (*Beckmesser*), M. Montariol (*David*), Signor Abramoff (*Pogner*), and M. Winogradow (*Kothner*). Signor Mancinelli conducted, and won special praise for the admirable work done by his orchestra. The stage manager was M. Lapissida, of the Brussels Monnaie, who had already superintended the production of the opera at that house.

did not attend, being, as usual, represented by the Prince of Wales. But more than a quarter of a century had now elapsed since the death of the Prince Consort, and there was growing evidence of Her Majesty's willingness to emerge somewhat from her retirement and to indulge more freely in the enjoyment of an art to which she was always conspicuously devoted. Welcome proof of this had been forthcoming in the previous May, when Queen Victoria went to the Royal Albert Hall to hear a performance of "The Golden Legend" conducted by Sir Arthur Sullivan. The idea now received further confirmation from the fact that Her Majesty began to take a renewed interest in the Opera; and, thanks to the glowing reports of various members of the royal family, her curiosity regarding the new Polish singers was roused to the highest pitch. This at last found expression in a "command" that, together with Mme. Albani, they should appear before Her Majesty at Windsor Castle.

I cannot do better than quote at length a note wherein M. Jean de Reszke gave me a full description of this, his first visit to Windsor. He says:

[Translated from the French.]

MY DEAR FRIEND:

The concert began with the air from "L'Etoile du Nord," which Edouard sang wonderfully. Then Mme. Albani and I sang the duet from "Lohengrin," after which the Queen expressed a desire to hear me in "Salve dimora" from "Faust." This I gave, and she appeared delighted. Next Mme. Albani sang an air by Handel, with the accompaniment for flute obbligato—I think "Sweet Bird" was the title, but you will know better than I the particular piece in question; and she sang it like a true *virtuose.* I accompanied Edouard in Denza's romance "A un portrait," with which the Queen was much pleased; then Edouard and I thundered out the unaccompanied duet from "Carmen," arranged by ourselves—great success![1] At Her Majesty's request, the concert ended with the duet from the "Traviata," sung by Mme. Albani and myself. The Queen, smiling and full of kindness, approached us and paid us many compliments. Among them she told me that I reminded her of Mario, only that my voice had more power. She refused to believe that I was the elder brother, and this discussion, in which Mme. Albani was called upon to arbitrate, greatly amused the Queen. Then, after the customary courtesies, the Queen retired. I found her extremely well, charming in manner, speaking French like a Parisian, and a genuine lover of music—as one could easily see by her eyes and in the movements of the head with which she emphasized the chief passages. In a word, this musical pilgrimage was anything but the solemn function which we at first feared it might be. Thanks to the amiability of the sovereign, there was not a vestige of fog at Windsor! Mancinelli accompanied. A thousand greetings.

JEAN DE RESZKE.

[1] The "Carmen" duet referred to in the above is a clever arrangement by the brothers, for two voices in "thirds" and "sixths," of the refrain "Dragon d'Alcala," sung by *Don José* just before his entry into the tavern of Lillas Pastia in the second act.

The summer of 1889 did not pass entirely without operatic rivalry. A feeble effort and an expiring one was that made at Her Majesty's by Mapleson in June, with Bevignani as conductor. The company, with two or three exceptions, was mediocre in the extreme, and the only débutante worth mentioning was the contralto, Signorina Bellincioni, younger sister of the soprano, who also, later on, created the rôle of *Santuzza* in "Cavalleria Rusticana." This season lasted exactly twenty-five days. A more interesting and more fortunate speculation was the series of representations of Verdi's "Otello" given at the Lyceum Theatre in July, under the direction of Mr. M. L. Mayer, with a complete Milanese troupe—principals, chorus, orchestra, and even *mise en scène*—expressly brought over from La Scala, where the opera was first produced in February, 1887. Tamagno and Maurel sustained their original parts, and for the former it was his London début. The performance, exceedingly fine on the whole, was admirably directed by Faccio, the famous *chef d'orchestre* of La Scala, who died a year or two later.

It was in this same season that Eugène Ysaye made his first appearance in London, playing the Beethoven concerto at the Philharmonic with such brilliant success that he was at once reëngaged for the next concert. Under the auspices of the same society, a successful début was made also by the young Russian pianist Loris Sapellnikoff, who

From a photograph

THE WATERLOO CHAMBER, WINDSOR CASTLE

AS ARRANGED FOR A PERFORMANCE OF "CARMEN" BEFORE H. M. QUEEN VICTORIA

played Tschaikowsky's pianoforte concerto in B flat minor, the composer conducting. Largely through the influence of Joseph Barnby, the quick development of the modern Flemish school found recognition in the production by the Royal Choral Society of Peter Benoit's oratorio "Lucifer." It created the impression, however, of a more or less disconnected series of tone-pictures, original in treatment, but lacking in spontaneous inspiration.

CHAPTER XIII

Opera in America and England—Progress at Covent Garden—Jean de Reszke's *Don José*—Harris and the Wagner performing rights—Début of Paderewski—The Critics and the Virtuoso—A new musical "Lion"—Great artist and true friend—An evening with Paderewski.

EARLY in the winter of 1889–90 a powerful opera troupe was formed by Mr. Henry Abbey to undertake a tour in the United States, and just before the new year it opened at Chicago with immense éclat. Among the leading artists were Adelina Patti, Emma Albani, Lillian Nordica, and Tamagno. Then for the first time did American opera-lovers hear the diva as *Juliette,* Albani as *Valentina* and *Desdemona,* Nordica as *Aida,* and Tamagno as *Otello.* Each in turn achieved success; but the chief triumph of the tour fell easily to Mme. Patti, who appeared always to overflowing houses, and received from the critics, especially in California, their loudest pæans of praise. Taken for all in all, this enterprise was noteworthy because it opened the eyes of American managers to the possibility of working independently of the European impresario. It showed them where to look for the lodestones best calculated to attract their own public; and thus it led to the establishment of the prevailing system, which, for a decade at least, I have described elsewhere by saying that "what Covent Garden does this year, New York does next." I need scarcely add that this aphorism has no application whatever to German opera, since the latter was "running alone" in New York while in London it was not out of swaddling-clothes. In 1890, however, the two branches in both cities were still separate and distinct. The time was yet to come when the three great schools of opera should be exploited by a single company of artists upon one and the same stage.

Gladly would I have written "four" instead of "three." But, alas, the development of the young English school was again progressing at too slow a rate for it to keep pace with its older and more powerful sisters. Not that Augustus Harris left a stone unturned to direct to a successful issue the policy and the task bequeathed him by Carl Rosa. He signalized the very first year after his old partner's death by arranging for the company to renew its Easter visit to Drury Lane. Rosa had commissioned Frederic Cowen after his return from Australia to write an opera expressly for him.[1] The libretto was supplied by Mr. Joseph Bennett, who, knowing the composer's fondness for Scandinavian color, founded his plot upon an

[1] Mr. Cowen had conducted the whole of the orchestral performances given in connection with the Melbourne Centennial Exhibition of 1888.

episode in the ancient Icelandic tale of "Viglund the Fair." Cowen's "Thorgrim" was duly produced at Drury Lane on April 22,—some thirteen and a half years after Carl Rosa had brought out his "Pauline" at the Lyceum,—with Zélie de Lussan, Barton McGuckin, and Frank Celli in the principal parts. The Prince of Wales, to whom the work was dedicated, attended the first performance with the Duke and Duchess of Edinburgh; and the composer conducted an admirable rendering of his opera. Yet, despite a cordial reception, "Thorgrim" failed quite to hit the mark, and the effect of its many beauties was lost because of a story too unattractive and too undramatic to appeal to the popular taste. In the course of this season, Gounod's "Roméo et Juliette" was given for the first time in English.

To be quite candid, as every "faithful chronicler" should be, it is necessary to record that such hold as opera in the vernacular had taken upon the metropolitan public was now beginning to relax. The attention of the main body of opera-goers was directed almost exclusively toward Covent Garden. And there, during the season approaching, we were to witness a demand for opera in French that amounted almost to a craze. The "Roméo" experiment was bearing fruit with a vengeance. As far as the requisite time for preparation would permit, no opera composed to a French text was henceforth to be sung in any but the French language. Curiously enough, "Faust" and "Les Huguenots" were still for a brief spell to be given in their Italian dress; but "Le Prophète," "La Favorita," "Hamlet,""Carmen," and even Goring Thomas's "Esmeralda" were all to be done in French for the first time. That this was a step in the right direction there can be no question. It was artistic in the abstract, and furthermore it greatly pleased the largest array of subscribers known since the "palmy days" of Covent Garden. The subscription for the opera season of 1890 amounted in the aggregate to nearly forty thousand pounds ($200,-000), and this for only ten weeks of five nights each. Artists' salaries were rising too; but for all that, Augustus Harris was finding that the "Royal Italian Opera," conducted on liberal principles, was commencing to pay extremely well.

Of the new French répertoire only two works required special study on the part of the Paris singers—namely, "Carmen" and "Esmeralda." Jean de Reszke was pretty forward with the rôle of *Captain Phœbus;* but Lassalle was equally backward with those of *Escamillo* and *Claude Frollo,* having had little time to devote to the study of new operas for London. As a matter of fact, he had only created the title part in Saint-Saëns's "Ascanio" at the Opéra on the 21st of March, and two days later he wrote me as follows:

[Translated from the French.]

PARIS, March 23, 1890.

MY DEAR FRIEND:

What a pity you could not come to the première of "Ascanio!" You would, I am sure, have been delighted with this music. It is a very remarkable work, no matter what the Parisian press may say of it. I am much afraid that it (the press) will deceive itself concerning this work, just as it made a mistake about "Carmen" and so many other compositions that constitute the glory of the French school. Personally, I have had a very, very great success, whereof, as you may guess, no one could be happier; but it does not blind me to the point of not attributing it primarily to the musical value of Saint-Saëns's wonderful work. The honor of being the chosen interpreter of such a master is great. I am happy and proud of it. Jean and Edouard beg me to convey to you their best regards. I unite with them in adding my most sincere greetings.

J. LASSALLE.

The result was that neither "Carmen" nor "Esmeralda" appeared in its Gallic guise until late in July. Indeed, "Carmen" was given only for Harris's "benefit" on the very last night of the season, when the demand for seats was so enormous that stalls sold for £4 ($20) apiece, and many hundreds of people were turned away from the doors. The only disappointment was Melba's non-appearance as *Michaela,* but this was almost forgotten amid the triumphs of Jean de Reszke and Lassalle, whose admirable impersonations were well matched by the fascinating *Carmen* of Zélie de Lussan. Being a kind of gala night, Augustus Harris imagined it would be interesting to have each of his three conductors engaged upon the one opera. Accordingly Mancinelli directed the first act, Bevignani the second, Randegger the third, and Mancinelli again the fourth. The effect upon the ensemble of the performance was simply disastrous, and, needless to add, the childish experiment was never tried again.

The *Don José* of Jean de Reszke has been variously criticized. I hold the opinion, however, not only that it was, and still is, a superb embodiment, but that it did a great deal to restore to the character the musical and histrionic value which it had gradually been losing in inverse ratio to the ever-growing prominence of the central figure of the opera. For this reason I quote some lines that I penned anent M. de Reszke's impersonation at the time:

> He showed us that it was as easy for one great artist to revive the importance and enhance the interest of a good rôle as for twenty mediocrities to drag it down to the level of their own talent. It goes without saying that the Polish tenor copied nobody's *Don José* in particular. He knew the traditions of the character, just as he learned those of *Sir Walter von Stolzing* by visiting Bayreuth. He read his Mérimée and carefully studied his libretto; but like an artist of individuality and resource, he also thought the part out for himself. The result, curiously enough, was a conception more closely resembling Campanini's than any we have seen since. It was free from the melodramatic exaggeration intc which other tenors had fallen. Take, as an instance, the last act. M. de Reszke did not make himself up like a starved ghost, neither did he rush about like a savage

animal in a cage. He looked the picture of despair, and he made his piteous appeal to *Carmen* with the tone of a man who is yearning for love, not for an excuse to commit murder. When at last driven to extremities, he did not gloat over his revenge nor chase his victim from corner to corner as a cat might chase a mouse. He simply stood at the entrance to the bull-ring, and when *Carmen* made her attempt to escape, he seized his dagger as by a sudden impulse and stabbed her as she was endeavoring to pass him. An instant later he was leaning over her lifeless body in tears, horror-stricken at the deed he had committed. This surely was the true reading of the episode. Nor was it the only scene upon which M. Jean de Reszke, with rare artistic insight, contrived to throw a new and consistent light. He depicted with wonderful subtlety and skill the gradual stages by which *Don José* is drawn under *Carmen's* fascinating influence. Fierce and absorbing passion revealed itself in his facial expression, his gestures, and, above all, the thrilling tones of his voice. Never before has the beautiful passage where *José* brings forth the flower that *Carmen* gave him and tells her how it cheered his lonely prison hours, been invested with such charm of voice and such tenderness and warmth of delivery.

Jean de Reszke did no less to elevate and enrich by his transcendent art the part of *Phœbus* in Goring Thomas's "Esmeralda." So did Lassalle that of the priest *Frollo,* and so, in a vocal sense at least, did Melba that of the heroine. These artists evinced a genuine interest in the opera, for they had taken an immense personal liking to the composer, and openly expressed their admiration for the talent and modesty of "ce cher Goringue." But in another direction unfortunate influences were at work. Notwithstanding its French origin and treatment, "Esmeralda" was in all essential matters an English opera, and as such the public knew and remembered it. Clothed in a foreign garb, it did not really appeal to connoisseurs, while the subscribers, as usual, gave infinitely more thought to the interpreters than to the work. That Goring Thomas's charming opera would have fared better—obtained an abiding-place in the active repertory—had it been presented in English by the same distinguished artists, is also a matter of doubt. Experience has proved that Covent Garden audiences do not care for opera in the vernacular, whether the work be of native or Continental origin; and it is the same, I believe, with the audiences of the Metropolitan Opera House in New York. Nor will the prejudice be overcome until the leading singers of the English-speaking countries are perfectly trained in the enunciation of their native tongue and can coax their compatriots into listening with pleasurable appreciation to first-rate native works rendered in the language "understanded of the people."

In 1890 all sorts of rumors were in the air concerning the future of Covent Garden Theatre. There was a heavy mortgage on the property, and the owner, Mr. A. Montague, was so uncertain what he would do with it that he would consent to let the opera-house only for a few weeks at a time. Augustus Harris, who that year added to his other trifling labors by accepting the honorable duties of Sheriff of London,[1] would gladly have taken a sub-lease of the theatre for a lengthened period, if only for the sake of being able to effect the many costly structural alterations and decorative improvements of which the place stood so badly in need. But Mr. Montague was in too vacillating a mood, and he would agree to nothing definite. Such was the position of affairs when our old friend Signor Lago came forward and offered to take Covent Garden for a six weeks' autumn season of Italian opera at cheap prices, dating from October 18. The offer was accepted.

This autumn enterprise was noteworthy for two or three things; chiefly for the revival of Gluck's "Orfeo," wherein the sisters Sofia and Giulia Ravogli made their débuts, and the contralto, by her nobly picturesque assumption of *Orfeo*, created a very striking and powerful impression. Further, Albani and Maurel resumed together the parts of *Elizabeth* and *Wolfram* which they had played in the production of "Tannhäuser" at this house in 1876. Last, but not least, Lago established his claim, under the clauses of the Berne Convention, to perform certain operas, such as "Faust"

[1] He was a liveryman (by purchase) of the City of London and Prime Warden of the Loriners' Company. He was the first theatrical manager upon whom the coveted shrieval dignity had ever been bestowed.

PADEREWSKI

and "Lohengrin," without payment of fees to other parties who declared that they owned the remaining rights in those books. It was in virtue of the "interest" vested therein by prior production at Covent Garden that Lago obtained that victory, and the result considerably upset the calculations of the Carl Rosa Opera Company and Augustus Harris, who had paid large sums for surviving rights in certain operas that now proved to possess only a limited value. Harris, in reply to an inquiry, had written me a note to say that, "Except 'Parsifal,' all Wagner rights for this country are ours, in all languages. No piece can be done at a concert, even, without permission from yours truly, Augustus Harris."

But the connection between the two undertakings was soon to be terminated. The new sheriff was fain to admit that even his Napoleonic grasp was not equal to the task of holding and directing the strands of such a huge coil of enterprises, to which, by the way, he had recently added the lesseeship of a theatre at Newcastle. Toward the end of 1890 he resigned his position as managing director of the Carl Rosa Company, and the splendid edifice which had taken fifteen years to build was now, for the first time, without an actual controlling head. Its fortunes, I am sorry to say, quickly began to suffer. The concern did not long continue to pay a dividend, and in a few years had become, what it is now, a mere shadow of its former prosperous self.

The early summer of 1890 was to witness the début of the successor to Liszt and Rubinstein, of the greatest of the *fin de siècle* group of great pianists—Ignace Jan Paderewski. This event created interest at the time among a very limited circle. It was anticipated with curiosity only by the critics and dilettanti who follow the trend of musical events in Paris. For several months we had been receiving vivid accounts of a young Polish pianist, "with a wonderful aureole of golden hair," who executed miracles upon the keyboard, who composed delicious minuets and played Chopin to absolute perfection. But London cares little, as a rule, for what Paris thinks of new artists, and it displayed anything but a burning impatience to hear Leschetizky's latest pupil. This fact was sufficiently demonstrated by the meagre audience which gathered at St. James's Hall on the 9th of May for the first of the four recitals announced by the composer of "Paderewski's Minuet." A more coldly critical assemblage perhaps it would have been impossible to find. Not a soupçon of magnetic current was in the atmosphere—not even the quickened pulse arising from the anticipation of "sensational effects."

When M. Paderewski appeared upon the platform there was a mild round of applause accompanied by an undercurrent of whispering and suppressed murmurs that had evident reference to his unwonted picturesqueness of aspect. The deep golden tinge of his hair seemed to accentuate the intense pallor of his countenance. One could plainly see that he was nervous; but in those deep, thoughtful eyes, in those firmly-set lips, in that determined chin, one could read also the strong, virile qualities of the self-contained, self-reliant artist, already accustomed to conquer audiences and to create magnetism in the most sterile space Exactly how he played that day—I mean, as compared with the Paderewski whose every mood was by and by to become familiar—it is rather hard for me to say. That he strove to be "sensational" I do not believe now, though at the time it was difficult to think otherwise. For surely his contrasts were startling in their violence, and the instrument fairly thundered under his execution of a forte passage. At times there seemed to be no restraint whatever. His magnificent technique enabled him to give free rein to his impulse and imagination, and *laissez-aller* was then the word. If you loved sensationalism in a pianist, here unquestionably was a virtuoso capable of providing an unlimited quantity of it.

And such was the prevailing impression in the minds of the aforesaid critics and dilettanti when they left St. James's Hall that afternoon. The former dwelt not upon the tenderness and poetry that Paderewski had revealed in his Chopin-playing, nor upon the romantic touches in his Schumann. They described as "eccentric" his reading of Handel and Mendelssohn, and preferred his interpretation of Liszt and Rubinstein. They liked best of all his rendering of his own "Trois Humoresques à l'antique," and the inevitable "Menuet," which had been enthusiastically encored. Altogether the press notices were marked by coolness and extreme caution. For my own part, I confess that I did not at first care to commit myself to a definite judgment. Yet I had found so much to admire, so much to marvel at, so much that was individual and supremely masterful in Paderewski's playing that I determined not to miss a single recital of the three still to come. The second drew a better audience, though nothing approaching a crowd; and this time the new pianist included Bach, Beethoven, and Schubert in his scheme, together with more Chopin and Paderewski. The "barometer" began to rise. At his third recital his fine performances of Beethoven's sonata in A flat, Op. 110, and Schumann's "Carnival" carried the mercury from "change" to "fair"; but there it remained, stationary for the season. In addition to the recitals he also gave an orchestral concert, at which he played his own concerto in A minor, Saint-Saëns's concerto in C minor, and Liszt's "Fantaisie Hongroise," the conductor being Mr. Henschel; and if it failed to arouse wide-spread interest, this parting shot served to hit the mark so truly that I, for one, no longer hesitated to acknowledge Paderewski as a really great artist.

The completion of the conquest was deferred, however, until the season of 1891. There had been opportunities in the meantime for reflection, and the public was now beginning to scent a veritable musical "lion." I used to receive letters from women readers asking all sorts of questions about the Polish pianist and begging for particulars that in no way concerned them. These of course went unanswered; for the English journalist is less generous than his American confrère in dispensing information about the private lives of artists. But the very existence of such curiosity told a tale. There would be no more "meagre audiences" when Paderewski played. As a matter of fact, his Chopin recital at St. James's Hall in July drew the largest crowd and the highest receipts recorded since the final visit of Rubinstein. He also appeared at the Philharmonic, at a Richter concert, and at an orchestral concert of his own, when he was heard in the greatest two of all pianoforte concertos: the E flat ("Emperor") of Beethoven and the A minor of Schumann. It was his superb rendering of these masterpieces that, in England at least, assured the fame of the gifted Pole; and it was this concert that led indirectly to my making his acquaintance.

I had been requested by his manager, Mr. Daniel Mayer, to undertake the writing of such brief analytical notes as the programme required, and, instead of following conventional lines or of describing these familiar works in detail, I contented myself with a more or less detailed contrast of the characteristic features of the two concertos. This appeared to have pleased and interested Paderewski; and when I was introduced to him after the concert he said some charming things in that charming manner which is so characteristic of the man. We quickly became close friends. I learned not only to appreciate the real magnitude of his gifts as a creative and executive musician, but also to gauge his rare intellectuality and to respect his broad-minded views as cultured artist and man of the world. During his many visits to London we saw a great deal of each other, and more than once he testified to his kindly regard for me.

An instance of this occurred in 1894. It was arranged that, toward the end of his English tour, M. Paderewski should dine one evening at my flat in Whitehall Court to meet a few well-known musicians; other friends were invited to come in afterward. The date—May 3—was fixed by the artist himself, and the guests at dinner further included Sir Arthur Sullivan, Sir Alexander Mackenzie, Sir Joseph Barnby, my beloved old master, Manuel Garcia, and the veteran 'cellist, Signor Alfredo Piatti. I was especially gratified to be the means of bringing Paderewski and Sullivan together. They were acquainted, I fancy, but had not met frequently; at any rate, the former wrote me:

> Inutile de vous dire que je serai absolument enchanté de passer une soirée chez vous, avec vous, et de recontrer Sir Sullivan [*sic*], que j'admire beaucoup.

Just before dinner a quaint sort of letter was placed in my hands. It was from some one in the famous pianist's entourage, reminding me that M. Paderewski was very fatigued after his heavy work in the provinces, and begging that I would under no circumstances ask him to play that evening. I was half amused, half annoyed by this unexpected communication, which, of course, I knew better than to regard as inspired by my guest of honor himself. It was also entirely superfluous, as I always made it a strict rule never to request an artist to perform in my house who did not come there for that purpose or with that expressed intention. However, I thought no more about it until after dinner, when I took an opportunity to inform Paderewski, in a whispered "aside," of the strange warning I had received. I assured him seriously that I had not had the slightest idea of asking him to play, and that my friends were more than satisfied to have the pleasure of meeting him and enjoying his society. He replied:

"Do you imagine I think otherwise? This is a case of 'Save me from my friends!' That I am tired is perfectly true. But when I am in the mood to play fatigue counts for nothing. And I am in that mood to-night. Are you really going to have some music?"

"Yes, Piatti has brought his 'cello, and he is going to take part in the Rubinstein sonata in D."

"Then I should like to play it with him; and

more beside, if he will permit me. Piatti and I are now old colleagues at the 'Pops,' and we always get on splendidly together."

What could I say?—save express my gratitude, and apprise my friends of the treat that was in store. It was the more welcome because it was virtually unexpected. An unalloyed delight was the performance of that lovely sonata by the "Prince of 'Cellists" and the greatest of living pianists. Both seemed to revel in the beauties of a work admirably designed for the display of their respective instruments, and the rendering was in every way perfect. After it was over, dear old Piatti, who rarely talked much, said to me in his quiet way, "I quite enjoyed that. I have played the sonata with Rubinstein many times, but it never went better than to-night." Later on he played again; and so did Paderewski—with Sullivan close by his side, watching with fascinated eyes the nimble fingers as they glided over the keys. That evening the illustrious pianist was inspired. Fatigue was forgotten; indeed, he seemed much fresher than on the preceding night, when he introduced his fine "Polish Fantasia" at the Philharmonic.[1] He went on and on from one piece to another, with characteristic forgetfulness of self, and it was well on to dawn before we parted.

The début of Leonard Borwick in 1890 is worthy

[1] This work was composed for and first performed by M. Paderewski at the Norwich Festival of 1893.

SIR CHARLES HALLÉ

From a photograph by Messrs. Bassano, London

LADY HALLÉ

From a photograph by Elliott & Fry, London

of mention, inasmuch as, like Fanny Davies, he embodies in a remarkable degree the unique qualities of the romantic school whereof their teacher, Mme. Clara Schumann, was admittedly the most spontaneous and finished exponent. The success of these two native artists was destined to afford great encouragement to rising students both in England and on the Continent. It also helped to create among the general mass of amateurs a taste for pianoforte-playing of a more warm-blooded type than had hitherto satisfied them. The days of Arabella Goddard and her *feux d'artifice* had now passed forever; and so, very nearly, had those of the coldly correct and scholastic Sir Charles Hallé. Let it be said, nevertheless, that the late musical knight accomplished much useful work in the oral education of the youthful and impressionable mothers of future generations of amateurs. He performed a still higher function, moreover, by diffusing a love of high-class orchestral music through the medium of his famous Manchester band (now conducted by Hans Richter), which enjoyed a tremendous vogue in the north of England, though it consistently failed to make money when brought to the metropolis, as it frequently was at that time. At the Popular Concerts Sir Charles was still a favorite, and I note that in December, 1890, he was taking part in a "Beethoven programme" with Lady Hallé (*née* Neruda), Louis Ries, Ludwig Straus, Alfred

Gibson, and Piatti for coadjutors. The old combination, even as late as that, was still intact. In the same month, by the way, Jean Gérardy made his first appearance in London, a marvelous 'cello prodigy of twelve, and destined to ripen into an artist of the first rank.

CHAPTER XIV

Adelina Patti at home—Life at Craig-y-nos Castle—Opening of the Patti Theatre: inaugural operatic performance—Preparing "wordless" plays—The diva as *La Tosca*—Her love of Wagner—Bayreuth by proxy and in reality—"The Queen of Song": an appreciation—How she reappeared at Covent Garden—A strange presentiment.

IN August, 1891, I paid my first visit to Craig-y-nos Castle, the lovely Welsh home of Mme. Adelina Patti. I had known the distinguished cantatrice personally some half-dozen years; but somehow I had always been content to worship from afar one who filled, by right of unrivaled gifts, the highest place in the temple of vocal art. The greatest vocalist of her sex that the world had brought forth since the middle of the nineteenth century; the brilliant "Queen of Song," honored by monarchs and princes, sought by the *crême* of aristocracy and wealth, quoted by poets and novelists, fêted and applauded alike in the Eastern and Western hemispheres—small wonder if this strangly unique being had inspired me from youth upward with feelings of the deepest veneration and amazement. Nor were those feelings to undergo the slightest tinge of modification during the period of ripening friendship and often close association that was now to follow. There 's a "divinity doth hedge" queens as well as kings; and Patti is one of those in whom familiarity may exercise a charm, but can never "breed contempt."

The immediate occasion of my first journey to Craig-y-nos was the inauguration of the elegant little theatre which Mme. Patti-Nicolini had recently built in the new wing of her castle. It had been settled in the spring that I was to be present. In July came the following note:

CRAIG-Y-NOS CASTLE, YSTRADGYNLAIS,
July 13, 1891.

DEAR MR. KLEIN:

I promised to send you a line with itinerary for journey from London to Craig-y-nos Castle,[1] which I enclose, and trust you will be good enough to let me know on which day we are to expect you, so as to send the carriage to the station to meet you. With our united very best regards,

Most sincerely yours,
ADELINA PATTI-NICOLINI.

P.S.—The opening of our theatre takes place on the 12th of August.

I went down on the 8th. It was so much more pleasant to be there for three or four days before

[1] It was then an eight hours' affair, involving two changes of railway and a journey from one station to another at Neath, followed by a drive to the castle from the station in Swansea Valley by the road which Mme. Patti expressly had cut along the mountain-side. The present journey by the Brecon route is much shorter.

the function. One could study the castle and its environs, and become accustomed to the ways of the household. My welcome was of the utmost cordiality. Mme. Patti's fame as a hostess had preceded and did not belie her; she kept an eye open for the comfort of each of her guests. The house party was a numerous one, including as it did the Spanish Ambassador, Sir Edward Lawson, Sir Augustus and Lady Harris,[1] poor William Terriss, the actor (asked to deliver the opening address in place of Sir Henry Irving, who could not come), the Eissler Sisters, Signor and Mme. Arditi, Antoinette Sterling, Giulia Valda, Durward Lely, Tito Mattei, Wilhelm Ganz, Franco Novara, and others.

The place has been described so often that I take it almost for granted the reader knows something of Craig-y-nos and its beauties. Enough that the scene is a bit of fairyland, a veritable "oasis in the desert," as some guide-books have called it, amid the long tracts of uninteresting country that constitute the watershed of the Swansea Valley. The castle itself is fitted up with every contrivance that modern luxury can afford. The winter garden, with its wonderful electric fountain, is of huge dimensions, and in summer the conservatory makes the most picturesque dining-room I have ever seen. In the French billiard-room stands the famous

[1] The worthy sheriff had just received the honor of knighthood in connection with the visit of Kaiser Wilhelm II to the City of London.

orchestrion, probably the finest instrument of its kind ever built. It possesses a rich, mellow organ tone, and executes the most complex compositions with extraordinary clearness. I may say, without exaggeration, that it was by the aid of her splendid orchestrion that Mme. Patti first began to comprehend the intricacies of Wagner's more advanced works. She now knows them by heart and enjoys them.

But, after all, the gem of the castle, apart from its mistress, is the theatre. It has been called "a Bayreuth theatre *en miniature*"—and justly. No side boxes or seats; a single gallery at the back; stalls sloping down to the orchestra so that the musicians are nearly out of sight; and a clever system of stage lighting by electricity. The pure Renaissance architecture is set off to great advantage by a singularly delicate scheme of color,—pale blue, cream, and gold,—to which the deep sapphire of the curtains supplies a most effective contrast. The walls and proscenium are tastefully decorated, and between graceful columns are inscribed in panels the names of the great composers. The scenery is painted by the best theatrical artists; while the act-drop, representing *Semiramide* driving her war-chariot, is a spirited achievement, beside furnishing an excellent portrait of the Queen of the Castle. Also to be noted is the novel mechanism for raising the floor of the auditorium to the level of the stage, whereby the *salle* is converted into a handsome ball-room. It is here, every Christmas

PATTI

AS JULIETTE

From a photograph by W. A. Smith, Swansea

PATTI, ABOUT 1861

From negative in the possession of F. H. Meserve, N. Y.

Eve, that Mme. Patti bestows her annual gifts upon the servants and tenantry of her estate.

With her professional career nearing its end, what, it may be asked, can have been the object of this great artist in enriching her home with such a structure as this? To practise and perform operas? Certainly not. True it is that on the memorable opening night now referred to the still youthful Patti, a picture of grace ablaze with diamonds, sang the first act of "La Traviata," followed by the garden scene from "Faust," with her husband, M. Nicolini, in his old part. Again, three days later, a performance was given of the balcony scene from "Roméo" and the third act of Flötow's "Martha"; this, like the first, being attended by a crowded audience of privileged friends and neighbors. But these were the baptismal representations. They consecrated the theatre, as it were, without precisely foreshadowing the main purpose of its existence.

The answer to this question was supplied by Mme. Patti herself early during that very sojourn at Craig-y-nos Castle: "I love the stage. I love to act and to portray every species, every shade of human emotion. Only I want freedom—more freedom than opera, with its restricted movements and its wear and tear on the voice, can possibly allow the actress. I care not whether it be comedy or tragedy, so long as I feel that I can devote my whole energy, my whole being, to realizing the character that I have to delineate. Even words trouble me; they take time to commit to memory, and their utterance fatigues a singer too much. Yet I want to act, to feel myself upon the boards, playing to amuse myself and a few chosen friends on each side of the footlights. What does there remain for me to do? What but to enact scenes and plays in 'pantomime'; to utilize the ancient art of the Italian mime and express every sentiment by means of gesture, action, and facial expression. I must have music, of course; I cannot do entirely without my own art and all its wealth of suggestive force. Give me only a dramatic idea, with music that aids in depicting it, and I will play you any part you choose, from one of Sarah Bernhardt's down to *Fatima* in "Bluebeard."

I understood. There was something more in this than mere whim or caprice. That Mme. Patti had already been demonstrating her marvelous talent for "dramatic pantomime" upon the stage of her new theatre I knew quite well. In a word, her histrionic powers, which had so conspicuously developed during the later years of her career, were now asserting their strength to a degree which in this case demanded active exercise. Knowing that I was an "old hand" at amateur stage work, she asked me if I would like to assist in one of the entertainments. I inquired which particular kind—the "Sarah Bernhardt" or the "Bluebeard"?

"Both," she replied, laughing. "We already have a capital arrangement of 'Bluebeard.' We can do that to-morrow or next day. Then if you like to write out a *scenario* of one of Bernhardt's plays, we will put it in hand and give it later in the month."

I suggested "La Tosca"—little dreaming that Puccini was then thinking of composing an opera upon Sardou's play. My hostess agreed. The casts were arranged and forthwith we set to work. In "Bluebeard" I played the lover. In "La Tosca" young Richard Nicolini, a professional actor, enacted the painter *Paul Cavaradossi,* and I took the part of *Scarpia.* The rehearsals were a delight. They frequently took place in the afternoon, and Mme. Patti entered into them as seriously as though they were for a public performance; interesting herself in every little detail and suggesting countless bits of effective "business." It was in course of these rehearsals that I began to realize what a consummate mistress she was of the art of the stage.[1] A bare idea, a mere hint, would suffice; whether comedy or tragedy was the theme, she would work upon it and elaborate it with wonderful skill. Once while we were rehearsing "La Tosca," Sir Augustus Harris quietly slipped in and took a seat in the dark auditorium. He watched the proceedings with the amusement of a master of the game enjoying a holiday. Mme. Patti soon perceived him, and she called out:

[1] In matters concerning scenery, costumes, and lighting it was the same, though herein Mme. Patti relied greatly upon the able assistance of Frank Rigo (the second *régisseur* of Covent Garden and the Metropolitan Opera House), who used regularly to spend his summer holiday at Craig-y-nos.

"Gus, what are you doing there? Why don't you come on the stage and help us?"

"My dear Adelina," answered Sir Augustus, "if this were an opera or a play I would with pleasure. But it is neither, and whatever it may be, there is no need of my help as long as you are there. I am just beginning to realize that if you had not been the world's greatest singer you could have been one of its best actresses." He meant it —and it was true.

The "Tosca" performance did not come off until August 29, after the impresario had left the castle. At the last moment we found the bill too long, so we determined to omit dramatic action and give it as a series of *tableaux vivants,* in which form it vastly pleased a large audience of friends from "The Valley." They missed, however, the thrilling effect of Mme. Patti's gliding, serpentine movements in the supper scene where she stabs *Scarpia;* and they could not guess that the dead *Minister of Police,* in the person of myself, was positively shuddering as he lay prone between the two lighted candles. I had been told to keep my eyes open and stare, but that tragic look upon the countenance of *La Tosca* as she placed the crucifix upon my breast was so terrible that if I had not closed them I should have had to jump up before the curtain fell. Throughout, Patti's attitudes were a wonderful study, and I feel sure Sarah Bernhardt and Ternina would have given much to have seen her remarkable impersonation.

A week prior to this event Mme. Patti had been honored by a visit from the late Prince Henry of Battenberg, who was staying at Clyne Castle, and who came out to lunch accompanied by Count Gleichen, Lord Royston (now the Earl of Hardwicke), and other friends. The Queen's son-in-law witnessed a repetition of the garden scene from "Faust," and altogether spent a most agreeable afternoon. A few days later we all went over to Swansea to take part in the annual concert given by Mme. Patti in aid of the local charities. The journey each way assumed the character of a triumphal progress, the entire route from the station to the concert-hall being lined by dense crowds. It was touching to witness the eagerness of the humble folk—men, women, and children—to catch a glimpse of the illustrious vocalist, who once every year came from her mountain home to aid the institution that succored their needy and suffering. The concert itself was memorable because on this occasion, for the first time in her life, the famous songstress delivered as an encore the soul-stirring strains of the Welsh national air, "Land of my Fathers"; and when, at her request, her enthusiastic auditors joined in the chorus, the effect was simply electrifying.

Altogether that delightful month at Craig-y-nos Castle was packed with excitement and bustle. It was my privilege during the next few years to spend there many weeks—visits not less enjoyable, but less eventful, and infinitely more restful. In the evenings we would sit and listen to the orchestrion, and when it had exhausted its round of Wagner excerpts I would occasionally supplement the selection upon the piano with fragments from the "Meistersinger," "Tristan," and the "Nibelungen." It was extraordinary to see the pleasure Mme. Patti took in this music. One year August Wilhelmj was there, and to please her he played his own transcription of the "Preislied" upon Nicolini's fine "Guarnerius," Clara Eissler executing the accompaniment upon the harp. To reward him Patti sang Gounod's "Ave Maria" to his violin obbligato, Clara Eissler again playing the harp part, while I took the harmonium. Never did the familiar piece go better. But the real reward came later when some one brought a copy of Wagner's "Träume" to the castle, and the diva, for the first time in her career, wedded her golden tones to one of Wagner's long-drawn melodies. By her request we worked at it together, but her German accent and phrasing were faultless, and, beyond marking the breathing-places, I had virtually nothing to suggest.

In the following season she sang "Träume" at one of the concerts at the Albert Hall, and so rapturously was this applauded that we subsequently took up the study of *Elizabeth's* Prayer ("Tannhäuser"). This suited her to perfection, and she rendered it with a depth of fervid expression and a wealth of glorious tone that have never been equaled. Further than this, however, Mme. Patti has not yet consented to pursue her active alliance with the music of Wagner. She loves to listen to it, but hesitates to impose upon her delicate organ the strain of singing it in public. During our Wagner chats she would often ask me about Bayreuth, and I begged her to seize the first opportunity of attending the festival. She did not do so, however, until after her marriage with Baron Cederström, who is extremely fond of traveling, and, beside taking his wife to Sweden every summer, introduces her to many interesting European resorts. The following letter tells its own tale:

Fåhrens Villa, near Saltsjöbaden, Stockholm,
August 5, 1901.

Dear Mr. Klein:

We have just arrived at this lovely place after spending a very pleasant time in Switzerland and at Bayreuth, and I must send you first these few lines to tell you how immensely I was impressed by the Bayreuth performances. I never could have imagined anything so perfect as the *mise en scène,* and I thought the "Ring" simply divine. There are no words to express it; it is all so wonderful and beautiful. I thought "Parsifal" was *glorious,* especially the last act, and I am indeed glad to have heard all these marvelous works.

After a three weeks' stay at Schinznach we went to Lucerne, where we had a most delightful time, taking long excursions every day. Can you imagine *me* going up the Rigi, Pilatus, the Bürgenstock, and similar places? I was well rewarded for my courage in mounting those perpendicular heights, for the view from the top was simply beyond description. . . .

We expect to remain here until the beginning of September, when we shall return to England, as my concert tour commences the first week in October. The Baron joins me in sending you kindest remembrances.

Yours very sincerely,
ADELINA PATTI-CEDERSTRÖM.

The days at Craig-y-nos were always full of interest and variety. It was an inestimable privilege to enjoy the daily society and conversation of Adelina Patti; to hear her ever and anon burst into song; to catch the ring of her sunshiny laugh; to come under the spell of a personal charm such as few women possess. She converses with equal facility in English, French, Italian, and Spanish, speaks German and Russian well, and by this time, I dare say, can carry on a fluent colloquy in Swedish. Her memory is extraordinary. She tells a hundred stories of her early life in America, dating from the age of seven, when she made her first appearance in public.[1] She tells how they used to stand her upon the table to sing; how she first

[1] The portrait of Adelina Patti at the age of nine forming the frontispiece of this book is taken from a daguerreotype in her possession, which she showed me at Craig-y-nos Castle a few years ago. The complete picture shows three little girls seated together at a table—Adelina in the centre and a playmate on each side. I was so much struck by the intelligence of the expression and the extraordinary maturity of the features generally—so like, even at that age, to the familiar face of later years—that I begged Mme. Patti to allow me to have a photographic enlargement made of the central figure. She kindly consented, and three copies were executed. Of these she herself owns one, the widow of Sir Augustus Harris has another, and I possess the third.

rendered "Casta Diva" by ear without a single mistake; and how, when her eldest sister, Amalia, was striving hard to master the shake, the tiny Adelina stopped her and asked, "Why don't you do it like this?" therewith executing a natural and absolutely irreproachable trill.

Patti tells you that she never studied the art of producing or emitting the voice. Nature, alone and unaided, accomplished that marvel. To keep the organ in perfect condition, she has but to run over the scales ten minutes every morning. Her vocalization is one of those miracles that cannot be explained. Its wondrous certainty and finish are assuredly not arrived at without some labor; but in the end the miracle seems to have accomplished itself. Her "ear" is phenomenal. She never forgets a tune, and will instantly name the opera or composition in which it occurs. Another mystery is the perennial freshness of her voice, which, after half a century of constant use, retains well-nigh unimpaired the delicious sweetness and bell-like timbre of early womanhood. No other such example of perfect preservation stands on record in the annals of the lyric art. To analyze its secret one can only say, here surely is a singer of marvelous constitution, heaven-gifted with a faultless method, who has sedulously nursed her physical resources, and has never, under any circumstances, imposed the smallest undue strain upon the exquisitely proportioned mechanism of her vocal organs.

And the triumphs of this incomparable artist have not "spoiled" her. The homage of kings, the adulation of friends, the applause of multitudes, have not robbed her of that unaffected simplicity, that freedom from ostentation, that yearning for home life and domestic tranquillity, which are among her most characteristic attributes. As evidence of this fact, I quote a portion of a letter which Mme. Patti wrote me from Nice in the spring of 1895. It was obviously not "intended for publication," but herein lies its chief value as a communication emanating from the friend rather than the artist:

When I gave my extra performance of the "Barbiere" my triumph was, if possible, even greater than usual, but on each occasion the success has been so enormous that it would be difficult to say which performance excited the greatest enthusiasm, or when I received the biggest ovation. It has, indeed, become a succession of triumphs the whole time. Do you not feel proud of your little friend, who was fifty-two last month, and has been singing uninterruptedly every year from the age of seven! I am really beginning to believe what they all tell me—that I am a wonderful little woman!

It is no exaggeration to say that every one, without exception, has been running after me, and loading me with invitations—in fact, to such a degree that I must honestly confess that I am getting decidedly tired of all the parties and gaieties we have been going through during the past few weeks. It has been an incessant lunching out, dining out, and receiving visitors from morning till night. I shall be very happy to see my dear Castle again and have a little peace and quietness.

It was just prior to this visit to the south of France that negotiations, in which I acted as intermediary, were concluded between Mme. Patti and Sir Augustus Harris for the diva's reappearance in opera at Covent Garden during the season of 1895. I had long devoutly wished for this consummation; but there were many obstacles to be removed, not the smallest of these being concerned with the Birmingham managers of the "Patti Concerts" throughout the United Kingdom, who were naturally afraid lest her return to opera should interfere with the financial success of the customary concerts at the Albert Hall. Ultimately these fears were allayed, and Mme. Patti confided to me that she would not be unwilling to consider an offer on certain terms from her old friend "Gus." I immediately set about arranging for an interview between them in London. This was not altogether an easy matter. The great prima donna was to spend only one evening in town on her way to the Riviera, and the busy impresario, with whom minutes reckoned as hours, was not readily to be moved —on an uncertain mission, as he deemed it —from one quarter of London to another. But, eventually, I persuaded him that Mme. Patti was really in earnest, and he consented to accompany me to Paddington Station to meet the express from South Wales.

It was a bleak January evening, and of course the train was late. This was the more unlucky because it happened that Tennyson's "King Arthur" was to be produced at the Lyceum that night, and we were both anxious to be there at the rise of the curtain; and, moreover, I had to write a notice of Sullivan's incidental music to the new play. We were already in evening dress, and as Harris was suffering from a cold I took care not to let him stand upon the draughty platform. We waited, therefore, by a warm fire at the station hotel and discussed current events. My companion was not in good spirits, while the fact that he was not in a sanguine mood was palpable from his frequent remark, "Klein, I can't believe Patti means to sing at Covent Garden this season." So I felt heartily glad when the train was signaled and the youthful little lady, vivacious as ever in bearing, but silent under a mountain of wraps wound round to protect her from the biting air, stepped buoyantly out of her saloon carriage and took Harris's arm to walk into the hotel. Not a word was spoken until we got to the private sitting-room. Then, greetings over, Mme. Patti, with an arch smile, asked Sir Augustus if he would like a little quiet conversation with her. He bowed graciously. The rest of us discreetly retired. Ten minutes later he came out of the room beaming with pleasure. "Make haste and say good-by. Adelina would like us to stay and dine, but we mustn't; we must get a 'snack' somewhere and then hurry to the Lyceum." In the hansom he added: "It 's all right. She sings at six performances, beginning the second week in June!" And we both felt as happy as school-boys.

PATTI

AS MARGUERITE

From a photograph by W. A. Smith, Swansea

PATTI

AS NINETTA

From a photograph by W. A. Smith, Swansea

In the late summer I was at Craig-y-nos once more. Work was all over for the season, and the indefatigable mistress of the castle, satiated with triumphs surpassing any that she had ever previously earned at Covent Garden, was only thinking how she could best amuse her guests and herself upon the stage of her beloved theatre. It was decided to do a new "play without words." Several subjects were proposed, but the choice eventually fell upon Mrs. Henry Wood's "East Lynne," which, as every one knows, was dramatized many years ago and makes a most effective play. The scenario was soon prepared and rehearsals started. There was ample talent available for the rather lengthy cast. Mme. Patti of course played *Lady Isabel* (afterward *Mme. Vine*); that talented amateur actor C. P. Colnaghi (since deceased) was the *Archibald Carlyle;* another well-known amateur, Augustus Spalding, played *Captain Levison;* and I undertook the part of *Richard Hare*. Music for the *mélodrame* was expressly composed (at lightning speed) by our hostess's distant relative André Pollonnais, the clever French musician who afterward wrote for her the pantomime play "Mirka," in which she appeared at Nice for the benefit of the local charities. M. Pollonnais also set to music the lines of a lullaby which I had written specially for Mme. Patti to sing in the scene where the supposed governess watches tenderly over her dying child in the nursery at East Lynne. This same lullaby she afterward sang in public in London and in other places.

The performance of the wordless "East Lynne" on August 17 was perhaps the most complete artistic achievement in this direction accomplished at Craig-y-nos Castle. Certainly it yielded the finest piece of acting on Mme. Patti's part that I have known her to give at her own theatre. It was also notable for a curious incident. Readers familiar with the novel or play will remember that when *Mme. Vine* revisits her former home she is dressed in widow's "weeds." Such a costume was worn by Mme. Patti, and very charming she looked in it. One person, however, objected strongly to her having donned a crape dress. That person was M. Nicolini. After the curtain had fallen he expressed himself on the subject in no measured terms, declaring that such attire "portait malheur," and that he did not like to see his wife in a costume which she might one day be compelled of necessity to wear. I pointed out to him that he might make the same complaint about the peignoir worn by *Violetta* when dying, or the prison garb of *Marguerite* in the last act of "Faust." But he refused to see it, and remarked, "Elles n'étaient jamais veuves, cettes femmes-là!" Which was perfectly true; and, having regard to subsequent events, his objection would appear to have been not altogether unjustifiable.

It was in June of the succeeding year that Mme. Patti honored me by being the centre of attraction at a dinner-party which I gave at Whitehall Court, followed by a large reception whereat some three hundred guests, well known in the musical, theatrical, and literary worlds, were bidden to meet the diva. The peculiarity of this function was that it collected a good many celebrities who, for various reasons, are seldom brought together. For this, no doubt, good luck was largely responsible. One may know and invite many famous folk to dine or sup during the London season; but it will rarely happen that ninety-five per cent. are disengaged and willing to come. In this instance I did not receive more than twenty refusals, all told. Thus it fell that when I took Mme. Patti in to dinner she found on her right her old friend Jean de Reszke, whom she had not met since the glorious "Roméo" time in Paris, eight years before. Edouard was, of course, there, facing his old confrère Nicolini, who chatted about his pet Cremona violins with the perennial Alfredo Piatti. Among others present were my father's old friend and pupil, Lord Suffield, and Lady Suffield (now lord and lady in waiting to King Edward and Queen Alexandra), Sir Edward and Lady Lawson, Sir Augustus and Lady Harris, and Miss Zélie de Lussan. Charles (now Sir Charles) Wyndham and Miss Mary Moore also came to dinner—or perhaps it was later in the evening; and with them the young American actress Miss Fay Davis, not then known on the stage, who recited some pieces with infinite piquancy and grace. Altogether it was an interesting gathering.

The feature of the musicale, however, was a performance of Schumann's pianoforte quartet (Op. 47) by four distinguished artists: Fanny Davies, Sarasate, Hollander, and Piatti—a combination rare even at the "Pops," and, above all, to be appreciated for the honor conferred by the great Spanish violinist, who seldom took part in a chamber work beyond the "Kreutzer" or some other duet-sonata. So anxious was he for the quartet to go well that he insisted upon a rehearsal, and from Paris fixed the date himself. Here is his note:

PARIS, 23—5—'96.

C'est entendu, cher ami, je partirai le 3 juin. Arrangez la répétition pour le 4 dans l'après-midi.[1]

Votre,

PABLO SARASATE.

What was more, he declined the invitation to dine in order that he might be able to eat his early meal at the Bristol, as was usual on evenings when he had to play. It is hardly necessary to add that the performance of the quartet was superlatively fine. From first to last it went with magnificent spirit; and it was listened to with keen enjoyment by an assemblage whose interest seemed evenly divided as to the music, the executants, and the foremost group of auditors, headed by the peerless "guest of the evening."

To-day Craig-y-nos Castle is the scene of fewer

[1] Translation: It is agreed, dear friend, I shall leave on June 3. Arrange the rehearsal for the 4th, in the afternoon.

entertainments upon a large scale. Still, the Baroness Cederström is as dearly attached as ever to her mountain home, and, when she is not traveling abroad or professionally, she spends practically her whole time there. She sings at twenty or twenty-five concerts every year (three or four in London, the rest in the provinces), and is received everywhere with the old-time ecstasy and enthusiasm. Nor can one feel astonished at the vast assemblages which gather at these familiar functions, since Adelina Patti yet retains her title, "The Queen of Song," by virtue of tones still pure, rich, vibrant, and exquisitely musical; by the magic of an art which no other singer of her day has exemplified with the same wondrous measure of beauty and perfection. This extraordinary survival of power and popularity makes it difficult to foretell even approximately when the great prima donna will bring her unexampled career to a close. She has now agreed to undertake a farewell tour in the United States; but it is not her intention to appear there in opera. Thus the American public will not have an opportunity to realize the full extent of that amazing development of her dramatic genius to which I have more especially made reference. But Patti is always Patti; and whatever the conditions, her final coming will be the occasion of a rapturous welcome from the citizens of the country in which she was reared.

CHAPTER XV

A meteoric opera scheme—Sullivan's "Ivanhoe"—How composed: how "run to death"—Début of Eugène Oudin—David Bispham appears in "La Basoche"—Oudin and Tschaikowsky: a singular coincidence—The Russian master's journey to Cambridge—First and last meetings—"Cavalleria Rusticana" at London and Windsor—Jean de Reszke's American début: his impressions.

THE early months of 1891 witnessed a very remarkable operatic experiment. New forces were at the back of it, and it was destined to mark the climax of the modern development of English opera. Had the scheme succeeded in its integrity, the operatic history of the next dozen years would have had to be rewritten; as it was, an individual artistic triumph was hampered by a Quixotic managerial policy, and the ambitious enterprise resulted in a regrettable failure.

The late Richard D'Oyly Carte was an excellent man in his own sphere of action at the Savoy Theatre. He thoroughly understood the business of mounting the unique comic operas of Gilbert and Sullivan, and of sending them round the globe in the hands of well-trained companies. But about the organization and management of serious opera he knew absolutely nothing. Shade of

DAVID BISPHAM
AS THE DUC DE LONGUEVILLE
From a photograph by Van der Werde, London

EUGÈNE OUDIN
AS THE TEMPLAR
From a photograph by Barraud, London

Carl Rosa! Imagine the fatuity of building a large and costly theatre on Shaftesbury Avenue,[1] bestowing upon it the high-sounding title of the "Royal English Opera," engaging a double company, and opening it with a repertory of—one work! Never was the initial error of placing the whole of the golden eggs in a single basket more surely followed by the destruction of the goose that laid them! Great was the faith of D'Oyly Carte in Arthur Sullivan. But not even the genius of that fine musician, as exemplified in his first grand opera, "Ivanhoe," was capable of withstanding so rude a test. Like one of the thoroughbred horses he loved so well, "Ivanhoe" ran a great race, achieved a "best on record," and then collapsed from sheer exhaustion. It has never raced since.

Sullivan wrote "Ivanhoe," so to speak, with his life-blood. He slaved at it steadily from May till December, and put into it only of his best. For weeks before he finished it he was inaccessible; the Christmas of 1890 was no holiday for him. The rehearsals had begun long before the orchestration was ready, and the opera was to be produced on January 31, 1891, at the latest. By the first week in the new year the score was completed. Then Sir Arthur told me I might come to Queen's Mansions to hear some of the music. To my great delight, he played several of the

[1] It has for the past eleven years been the popular place of amusement known as the Palace Theatre of Varieties.

numbers for me. I found them picturesque, dramatic, original, and stamped throughout with the cachet which the world understands by the word "Sullivanesque." I was particularly struck by the Oriental character of the harmonies and "intervals" in *Rebecca's* song, "Lord of our chosen race," and I told Sullivan that I thought nothing could be more distinctively Eastern or even Hebraic in type.

"That may well be so," he rejoined. "The phrase on the words 'guard me' you especially refer to is not strictly mine.[1] Let me tell you where I heard it. When I was the 'Mendelssohn scholar' and living at Leipsic, I went once or twice to the old Jewish synagogue, and among the many Eastern melodies chanted by the minister, this quaint progression in the minor occurred so frequently that I have never forgotten it." It certainly comes in appropriately here.

The libretto of "Ivanhoe" was from the fluent pen of Julian Sturgis, the author of "Nadeshda." It won praise as a skilful and fairly dramatic adaptation of Scott's novel and a polished example of poetic lyric-writing. The work generally I described at the time as "one which rivets the attention of the spectator from the moment the curtain is raised; which is strong and sympathetic

[1] The passage in question is this:

in action and picturesque in story; which is rich in melody and replete with musical interest and contrast; and which, finally, is presented amid a wealth of surroundings and with a perfection of executive detail such as English opera never enjoyed before." It was acclaimed with the utmost warmth by an audience that included the composer's ever-constant friends and patrons, the Prince and Princess of Wales, and the Duke and Duchess of Edinburgh. The cast on the first night comprised Marguerite Macintyre (*Rebecca*), Esther Palliser (*Rowena*), Ben Davies (*Ivanhoe*), Norman Salmond (*Richard Cœur de Lion*), Ffrangcon Davies (*Cedric*), Charles Kenningham (*De Bracy*), Avon Saxon (*Friar Tuck*), Charles Copland (*Isaac of York*), and that gifted American barytone, Eugène Oudin, who made a brilliant début in the part of the *Templar*. The composer held the baton.

The opera was at once scheduled "for a run," with two distinct casts, the alternative group including Miss Thudichum as *Rebecca,* Lucile Hill as *Rowena,* Franklin Clive as *King Richard,* Joseph O'Mara as *Ivanhoe,* and Richard Green as the *Templar*. The strain of this test was marvelously borne. For no fewer than one hundred and sixty consecutive representations did "Ivanhoe" draw large and enthusiastic audiences—far and away the longest unbroken run ever accomplished by a serious opera. Then, at the end of July, it was withdrawn, and the house closed until November, when an English version of André Messager's successful comic opera "La Basoche" was brought out. This did fairly well, but it is noteworthy to-day only from the fact that it enabled Mr. David Bispham, by his clever singing and acting, to make a deep impression at his first appearance upon the London stage.[1] D'Oyly Carte now doubtless imagined that he possessed the foundation of a repertory, and he revived "Ivanhoe" to run alternately with "La Basoche"—Barton McGuckin filling the title-rôle, while Medora Henson was the *Rowena*. But the public quickly undeceived the too sanguine manager. It stayed severely away. The drawing power of Sullivan's beautiful opera had been exhausted; and on January 16, just a fortnight short of twelve months after its auspicious opening, the "Royal English Opera" was finally closed—the strangest commingling of success and failure ever chronicled in the history of British lyric enterprise!

[1] The brilliant stage career of David Bispham virtually had its beginning with his singularly picturesque embodiment of the *Duc de Longueville* in "La Basoche." There was about it an element of fantastic *bizarrerie* that was singularly attractive, and which at once drew attention to the unique personality of the artist. From that time forward, in whatever branch of his art he has elected to labor, David Bispham has consistently earned distinction and applause; and his success has been equally emphatic on both sides of the Atlantic. His gift of versatility is extraordinary. Alike in serious and comic characters, in Wagnerian music-drama and light French opera, in oratorio and Lieder, in declamation both spoken and sung, he has proved himself a thoroughly intellectual, accomplished, and original artist.

From a photograph by Eugène Oudin

JEAN DE RESZKE LASSALLE EDOUARD DE RESZKE

"BIRDS OF A FEATHER"

Yet, had there been nothing else, this venture would have been remarkable on account of the unusual number of American singers who made their débuts in the two operas. Many of them subsequently were to earn wide repute, while two at least—Eugène Oudin and David Bispham—were to achieve universal fame. I can recall few instances of a popularity so spontaneous as that vouchsafed to Eugène Espérance Oudin. Alike as artist and as man he rapidly became a general favorite. Among his warmest admirers was Jean de Reszke; and I remember how profoundly he interested the famous tenor by his exquisite *mezza voce,* his perfect union of the "registers," and the rare ease with which he produced his upper notes. His voice was singularly sweet and sympathetic in quality, yet not lacking in dramatic power; and none who saw him as the *Templar* will readily forget the extraordinary dignity of his assumption or the intense passion of his singing. His rendering of the fine air, "Woo thou thy Snowflake," was to my mind the vocal feature of the opera.

Oudin had made himself a name both as a church singer and in opera before leaving the United States; but in London he seems at once to have risen to a higher plane, for there was need just then of a barytone possessing his special gifts. Thanks to his parentage, he had a pure French accent, and sang delightfully in that tongue. He also worked for some time with me at German Lieder, and made quite a hit at the Philharmonic by his admirable declamation in the "Hans Heiling" air. His versatility was further demonstrated by a number of translations of French lyrics, all very neatly and smoothly done. He had quite a passion for amateur photography, and loved to obtain unconventional pictures of all the artistic celebrities who would consent to "sit." Among these was the group of the two de Reszkes and Lassalle at their breakfast-table at the Continental, of which he sent me a copy accompanied by this note:

31 LINDEN GARDENS, W., October 21, 1893.

MY DEAR KLEIN:

I send you per same post a print (proof) from my negative, "Birds of a Feather," with every compliment. I shall not forget that it was through you and in your house that I first met the great singers who have since become my friends.

It is an extraordinary coincidence, I think, that I should have put down for my part in the "Pops" this afternoon (and as long as a fortnight ago) four of my favorite Gounod songs.[1] Also that I am singing at the offertory in St. George's, Albemarle Street, to-morrow morning, under promise a fortnight old, the same master's "There is a green hill."

Faithfully and fraternally yours,

EUGÈNE OUDIN.

Alas! only eighteen months later I stood in the same church in Albemarle Street grieving be-

[1] The death of Gounod had been announced three days previously.

side the bier of that sweet singer himself. He had fallen a victim to a mistaken sense of duty, literally wearing himself to death by nursing a friend who lay sick in his house. That was indeed a sad and premature cutting off of a useful life. I had spoken to Oudin at the Birmingham Festival (October, 1894), and remarked upon his thin, careworn aspect. Yet how beautifully he had sung the music of *Dr. Marianus* in the third part of Schumann's "Faust"! It was all he had had to do at the festival; but it was enough, he had made his mark. Then he went home, and in a month's time was no more.

The premature decease of Eugène Oudin is always associated in my mind with that of Tschaikowsky. The reason lies in a rather curious chain of circumstances. In the autumn of 1892 the Russian master's opera "Eugény Onégin" was produced in English at the Olympic Theatre, under the management of Signor Lago, with Eugène Oudin in the title part. It met with poor success, and after a few nights was withdrawn.[1] In the June of 1893, Tschaikowsky came to England to receive the honorary degree of "Mus. Doc." at Cambridge University; the same distinction being simultaneously bestowed upon three other celebrated musicians—Camille Saint-Saëns, Max

[1] The whole undertaking was ill-timed and ill-placed. One of its few creditable features was the début in England of the barytone Mario Ancona, who sang first in "La Favorita" and afterward in "Lohengrin." He was engaged the following season for Covent Garden.

Bruch, and Arrigo Boïto. By a happy chance I traveled down to Cambridge in the same carriage with Tschaikowsky. I was quite alone in the compartment until the train was actually starting, when the door opened and an elderly gentleman was unceremoniously lifted in, his luggage being bundled in after him by the porters. A glance told me who it was. I offered my assistance, and, after he had recovered his breath, the master told me he recollected that I had been presented to him one night at the Philharmonic. Then followed an hour's delightful conversation.

Tschaikowsky chatted freely about music in Russia. He thought the development of the past twenty-five years had been phenomenal. He attributed it, first, to the intense musical feeling of the people which was now coming to the surface; secondly, to the extraordinary wealth and characteristic beauty of the national melodies or folk-songs; and, thirdly, to the splendid work done by the great teaching institutions at St. Petersburg and Moscow. He spoke particularly of his own Conservatory at Moscow, and begged that if I ever went to that city I would not fail to pay him a visit.[1] He then put some questions about England and inquired especially as to the systems of management and teaching pursued at the Royal

[1] I did visit Moscow in the summer of 1898, and, on presenting my card as an English friend of the lamented master, was received by the Conservatory officials with every attention and cordiality.

GOUNOD

TSCHAIKOWSKY

From a photograph by Reutlinger, Paris

Academy and the Royal College. I duly explained, and also gave him some information concerning the Guildhall School of Music and its three thousand students. It surprised him to hear that London possessed such a gigantic musical institution.

"I don't know," he added, "whether to consider England an 'unmusical' nation or not. Sometimes I think one thing, sometimes another. But it is certain that you have audiences for music of every class, and it appears to me probable that before long the larger section of your public will support the best class only." Then the recollection of the failure of his "Eugény Onégin" occurred to him, and he asked me to what I attributed that—the music, the libretto, the performance, or what? I replied, without flattery, that it was certainly not the music. It might have been due in some measure to the lack of dramatic fibre in the story, and in a large degree to the inefficiency of the interpretation and the unsuitability of the locale. "Remember," I went on, "that Pushkin's poem is not known in this country, and that in opera we like a definite dénouement, not an ending where the hero goes out at one door and the heroine at another. As to the performance, the only figure in it that lives distinctly and pleasantly in my memory is Eugène Oudin's superb embodiment of *Onégin.*"

"I have heard a great deal about him," said Tschaikowsky; and then came a first-rate opportunity for me to descant upon the merits of the

American barytone. I aroused the master's interest in him to such good purpose that he promised not to leave England without making his acquaintance,—"and hearing him sing?" I queried. "Not only will I hear him sing, but invite him to come to Russia and ask him to sing some of my songs there," was the composer's reply as the train drew up at Cambridge, and we alighted. Tschaikowsky was to be the guest of the Master of Merton, and I undertook to see him safely bestowed at the college before proceeding to my hotel. Telling the flyman to take a slightly circuitous route, I pointed out various places of interest as we passed them, and Tschaikowsky seemed thoroughly to enjoy the drive. When we parted at the college, he shook me warmly by the hand and expressed a hope that when he next visited England he might see more of me. Unhappily, that kindly wish was never to be fulfilled.

The group of new "Mus. Docs." was to have included Verdi and Grieg, but these composers were unable to accept the invitation of the University. However, the remaining four constituted a sufficiently illustrious group, and the concert at the Cambridge Guildhall was of memorable interest. Saint-Saëns played for the first time the brilliant pianoforte fantasia "Africa," which he had lately written at Cairo; Max Bruch directed a choral scene from his "Odysseus"; and Boïto conducted the prologue from "Mefistofele," Georg Henschel singing the solo part. Finally, Tschaikowsky directed the first performance in England of his fine symphonic poem, "Francesca da Rimini," a work depicting with graphic power the tormenting winds wherein Dante beholds *Francesca* in the "Second Circle" and hears her recital of her sad story, as described in the fifth canto of the "Inferno." The ovation that greeted each master in turn will be readily imagined. A night or two later I met Boïto at a reception given in his honor by my friend Albert Visetti, and the renowned librettist-composer did me the pleasure of accompanying me to the last Philharmonic concert of the season, at which Max Bruch conducted a couple of works and Paderewski played his concerto in A minor.

Tschaikowsky and Eugène Oudin duly met. The latter sang the "Sérénade de Don Juan" and other songs of the Russian master, and so delighted him that the visit to St. Petersburg and Moscow was immediately arranged. Its success and its attendant sorrow are alike set forth in the following letter:

HOTEL DE FRANCE, ST. PETERSBURG,
November 8, 1893.

MY DEAR KLEIN:

You have, of course, read and commented on the terribly sudden demise of Tschaikowsky. You can imagine its effect on me! I missed him in Petersburg on my way to Moscow, and there received his message that he would not fail to be present at my début in the latter city. Instead came a telegram of sudden sickness, danger passed, and hope. This was on Saturday last. On Monday morning a telegram came to speak of—death!

On Wednesday last he was sound and well; he drank a glass of unfiltered water from the Neva, and cholera laid him low! It is awful! The musical societies throughout Russia are in mourning, and the concert which was to have been my début in Petersburg (next Saturday, the 11th) is postponed for a week. It will be made up entirely of works of the dead master. I shall sing the "Arioso" from "Onégin" and some of his romances, and the joint recital will take place the following day.[1]

So my visit here is prolonged most unexpectedly.

My début in Moscow was a magnificent success. I was recalled and encored again and again, . . . and the notices are very fine.

Yours in haste, but ever fraternally,

EUGÈNE OUDIN.

And now to return to 1891. So far I have spoken only of "Ivanhoe" and "La Basoche." At Covent Garden we had the heaviest opera season on record. Twenty operas were mounted, none of them novelties, but six for the first time under Harris's directorate; and ninety-four representations were given in sixteen weeks. The total receipts amounted to £80,000 ($400,000), and the impresario made a profit. It is interesting to note how the repertory and the personnel were begin-

[1] Oudin was accompanied on this trip by his wife, a talented singer who frequently appeared with him at his London recitals, but who, on the death of her husband, relinquished her career as a vocalist and became a teacher.

VAN ROOY
AS WOTAN
Copyright by A. Dupont, N. Y.

PLANÇON
AS MEPHISTOPHELES
Copyright by A. Dupont, N. Y.

ning to settle down into the mold or formula with which the American public was soon to become so familiar. Take the operas—twelve performances of "Faust"; nine of "Lohengrin"; eight each of "Les Huguenots" and "Roméo et Juliette"; seven of "Carmen"; six of "Orfeo"; five each of "Don Giovanni," "Tannhäuser," and "Rigoletto"; four of "Otello" (with Jean de Reszke in the title-rôle), "Traviata" and "Manon"; three of "Le Prophète" and "Mireille"; two of "Mefistofele," "Die Meistersinger," "Lucia," "Martha," and "Aida"; and (poor Beethoven!) one of "Fidelio." Again, among the fifteen new-comers of the season were Emma Eames, Sybil Sanderson, Van Dyck, and Plançon, forming part of a company of no fewer than forty artists, which included Jean and Edouard de Reszke, Lassalle, Maurel, Ravelli, Devoyod, Isnardon, and Montariol; with Nordica, Melba, Albani, Zélie de Lussan, Rolla, Regina Pinkert, Bauermeister, Giulia Ravogli, and the French contralto Mme. Richard. Altogether a very remarkable collection, and in its make-up thoroughly suggestive of the Metropolitan Opera House, New York.

On the second night of the season (April 7) Emma Eames made her London début as *Marguerite* in "Faust," that being her first appearance on any stage save the Paris Opéra, where she had been a favorite for the two preceding years. Her singularly rich, flexible soprano voice, her refined and expressive singing, and her graceful bearing won for her warm admiration and instantaneous success. She looked Goethe's heroine to the life, and her conception of the character charmed alike by its naturalness and its tender womanly feeling. Four nights later she essayed the part of *Elsa,* for the first time, to the *Lohengrin* of Jean de Reszke, and again succeeded in creating a highly favorable impression. Later on she made a hit as *Juliette* and gave a delightful rendering of the music of *Mireille,* both of which characters she had studied under the personal guidance of Gounod. Her *Mireille* was, I recollect, a particularly captivating performance, and it is perhaps a little odd that it should not have subsequently filled a more conspicuous place in the répertoire of this talented American artist.

Equally unprecedented was the amount of operatic work done in the autumn. Besides D'Oyly Carte's hapless enterprise, a French season was given by Augustus Harris at Covent Garden with the *concours* of artists of the Paris Opéra-Comique, comprising the graceful Mlle. Simonnet, that fine singer Mme. Deschamps-Jehin, M. Engel, M. Bouvet, and M. Lorrain. They gave for the first time there Alfred Bruneau's clever opera, "Le Rêve," and Gounod's "Philémon et Baucis." Yet a third venture was an Italian season given by Signor Lago at the Shaftesbury Theatre. This was notable chiefly for the first production in England of Pietro Mascagni's "Cavalleria Rusticana," which, I need scarcely say, created a sensation. The performance (conducted by Arditi) was not to be compared with those subsequently heard at the leading opera-house, but it served; and the fame of the young Italian composer spread with marvelous rapidity. It should be noted that Marie Brema here made a modest but effective début in opera as *Lola;* while the cast further comprised Adelaide Musiani (*Santuzza*), Grace Damian (*Lucia*), Brombara (*Alfio*), and Francesco Vignas (*Turiddu*).

These artists gave a performance of "Cavalleria Rusticana" before Queen Victoria in the Waterloo Chamber at Windsor Castle on November 25, 1891. Her Majesty was greatly impressed by the new opera, and in the following summer, after Mme. Emma Calvé had made her London début as Mascagni's Sicilian heroine, the Queen commanded her to sing at Windsor, together with the tenor De Lucia; Signor Tosti being at the piano. The two artists gave a selection from "Cavalleria," and, by Her Majesty's permission, went through their scene with action and gestures precisely as though they were performing it upon the stage. So earnestly did they throw themselves into their parts, and with such characteristic sentiment did they sing, that the venerable sovereign was deeply touched, and presented the artists with handsome mementos before they left the castle. I may note, by the way, that "Cavalleria Rusticana" was first performed in English by the Carl Rosa Company at Liverpool on January 14, 1892.

This same winter season was marked by operatic events of the greatest import to the United States. Encouraged by his previous successes, Henry Abbey determined to do things on a yet grander scale, and, with the aid of new associates, launched out upon a double enterprise of formidable magnitude. One of those associates was destined thereafter to play an important part in the direction of opera on both sides of the Atlantic—I refer to Maurice Grau. For the moment Abbey held the guiding reins, and nobody knew exactly how much he owed to the energy and tact of his junior partner. At the same time, the experience earned by Maurice Grau during this period was of inestimable value to him. He became familiar with the countless nuances of operatic management; he acquired his characteristic habit of blunt, straightforward dealing with artists of every rank; he developed his excellent business qualities, and learned the knack of gauging to a nicety the requirements of public taste. A finer practical schooling in the delicate duties of an impresario could not possibly have been devised. Nor could anything have been more timely.

For the moment had now arrived when the American manager was to keep in closer touch with the London stage; when the "tricks and manners" of Covent Garden were to be immediately imitated at the Metropolitan Opera House; when the same collections of artists and works were to serve for both countries. The double

EMMA EAMES
AS JULIETTE

venture run by Abbey consisted of a big series of Patti concerts and a five months' season of grand opera with a company headed by Jean de Reszke. The renowned prima donna awakened, as usual, the utmost enthusiasm. At each concert a scene, in costume, from an opera was given, Mme. Patti being supported by Del Puente, Novara, and other artists, with Arditi as conductor. On the other hand, the débuts in America of Jean and Edouard de Reszke were at the outset more successful in an artistic than a financial sense. It seems to have taken time for the public to realize that in the new Polish tenor a really great artist had come upon the scene. A small section of the press also appears to have hesitated, though not the leading critics of New York and Chicago, who quickly proclaimed the advent of a star of the first magnitude. That M. de Reszke himself was, on the whole, gratified by his reception may be gathered from the following letter:

[Translated from the French.]

Auditorium Hotel, Chicago,
December 9, 1891.

My dear Friend:

I beg to inclose some press cuttings from this place in order that you may learn of the success of your friends in America. I have sung twice in "Lohengrin," twice in "Faust," twice in the "Huguenots," once in "Roméo," twice in "Otello," and once in "Lohengrin" at Louisville. That makes ten representations in a month. The public is very warm, very enthusiastic toward us. Edouard, for his part, besides the operas with me, has sung *Leporello* and in "Sonnambula." You would confer on us a great pleasure by showing the cuttings to Harris, to Higgins, and to your colleagues, in order that London may know how the artists of its choice have been winning honors here. I sing to-morrow "Aida," with Lilli Lehmann, for my farewell in this city; then on Thursday I leave for New York, where I am to make my début on Monday in "Roméo." Trusting you are in good health, with a hearty hand-shake, believe me,

Your devoted and ever grateful,

JEAN DE RESZKE.

In New York the brothers were met by their friend Lassalle, who made his first appearance as *Nelusko* in "L'Africaine"; while, as *Selika,* Lillian Nordica also rejoined the company and her former comrades. That night was the most brilliant of the season, and the cable messages to Europe told of unequivocal success all round. Yet the "business," it appeared, was by no means first-rate, and, in the end, the *entrepreneurs* must have fared but moderately. The *revanche,* however, was to come in the succeeding years, when the American public knew Jean de Reszke better and learned to appreciate the true majesty of his transcendent gifts. He, for his part, quickly reciprocated the warm feeling shown him by American audiences, and would frequently assure me how profoundly he esteemed their good opinion. To show this I quote an interesting letter he wrote me from Chicago in 1894, immediately after the production of Massenet's "Werther":

[Translated from the French.]

CHICAGO, March 31, 1894.

MY DEAR FRIEND:

In an artist's life every new rôle is a stage in that long journey toward the summits of art, toward the beautiful, the infinite. "Werther," the other night, was for me one of those unanimous successes wherein the heart—the science of causing it to beat in one's audience and before one's audience—stood in true proportion to every artifice. The true path—that of emotion—that goal for which I am striving all my life—was reached in the presence of a public which did not understand the words, but which divined by instinct that my conception of the character arose from that simplicity, that pure, unexaggerated truthfulness which age and maturity alone can confer upon the thinking artist. . . . I am sending you the cuttings from the newspapers here; show them to Harris, who, I hope, will mount the opera for me. Mancinelli conducted the orchestra admirably. Eames and Arnoldson are two adorable little sisters. In a word, I believe that to the cultivated London public, accustomed as it is to novelties, it will come as a delightful surprise. I sing regularly three times every week, and my voice is excellent. At this present moment I am reaching my forty-first performance. Accept, my dear friend, from Edouard and myself, a thousand affectionate remembrances, together with a hearty shake of the hand.

Your devoted,

JEAN DE RESZKE.

Three months later, Harris did mount "Werther" at Covent Garden, with the Chicago cast, for the rentrée of Jean de Reszke; but the opera failed to please. Not even the genius of the artist could invest with enduring interest a work consistently sombre, undramatic, and dull. Yet, taken individually, his impersonation was, in its way, one of the supreme achievements of his career. His voice at this period was at its very finest; nor shall I ever forget his wonderful singing and acting in the duet of the third act, where "his beautiful tones fairly compassed the entire gamut of passionate longing and despair."

CHAPTER XVI

German opera at Covent Garden—Mahler as conductor—Débuts of Alvary and Schumann-Heink—A growing repertory—Victor Maurel and Manuel Garcia: The renowned teacher vindicated—Début of Clara Butt—Leoncavallo and Mascagni in London—How "Cavalleria" was first rehearsed at Rome—"I Rantzau"—Mascagni at Windsor Castle—More State Performances.

"CHI va piano va sano, ed anche lontano." The old Italian proverb applies with some force to the progress made by Sir Augustus Harris toward the development of the important branch of opera which yet awaited his attention. The popularity of French opera in the French language would seem to have been the natural stepping-stone to German opera in the German language. But I am not quite sure that Harris found his subscribers as ready as he himself was to risk the step. Annual pilgrimages to Bayreuth had not yet become a favorite amusement of the British aristocracy. Lady de Grey and her friends were said to be inclined to look askance at any proposition for the enlargement of the opera scheme beyond the lines which had hitherto proved so successful. However, it is to be presumed that the opposition, if there was any worth speaking of, speedily broke down; for in the early spring of 1892 the impresario boldly announced his intention of giving a series of German performances at Covent Garden in mid-season, with the aid of a special troupe of German artists engaged through the medium of the Hamburg manager, Herr Pollini.

By the press and the public this intimation was received with such unqualified satisfaction that Sir Augustus immediately followed it up with a further announcement to the effect that he would set apart seven Wednesdays in June and July for a subsidiary subscription, covering performances of "Der Ring des Nibelungen," with "Tristan und Isolde" and "Fidelio." This was an adroit move. Wednesday was not yet a regular subscription night at the opera, and by thus utilizing it Harris not only secured a perfect guarantee against loss, but offered his German supporters the opportunity of displaying themselves in grand- and pit-tier boxes, which they could not otherwise have obtained for love or money. The bait was greedily seized and a splendid subscription resulted.

Ultimately, too, the company engaged for these representations proved worthy of the establishment to which it became temporarily allied. I was very anxious to see Richter filling the conductor's place, and at my suggestion Harris made an effort to obtain the great man's services. But in vain; he was already definitely engaged for the concerts of the forthcoming Musical Exhibition at Vienna. In these circumstances, Herr Pollini recommended a young conductor named Mahler, who had been doing excellent work at Hamburg. Harris at once made terms with him; and thus for a single season did London afford hospitality to the talented musician who was shortly after to succeed Hans Richter as *chef d'orchestre,* and eventually to become director, of the Imperial Opera House at Vienna.

It was arranged that Mahler should come early in the season. Ten years had elapsed since the "Ring" or any section of it had been performed in a London opera-house, and in order not to interfere with the other work it was deemed advisable to procure a separate orchestra to rehearse and accompany the Wagner music-dramas. I made Mahler's acquaintance soon after his arrival. Smaller of stature than Anton Seidl, his clean-shaven, studious countenance nevertheless reminded me of the accomplished conductor whom I had seen at Her Majesty's in 1882; nor was he unworthy to be compared with him in temperamental qualities, well-balanced force, and rare concentration of energy. For a man who knew so very little English, I never came across any one so bent on speaking that language and no other. I met Mahler frequently at Harris's office, but could never induce him to carry on a conversation in German. He would rather spend five minutes in an effort to find the English word he wanted than resort to his mother tongue or allow any one else to supply the equivalent. Consequently, a short chat with Mahler involved a liberal allowance of time. For the same reason, his orchestral rehearsals proved extremely lengthy and, to the spectator, vastly amusing. In order to familiarize his men with their exacting task, he would take his band in sections, and spend hour after hour going over the various scenes of the tetralogy and "Tristan." He knew his scores virtually by heart, and infused into his executants that unity of spirit which only a born conductor can inspire. So it came about that the performances given under his direction were distinguished by a highly creditable excellence of ensemble.

Absurd as it may seem, the "Nibelungen" dramas were given out of their proper order because a certain great Bayreuth artist insisted upon making his English début in a particular character. Herr Max Alvary wished to be seen for the first time here in his fine impersonation of *Siegfried;* consequently, we had to have "Siegfried" first; then "Rheingold" and "Walküre," and then "Götterdämmerung" to wind up with. I know not whom to blame the more, Alvary for demanding such a piece of vandalism, or Harris for allowing it; but in either case "de mortuis nil nisi bonum," and there I halt. Certainly Alvary was an ideal *Siegfried;* and he had no less an ideal *Brünnhilde* in Rosa Sucher, who unfortunately was recalled to Germany after a night or two.

From a photograph by E. Bieber, Berlin

ALVARY
AS SIEGFRIED

Her place was taken by the gifted and lamented Frau Klafsky, whom I admired as a truly great Wagnerian artist. Other notable débutantes were the popular Frau Schumann-Heink, Fräulein Bettaque, Frau Ende-Andriessen, Fräulein Traubmann, beside Greve, Lieban (inimitable *Mime*), and Zoltan Döme, who shared the leading rôles with the veterans Reichmann and Wiegand.

So extensively did these German representations draw that Sir Augustus determined to give some of them on off-nights at Drury Lane, moving the scenery back and forth from one house to the other. The device paid him well, and, beside the Wagner works, he added to his repertory Nessler's "Trompeter von Säkkingen," with Reichmann, Wiegand, Lorent, Landau, Bettaque, and Schumann-Heink in the principal parts. Altogether the experiment proved a complete success, and set at rest all doubts as to the wisdom and desirability of mixing the undiluted German with those other operatic elements which Sir Augustus Harris (dropping the traditional "Italian") had this season for the first time combined under the new official title of "Royal Opera, Covent Garden."

Relieved of his shrieval duties, the genial impresario now set to work to beat all previous records; and he fairly accomplished the task. Apart from the German venture, he produced no fewer than three novelties, viz.: Mascagni's "L'Amico Fritz," Bemberg's "Elaine," and Isidore de

Lara's "Light of Asia," this last being an Italianized stage version of a setting, in cantata form, of portions of Sir Edwin Arnold's poem. None of these earned more than passing favor, albeit "L'Amico Fritz," in virtue of Mascagni's charming treatment of a delicious pastoral story and Calvé's exquisite embodiment of *Suzel*, deserved a better fate. But not even the united efforts of Jean de Reszke, Plançon, Melba, and Deschamps-Jehin could awaken more than a shadowy interest in M. Bemberg's saccharine opera. The general repertory was much the same as in the previous year, only more extensive; while lingual incongruities were perhaps more flagrant than ever. For example, we would hear in alternation the "Flying Dutchman" in Italian (with Lassalle as *Vanderdecken*); "Tannhäuser" in German; "Lohengrin" in Italian (Van Dyck singing the title-rôle in French); an English opera, "La Luce dell' Asia," in Italian; "Le Prophète" in French, with an Italian chorus; and so forth. Evidently, this feature of the bad traditions of old had yet to be improved; but in other respects the work done and the progress made were alike remarkable. In the course of the year 1892 Augustus Harris mounted at Covent Garden and Drury Lane theatres as many as thirty operas, giving a grand total of one hundred and fifty representations.

In the midst of this abnormally busy season, M. Maurel elected to deliver a lecture at the Lyceum Theatre on "The Application of Science to the Arts of Speech and Song." It was partly an amplification of a *conférence* given shortly before at Milan and published at Paris under the title of "Le Chant renoué par la Science," wherein the distinguished barytone promised a book that should more or less completely revolutionize the art (or "science") of singing. For that book an impatient world is still waiting. The lecture, however, duly came off, and, apart from mere promises, its main feature proved to be an exceedingly virulent tirade against the *coup de la glotte*.[1] This would not have mattered much had it not happened that Manuel Garcia himself was present, and had to "possess his soul in patience" while M. Maurel executed some ridiculous imitations of what he considered to be the indispensable vocal concomitants of the *coup de la glotte*—a term derided only by certain Paris teachers who have misunderstood and misdirected its use. Age and dignity alike compelled Signor Garcia to sit still and treat with silent contempt this ill-timed and unjustifiable attack upon his method. When the lecture was over, however, I offered him the columns of the "Sunday Times" as a medium for replying to M. Maurel's assertions. On the spur of the moment, he accepted and sent a short account of the lecture, written in his own terse, trenchant manner. Then, thinking better of it, he decided not to take any personal part in the discussion, and requested me not to print his "copy."

[1] See reference to this subject on page 27.

This threw the onus of reply upon me; and the answer proved so far effectual that M. Maurel was moved to make a protest, in other London papers, against any contradiction of his "scientific argumentation," save by M. Garcia himself, and not even then unless supported by something beyond "simple denial." Accordingly, the maestro then consented to write a letter to the "Sunday Times," confirming the statement that he had found M. Maurel's illustrations of the *coup de la glotte* "extremely exaggerated," but declining that gentleman's invitation to discuss the subject-matter of his lecture, and adding that "it would be utterly impossible to argue upon theories which still remain to be revealed." Here the incident closed, and, as I have already said, the singing world is still awaiting the revelation of M. Maurel's precious theories. Meanwhile, however, there are people who still think it their duty to assume the Maurelesque attitude, and boldly impeach a method for which no adequate substitute, real or imaginary, has yet been found. It is chiefly with the view of showing the hollowness of the attacks occasionally leveled at the *coup de la glotte* that I have recalled an episode which otherwise might have been allowed to dwell in oblivion.

During the early "nineties" Sir Augustus Harris was the proprietor of the "Sunday Times." For some time he had been bent on possessing a newspaper, and would have actually started a new one on his own account had it not happened that

Copyright by A. Dupont, N. Y.

CALVÉ
AS CARMEN

the old weekly came into the market once more. I was responsible for his buying it, and, as matters turned out, neither he nor I had occasion to regret the step, despite the obvious delicacy of a position which, under ordinary conditions, might have involved the independence of a critic. I am bound to say, however, that Harris allowed me my full freedom; and, inasmuch as I had all along been an ardent supporter of his enterprise, my attitude was in no way influenced or disturbed through his temporary connection with the paper. He eventually sold it—for exactly the same sum, I believe, that he paid for it—to the present proprietor, Mrs. Frederic Beer.

During the winter of 1892–93, the indefatigable impresario revived the *bal masqué* at Covent Garden, thus furnishing the *jeunesse dorée* of the English metropolis with a form of entertainment which has ever since been keenly appreciated and regularly kept up. It is a common saying that the English take their pleasures sadly; but I may assert, without fear of contradiction, that these fancy-dress balls are a good deal less artificial and more spontaneous in their gaiety than the *bals-masqués* held in the opera-houses in Paris and Brussels. That, I admit, is about all there is to be said in their favor.

It was during the same winter that Clara Butt made her first appearance in public. The need for a new concert contralto of the first rank had become pressing. Trebelli had died suddenly at

Étretat the previous summer; and in the February of 1894 an even more sudden attack of heart disease closed the career of Janet Patey as she was leaving the platform at a concert at Sheffield. It was curious that midway between these two sad events there should have appeared upon the scene the artist who, whatever her vocal attributes as compared with those of her gifted predecessors, indisputably holds at the present time the position of leading English contralto.

Miss Clara Butt made her début, while yet a scholar of the Royal College of Music, in a performance of Gluck's "Orpheus," given by the pupils of the college at the Lyceum Theatre in December, 1892. Her unusually lofty stature lent to the embodiment of *Orpheus* a dignity and impressiveness that were at least equaled by the organ-like sonority and volume of her ample tones. Then she could neither act nor sing; but there was intelligence in her work, there was an evident faculty for imitation, and, above all, there was glorious material in her powerful, luscious voice. She continued her studies for some time in London and afterward in Paris, striding always toward popularity by a "royal road" that few young singers are fortunate enough to find. To-day she is a much improved vocalist, well up in the traditions of oratorio, and needing only complete control of her organ and fuller resources of expression and color to attain the highest level of artistic efficiency. Her husband, Kennerley Rumford, has a sympathetic light barytone voice with a style marked by admirable refinement and distinction.

A posthumous light opera by Goring Thomas, called the "Golden Web," ran for a time at the Lyric Theatre in the spring of 1893, after a trial production by the Carl Rosa Company at Liverpool. It was a charming example of the Auber school, and was ably conducted by Mr. Herbert Bunning—himself a composer of recognized merit, whose opera "La Princesse Osra" was to be mounted at Covent Garden nine years later. That this Englishman will one day make a big mark in the world of music I instinctively feel. His is a singularly graceful talent, and of orchestral effects he is a consummate master. When he comes across a really good libretto we shall perchance discover in him the successor to Arthur Goring Thomas. Another light-opera début at this period was that of the clever Spanish pianist and composer, Señor Albeniz, who conducted his "Magic Opal" during a run of considerable duration. A vastly superior work, however, was his "Pepita Jimenez," an exquisitely poetic opera founded upon Juan Valera's famous novel by Frank B. M. Coutts. I witnessed the production of "Pepita Jimenez" at the Liceo Theatre, Barcelona, in January, 1896, and admired it so much that I often wonder why the little *chef d'œuvre* has traveled no farther.

The features of the season of 1893 were the first

visits to London of Leoncavallo and Mascagni, and the production there of their respective operas, "Pagliacci" and "I Rantzau." The fame of Leoncavallo's sensational opera had preceded it, and the public expected something remarkable. They were not disappointed. I have rarely seen an audience so breathless with excitement over the development of an opera plot. The effect of the little tragedy was augmented by the burning intensity of De Lucia, whose portrayal of the hapless *Canio's* anguish and suffering was a triumph of realism. His touching soliloquy at the end of the first act was delivered with an abandonment of feeling that completely carried away his auditors. Very fine, too, was Ancona's rendering of the already famous Prologue; deliciously pure and sweet was Melba's vocalization in the *ballatella* for *Nedda;* excellent were the new-comers Richard Green and Bonnard as *Silvio* and *Peppe;* while Mancinelli's conducting left not a point undiscerned throughout. Leoncavallo, modest and unassuming, waited quietly in the background till the end, and then had to be forced on to the stage by the artists to acknowledge the ovation that awaited him. This was quite early in the season (May 19), and Leoncavallo remained in London for several weeks. I found him to be a man of great culture and strong intellect. He is a poet as well as a musician, and in both arts he reveals the grasp of a profound thinker.

Mascagni belongs to a different type. In Leon-

From a photograph by Guigoni & Bossi, Milan

PIETRO MASCAGNI

cavallo there is a dash of the refined and diplomatic Frenchman; in the composer of "Cavalleria Rusticana" one perceives, within as well as without, the impulsiveness, the impetuosity, the strong racial temperament of the full-blooded Italian. Quick as lightning in speech and gesture, excitable to the last degree, Mascagni carries his heart upon his sleeve, making no effort, apparently, either to conceal his sentiments or his thoughts. Here, plainly stamped, are the frank nature, the dogged perseverance, of the man who, under the most terribly adverse circumstances, was able to compose an opera which exhales the very essence of warm Southern passion, the very breath of free peasant life, the very spirit of Sicilian jealousy and revenge. Sordid and repulsive the story is and always must be; yet the music never fails to lift it from out the depths of its dramatic coarseness, and imparts to it a glamour and an intensity of color that few can resist. More than once has Mascagni told the tale of the pecuniary worries and the physical sufferings that he and his family underwent while he was writing the score of "Cavalleria" in his effort to win the prize offered by the Milanese publisher Edoardo Sonzogno. No wonder the news that he had won it nearly bereft him of his senses.

One day, at a dinner given by De Lucia (at the house of his friend Mazzoni in Charlotte Street, Bedford Square), Mascagni told us the sequel. And if the story of the composition was touching, the less familiar account of his journey to Rome and the staging of "Cavalleria" at the Costanzi Theatre was unquestionably as quaint and striking. At the time the news of his success reached him, he was residing in the small Sicilian town of Cerignola, where he filled the post of municipal conductor and organist at a tiny salary. Now the Sonzogno prize had not been awarded to Mascagni's opera alone: it was divided between two (if not among three) of the competitors. Consequently, there was considerable doubt as to which of the successful works would be mounted first, or when and where the performance would be. Quite unexpectedly, one morning early in May, 1890, Mascagni received an intimation that "Cavalleria Rusticana" had been placed in rehearsal at the Costanzi, and that his presence was forthwith required in Rome.

The request came to hand at an unfortunate moment. So straitened were his circumstances that he actually did not possess sufficient cash to meet the expenses of the journey. However, he contrived to borrow the necessary sum from a friend, and arrived in Rome the next day but one, in good time for the rehearsal. I should like to quote Mascagni's own words in describing what took place at the theatre, but to give them in cold English, without the aid of his eloquent gestures and his wonderful undercurrent of mimicry and "asides," would be to deprive them of half their significance. Enough that he had barely stepped inside the stage door before he felt himself upon "hot coals." Not a soul knew him. He had to introduce himself to the manager, who in turn presented him to the company as "the young composer who had been fortunate enough," and so on. Every one was studiously polite. The celebrated tenor Stagno, who was to honor him by creating the rôle of *Turiddu,* made a frigid bow; and the popular Gemma Bellincioni, who had accepted the part of *Santuzza,* offered him at least three fingers of her right hand. In short, it was a trying moment—particularly so for a youthful musician who was nervous, anxious, and —not over well fed.

When the rehearsal began, it quickly became evident that the principals had already invented and arranged most of their "business," and had no thought of submitting their ideas to Mascagni for his approval. Once or twice it was, "Maestro, do you like this?" or "Do you care for that?" But, generally speaking, his opinion was not sought; and, although his experience as musical director of a touring operetta company might have enabled him to drop a useful hint, he wisely refrained from interfering where such tremendously distinguished artists were concerned.

In point of fact, too, he was like a man in a dream—a veritable dream of paradise. Only once did he venture to ask a question, and that was at the outset of the rehearsal, when Stagno called for a chair just as he was about to begin the Sicilian serenade which *Turiddu* is heard singing in the prelude. With all humility he begged to inquire what the chair was for. (His imitation of the tenor's tone and attitude when he replied was exquisite.)

"Pardon, *caro maestro!* This is my own little affair. When I want to sing an air *con brio* I always like to think of 'La donna è mobile,' which I sing so well because I am all the time holding on to the back of a chair. Now, when I sing your serenade the curtain is down. Very well; no one sees me. I intend therefore to have my chair here to sing it just as if it were the 'Rigoletto' air. You will see, the effect will be superb!"

It did not seem to have occurred to Stagno that the serenade in "Cavalleria" is heard approaching from the distance and gradually dying away again. But never mind; he wanted his chair, and Mascagni was very glad to let him have it. For the rest, the rehearsal passed off satisfactorily enough, and the opera went extremely well on the 18th. How it created a furore that was to convert Mascagni into an idol and carry his name and music to the farthest corners of the civilized globe are facts that need no narration here. His début at Covent Garden took place on June 19, 1893, when he conducted "L'Amico Fritz" with Calvé, De Lucia, Pauline Joran, and Dufriche in the cast. He was rapturously greeted by an audience which included so many "royalties" that there was not room for half of them in the Queen's box. As a matter of course, he speedily became the "lion" of the season.

The elements were thus ripe for a fresh triumph when the time came for the production of "I Rantzau" on July 7. Mascagni's third opera had seen the light at Florence only in the previous November. The book appeared to offer a promising combination, being written by the librettist of "Cavalleria Rusticana" and founded upon a novel, "Les Deux Frères," by MM. Erckmann-Chatrian, the authors of "L'Amico Fritz." Unfortunately, the material of the plot proved altogether inadequate for a four-act opera, while the love interest which so largely predominated in "L'Amico Fritz" was here subordinated to the events of a sordid quarrel between two wilful, ill-tempered brothers. Moreover, Mascagni treated the quarrel in an intensely tragic vein, which is nowhere more strikingly exemplified than in the long and elaborate finale to the first act. This ambitious piece of writing I have described as strong, rugged, original, and clever. "Nevertheless, a big effort of the imagination is required to suppose an entire village so upset by a squabble over a field as to stand in two sections in the open piazza, shouting at each other for ten minutes by the clock!" Even a street row in Nuremberg, aroused by a matter of genuine public interest, was depicted by Wagner in less time than that.

So, despite the presence and coöperation of the genial young composer, "I Rantzau" was not a success. The principal parts were sung by Melba, De Lucia, Ancona, David Bispham, and Castelmary, and the opera was mounted in thoroughly efficient style. In the following week Mascagni found some consolation for this disappointment in the congratulations of the Queen, before whom he conducted the second act of "L'Amico Fritz" and "Cavalleria Rusticana." I had the pleasure of accompanying him to Windsor on this occasion. We had barely arrived at the Castle in the afternoon before Her Majesty sent for the composer, and bestowed upon him the unusual honor of an audience in the private apartments just before going on her customary drive. The Queen, speaking sometimes in Italian, but mostly in French, reminded him that she had already heard "Cavalleria," and expressed the deepest interest in his music. We took dinner with the members of the household, and the performance began at half-past nine.

Her Majesty, who was accompanied by Princess Henry of Battenberg, Prince and Princess Christian, Princess Henry of Prussia, Princess Louis of Battenberg, and the Grand Duke of Hesse, enjoyed the representation immensely, and directly afterward sent for Signor Mascagni, together with Mme. Calvé, Sir Augustus Harris, Signor Vignas, and Signor Ancona, all of whom received handsome souvenirs. The composer was presented with a portrait of Her Majesty in a silver frame bearing the autograph inscription, "Victoria R. I., July 15, 1893." In connection with this function I may mention, as a circumstance without precedent in operatic management, that Harris simultaneously gave in London two other representations,—namely, "Faust" at Covent Garden, and "Die Walküre" at Drury Lane,—employing altogether upward of five hundred persons in the three performances.

In the same month, also, Sir Augustus gave, by royal command, a State performance at Covent Garden, in honor of the marriage of the present Prince and Princess of Wales, when "Roméo et Juliette" was given with a cast including Jean and Edouard de Reszke, Plançon, and Melba, Mancinelli conducting. This was the third royal gala representation at the opera within five years. As already noted, the first had been for the Shah of Persia, and the second was in honor of the Emperor and Empress of Germany. At each of these celebrations the decoration of the auditorium was upon an increasing scale of gorgeous and lavish splendor; but not so that of the vestibule or grand staircase, nor even that of the foyer, since the impresario disliked the idea of spending large sums upon beautifying a building of which he was still only a yearly tenant. Hence an amusing bit of good-humored criticism from the Prince of Wales (now King Edward VII) on the night of the Kaiser's visit in 1891. During one of the intervals Harris was sent for and presented to their Imperial Majesties. Before leaving, he availed himself of the opportunity quietly to ask the Prince of Wales whether he was pleased with the decorations. His Royal Highness replied that he was delighted; then, taking the manager apart, he added in an undertone:

"Delighted with everything, Harris, but the old carpet in the foyer. It has been there so many years! Really, it was too bad not to put down a new one for a night such as this!"

Needless to add that the hint was acted upon long before the next gala night.

By the way, on the occasion of the Kaiser's State visit to the opera there was very nearly a big disappointment. Toward midday Sir Augustus received notice from Jean de Reszke that he was suffering from a bronchial attack and would be unable to sing. The tenor had undertaken to appear in scenes from "Lohengrin," "Les Huguenots," and "Roméo," and consequently his indisposition was a very serious affair. Being by chance at Covent Garden when the news arrived, I undertook to go round to the Continental and see if anything could be done before definitely altering the programme. I found M. de Reszke unwell, indeed, but by no means voiceless. Whereupon I laid before him arguments in favor of his making a superhuman effort to sing, rather than wholly disappoint so mighty and puissant a personage as the Emperor William II. I sug-

SUZANNE ADAMS

AS MARGUERITE

From a photograph by Marceau, N. Y.

ALVAREZ

AS OTELLO

Copyright by A. Dupont, N. Y.

gested that if he could not appear in all three excerpts, he might at least sing in one, which would be a great deal better than not appearing at all. Ultimately, the considerate artist gave way, and I returned to Harris the triumphant bearer of the following characteristic note:

[Translated from the French.]

My dear Friend:

Klein has just asked me to sing at least one act of the three that I had promised you. Consequently I choose that of *Roméo* as the least fatiguing. Look upon this, my dear friend, as an evidence of my desire to spare you a portion of the trouble occasioned by my indisposition. And in doing so I risk hurting my voice! Make an announcement. A thousand greetings!

Jean.

Two English novelties were added to the repertory of Covent Garden during the last month of the season; but neither was sung in the vernacular, and neither attained to more than a *succès d'estime*. Isidore de Lara's "Amy Robsart" was set to a French libretto founded by Sir Augustus Harris and Paul Milliet upon Scott's "Kenilworth"; and the principal interpreters were Alvarez, Lassalle, Bonnard, Castelmary, and Emma Calvé, Bevignani conducting. Villiers Stanford's "Veiled Prophet," originally composed to the English text of William Barclay Squire (who derived it from Moore's "Lalla

Rookh''), had been produced in German at Hanover in 1881, and was now sung to an Italian version by Mazzucato. The cast comprised Lillian Nordica, Lucile Hill, Vignas, and Ancona, and the composer conducted. In addition to these works, Harris mounted Bizet's ''Djamileh,'' Emil Bach's ''Irmengarda,'' and (at Drury Lane) Halévy's ''La Juive.'' The German performances, which did not begin until the end of June, were given under the direction of the celebrated Mayence conductor, Emil Steinbach. Again was Max Alvary the principal tenor; while among the more notable recruits were Frau Moran-Olden, Frau Reuss-Belce, Fräulein Meisslinger, and the talented Polish contralto, Fräulein Olitzka.

CHAPTER XVII

A double artistic jubilee—August Manns honored—Garcia's "Hints on Singing"—Opera in 1894—New orchestral institutions—Opening of Queen's Hall—A procession of famous conductors—Richard Strauss—With Seidl at Bayreuth—A Wagner anecdote—Covent Garden in 1895—New pianists.

THE English jubilee of Joseph Joachim and Alfredo Piatti was celebrated on March 22, 1894, by a reception at the Grafton Galleries, which the leading journal declared to be the most interesting event of its kind that had taken place in London since the memorable Liszt reception at the Grosvenor Gallery eight years before. For the organization of this function I was largely responsible as honorary secretary of the executive committee; and my duties constituted a veritable labor of love, a glad tribute to the two great artists who, by a remarkable coincidence, had made their first appearance before the British public within a few weeks of each other in the spring of 1844.

Unlike Liszt, neither of the honored guests on this occasion performed a solo upon his instrument. The only music was that furnished by what the late Lord Leighton was pleased to describe as "a good band."[1] The formal proceedings of the evening consisted of nothing more than the presentation of illuminated addresses,—one read by Sir Alexander Mackenzie, the other by Sir George Grove,—to which each artist in turn made an extempore reply. The addresses naturally laid stress upon the ties of friendship and affection that united the recipients to British lovers of music, and they gave expression to the deep admiration felt by the latter, as well as their gratitude to the distinguished artists for the inestimable benefits that had accrued to the cause of music in England through their yearly presence there. The replies, both delivered under the influence of profound emotion, were essentially characteristic of the modesty and single-hearted devotion of the two musicians. Piatti created much amusement by his reference to a "little fat boy in tight trousers," whom he saw make his first appearance in

[1] In this respect the Berlin celebration of Dr. Joachim's jubilee was, of course, far more interesting. Then a grand concert was given, at which every member of the orchestra was a former student of the Hochschule, every individual fiddler a pupil of the "King of Violinists"; while, to make things perfect, the hero of the night was ultimately persuaded to take his violin and bow from three of his fair musical children and delight his excited auditors with a solo by Bach. I went over expressly to attend that unique and brilliant function. The orchestra was directed by Herr Steinbach, and as long as I live I shall never forget the magnificent quality of the tone of those violins or the superb *élan* that marked the performance of Weber's "Euryanthe" overture. Every player was an artist of repute, and the total value of the stringed instruments was computed at a quarter of a million dollars.

PIATTI

From a photograph by Messrs. Bassano, London

JOACHIM

From a photograph by Elliott & Fry, London

London in 1844. "He had blooming cheeks and a short jacket, and he stepped up on the platform at the Philharmonic Concert and played Beethoven's violin concerto in such style that everybody was astonished. It was my good fortune to be very much associated with the little boy in after years; and his name was that of my friend, the great artist, Joseph Joachim."

The renowned violinist, for his part, referred to his introduction by Mendelssohn to that hospitable land, and to the great advance which the English people had made in their appreciation of chamber music, and instrumental music generally, during the past fifty years. He remembered how once in those far back days, when he had suggested that he should play at a concert Beethoven's lovely romance in F, he was informed there was a danger that the composition would be thought too classical. Now the quartets of the great masters were constantly played, and a large section of the people heard them with delight. If he had helped in any way toward the advance that had taken place, he was proud and happy; for he looked upon England as his second home, where he had met with no envy, but only the kindest appreciation, and to which country he was bound by the closest ties of friendship. These words will not be quickly forgotten by an assembly that was, indeed, of a nature to do honor to the occasion. Art was represented by Lord Leighton, P. R. A., Mr. Alma Tadema, R. A., and Mr. J. C.

Horsley, R. A.; the law by the Lord Chancellor, Judge Meadows White, Q. C., and Sir George Lewis; and music by, among others, Sir Arthur Sullivan, Sir Joseph Barnby, Sir John Stainer, Sir Charles and Lady Hallé, Sir Charles Hubert Parry, Sir J. F. Bridge, Mr. Edward Lloyd, Mr. Santley, Mr. Louis Ries, Mr. Ludwig Straus, Mr. S. Arthur Chappell, Professor Villiers Stanford, Mr. August Manns, Mr. F. H. Cowen, Mr. W. H. Cummings, Miss Agnes Zimmermann, Miss Fanny Davies, Mr. Leonard Borwick, Mr. Alfred Gibson, Dr. C. Harford Lloyd, and Mr. Franklin Taylor.

It was my good fortune to undertake similar administrative duties in connection with the successful reception held at the same galleries in May, 1895, to celebrate the seventieth birthday of the popular Crystal Palace conductor, August Manns. In this instance the members of the Crystal Palace band volunteered their services out of compliment to their chief, who directed an interesting programme; while an address was read and presented by his old colleague, Sir George Grove, eulogizing the veteran conductor for the noble attitude he had assumed toward British music and British musicians. Furthermore, Queen Victoria's musical second son, the late Duke of Saxe-Coburg and Gotha, attended the reception, and pinned upon Mr. Manns's breast the Coburg Order for "Kunst und Wissenschaft."

Apropos of birthday honors, I may also mention

that on March 17, 1894, Manuel Garcia entered upon his ninetieth year; and his brother professors at the Royal Academy of Music seized the opportunity to present him with a silver tea- and coffee-service, accompanied by an illuminated address. Later in the same year, the venerable maestro brought out his second and last text-book upon the art wherein he had labored with such distinguished success for nearly three quarters of a century. In the compilation of "Hints on Singing," as this instructive catechism is called, I was fortunately able to render Signor Garcia material assistance; and the help thus gladly tendered finds gracious acknowledgment in the preface. The "Hints" are published in the United States as well as in England, but have not yet attained the wide recognition that they deserve.[1]

The bewildering rapidity with which novelty succeeded novelty during the Covent Garden sea-

[1] The following quotation from the preface of "Hints on Singing" affords an admirably succinct statement of Signor Garcia's views upon the degeneracy of the *coloratur* singer: "At the present day the acquirement of flexibility is not in great esteem, and were it not, perhaps, for the venerable Handel, declamatory music would reign alone. This is to be regretted, for not only must the art suffer, but also the young fresh voices, to which the brilliant florid style is the most congenial; the harder and more settled organs being best suited for declamation. It would not be difficult to trace the causes of the decline of the florid style. Let it suffice, however, to mention, as one of the most important, the disappearance of the race of great singers who, beside originating this art, carried it to its highest point of excellence. The impresario, influenced by the exigencies of the modern prima donna, has been constrained to offer less gifted

son of 1894 has had no parallel either before or since. Within the space of three weeks (June 10 to June 30) Sir Augustus Harris mounted Massenet's "Werther" and "La Navarraise," Alfred Bruneau's "L'Attaque du Moulin," and Frederic Cowen's "Signa"; the second of these being given for the first time on any stage. Both the French composers came over to superintend the production of their works. Massenet was as much disappointed by the comparative failure of "Werther" as he was delighted over the enthusiasm that greeted that "blood-and-thunder" little music-drama "La Navarraise," which, however, owed its temporary vogue chiefly to the genius of Emma Calvé. "L'Attaque du Moulin" won a more genuine artistic success, even if it did not secure a permanent place in the repertory, and an ineffaceable impression was made by the gifted mezzo-soprano, Mlle. Delna, who then appeared here for the first time. Her *Marcelline* was a superb creation; and Bouvet's embodiment of the kind-hearted old miller, *Père Merlier,* was also extremely fine. The performance, directed by Philippe Flon, was of astonishing excellence. M. Bruneau assured me he found it equal in every respect to that at the Opéra-Comique, and he—

and accomplished *virtuose* to the composer, who in turn has been compelled to simplify the rôle of the voice and to rely more and more upon orchestral effects. Thus, singing is becoming as much a lost art as the manufacture of mandarin china or the varnish used by the old masters."

professional critic as well as composer—is by no means easy to please.

Mr. Cowen's "Signa" was not sung in English. Originally composed to a libretto by the late Gilbert à Beckett (founded on Ouida's novel), and intended for the defunct Royal English Opera, it had been produced in November, 1893, at the Dal Verme Theatre, Milan, where it was, of course, sung in Italian. It was now given at Covent Garden with the same foreign text, the principal parts being filled by Mme. de Nuovina, Ben Davies, and Ancona, while the composer conducted. So with another English novelty, "The Lady of Longford," produced later in the season: the book was by Augustus Harris, and the music had been set to it by Emil Bach; but for the performance Paul Milliet, a Parisian librettist, was called in, and the opera was sung in French by Emma Eames, Alvarez, and Edouard de Reszke. Neither of these productions attained to more than passing favor.

To the above record must be added two new Italian operas, Verdi's "Falstaff" and Puccini's "Manon Lescaut," both of which were brought out early in the season; and so well did the former please that no fewer than eight performances were given of the old master's exquisite musical comedy. The German representations, as in the previous year, took place at Drury Lane, Klafsky and Alvary again heading the list of artists, with a new conductor, Herr Lohse, who returned to London in the same capacity in 1902. The features of the Carl Rosa season were a stage version of Berlioz's "Faust"; a new romantic opera, "Jeanie Deans," written by Joseph Bennett and composed by Hamish MacCunn; and the first production in England of Humperdinck's "Hänsel und Gretel." At Covent Garden and Drury Lane alone, however,—that is to say, quite apart from the Carl Rosa productions,—ninety-two performances of twenty-seven operas were given in eleven weeks, and of these works seven were mounted for the first time in London.

Amid this orgy of operatic activity, another notable development was in progress. I refer to the growing taste for orchestral music of the highest class. It was welcome for more than one reason. Accurately reading the signs of the times, it was impossible to shut one's eyes to the fact that oratorio was on the downward path; that the once characteristic English love for choral music was distinctly waning. Without the Royal Choral Society in London, without the prosperous provincial festivals and the legion of small choral societies in all parts of the kingdom, the oratorio and the cantata to-day might be looked upon in the light of a "negligible quantity." The vast majority of metropolitan music-lovers would never miss them. It is more difficult to account for this than for the decline of institutions like the Crystal Palace and the Popular Concerts. The latter have lost their hold upon the public as the centre of artistic movement has shifted from one scene to another, as the old supporters have died out, or as the famous performers most intimately associated with these enterprises one by one have disappeared from the platform.

The opening of the new Queen's Hall, in Langham Place, added a locale of much-needed intermediate size to the number of London's concert-rooms. Any hope that it might be put to profitable use for choral performances was fairly dispelled by the experiences of a season or two. On the other hand, under the energetic management of Mr. Robert Newman, the popularity of orchestral music largely increased. In this direction the appetite of the public seemed to grow by what it fed upon, and the advent of a new and talented English conductor in the person of Mr. Henry J. Wood added just that touch of personal magnetism, of attractive individuality, without which the finest collection of instrumental performers may appeal in vain. In a word, the Queen's Hall band and their leader quickly won renown, and their concerts were soon to be regarded as synonymous with well-chosen schemes, interesting novelties, and admirable performances.

Nor did the effect of this growing love for orchestral music end here. It brought augmented support to the Philharmonic Society, and it led to the establishment at Queen's Hall of an annual series of concerts in frank imitation of those given at St. James's Hall under the direction of Hans

Richter. For this undertaking, managed by Mr. Alfred Schulz-Curtius, London was favored, season after season, with a veritable procession of more or less renowned foreign conductors. First and foremost, in 1894, came Felix Mottl, the gifted Karlsruhe Kapellmeister; then, later in the same year, the youthful and ambitious Siegfried Wagner. In 1895 the late Hermann Levi paid a solitary visit; subsequently came Felix Weingartner, Nikisch, and Richard Strauss. But for at least two or three concerts every year until the enterprise was abandoned did Felix Mottl direct performances of Beethoven symphonies and Wagner excerpts that were distinguished by a very high order of merit. During the same period, in a fitting spirit of emulation, Mr. Robert Newman secured the services of the famous French conductors MM. Lamoureux and Colonne. At first these musicians brought over their own orchestras, and some magnificent work was done by both. The plan, however, proved too expensive, and, while M. Colonne did not repeat his visit, his accomplished rival was content, after one or two seasons, to utilize, when he came, the excellent material of the Queen's Hall band. This he did until just before his death, which occurred in 1899.

It was at the concert conducted by Hermann Levi on April 25, 1895, that that fine artist, Milka Ternina, made her London début. This was the only occasion on which I ever heard her sing "off the key." The high English pitch was still employed

From a photograph by Davis & Sanford, N. Y.

TERNINA

then at Queen's Hall, and it frequently upset her intonation; beside, her singing lacked the freedom and inspiration that it acquires in a stage performance. I remarked at the time: "Fräulein Ternina has a splendid voice, and is a singer of remarkable intelligence; but it is evidently only in combination with her qualities as an actress that she can display these rare gifts in their true light." And my words were fully borne out when the Munich soprano made her first appearance at Covent Garden, three years later, in her superb embodiment of *Isolde*. Her triumph in that instance was brilliant and complete.

Siegfried Wagner came twice to London. In the autumn of 1894 he challenged criticism as a conductor only, and was "let off" pretty lightly. He wielded the baton with his left hand, but his beat was firm and distinct, and his readings, if colorless, were intelligent and clear. In the summer of 1895 he appeared as a composer, and presented to the world, for the first time, a symphonic poem written after Schiller's "Sehnsucht." This work revealed promise, but it was "the promise of the child who tries to run before he can walk, the prematurely exposed talent of the artist who represents on canvas some great problem of human life before he has mastered the art of mixing his colors." At the same concert he gave a practical demonstration of his father's ideas concerning the interpretation of Beethoven's "little" symphony in F. On the other hand, his reading of the "Der

Freischütz'' overture was ''simply remarkable for wilful eccentricity and a flagrant disregard for the obvious intentions of the composer.''

Richard Strauss paid his first visit to England in December, 1897. His songs and chamber pieces were tolerably well known, but of his orchestral works only three had so far been heard in London—namely, the symphony in F (April 12) and the symphonic poems, ''Till Eulenspiegel'' and ''Also sprach Zarathustra.'' He now brought with him the ''Tod und Verklärung,'' wherein is depicted the death struggle of a man before whose mental vision there passes the panorama of a wasted life, followed by the man's transfiguration, as his redeemed soul passes out of earthly existence into a higher state. The second section of this remarkable work made an especially deep impression, and at the close the composer was overwhelmed with applause. Strauss's gifts as a conductor were made manifest in very positive fashion. In his own music startling contrasts, powerful crescendos, and exciting climaxes naturally abounded. In the interpretation of Mozart and Wagner he displayed an admirable command of dynamic effects, ranging from the most delicate to the most sonorous; and in everything alike he revealed the intellectual insight and authority, the artistic culture, the magnetic force, the strong individuality of a musician of genius.

The name of Anton Seidl may perhaps be missed from the group of leading German conductors enumerated above. As a matter of fact, however, Seidl scarcely had an opportunity of displaying his powers in London as a concert conductor. His appearances there were solely in connection with opera—the "Nibelungen" performances at Her Majesty's in 1882, and the German representations at Covent Garden in 1897. In the course of the latter I saw him frequently, and one night he accompanied me to a Richter concert at St. James's Hall. He had not seen his great Viennese rival upon the platform for many years, and was especially curious to hear his rendering of Tschaikowsky's "Pathétique" symphony. He was delighted with every feature save one. Directly after starting the second (5-4) movement, Richter laid down his baton and allowed the band to proceed without guidance to the end of the piece. Seidl knit his brows and looked stern, but did not utter a word till the room was ringing with applause. Then he turned to me and said: "I wish he had not done that. It was to show that, in spite of the awkward rhythm, his men could keep perfectly together without the beat, and maintain the necessary precision all through the movement. So they did; but the result was a very machine-like performance. It was much less crisp and animated than it would have been if Richter had conducted it with his arm *as well as with his eyes!*"

The last time I saw Seidl was at Bayreuth in 1897. He was conducting "Parsifal" that summer; and what a glorious treat it was to listen to the orchestra under him, immediately after the blurred and ponderous execution of the "Nibelungen" under Siegfried Wagner! On one of the "off days" of the festival, Seidl invited his friend Francis Neilson and myself to lunch with him at the "Schwarze Adler."[1] The usually quiet, reserved musician was disposed to "come out of his shell" that afternoon, for when lunch was over he developed a communicative mood such as neither Neilson nor I had ever observed in him before. He told us story after story of his early experiences with Wagner, dating from the time when he first went to Bayreuth in 1875 for the purpose of acting as his secretary and of assisting to make a "clean copy" of the score of the "Ring." His preliminary interview with the master in the library at Wahnfried was among his more vivid recollections. When he entered the room he thought no one was there but himself. So he

[1] Anton Seidl was at that period setting to music for the stage the first part of a trilogy entitled "Manabozo," written by Francis Neilson, and founded upon the myths of the North American Indians. The fact was kept secret, and nobody seems to have heard any of the music but Mr. Neilson (now stage manager of the Royal Opera, Covent Garden), who declared that it possessed beauty and originality of no mean order. I understood that the first part of the trilogy had been fully sketched and was partially scored for orchestra; but what became of the score I am unable to say. The poem of "Manabozo" was published separately in London in 1899 by John Macqueen, Norfolk Street, Strand, and was dedicated by the author to the memory of Anton Seidl. The preface states that this work was Seidl's "dearest aim," and that his "confidence and belief in the subject and its potentialities" were extraordinary.

pulled out his letter of introduction and inwardly rehearsed for the twentieth time the little speech which he had prepared. Suddenly, from out of a dark corner, where he had been reading or searching for a book, there sprang into view—Richard Wagner! The apparition so completely upset poor Seidl's equanimity that he found himself unable to utter a single sentence of his speech. Even in reply to the master's questions he could barely manage to blurt out a monosyllable. At last Wagner dismissed him with the remark, "If you work as well as you hold your tongue you will do." And from that time forward his capacity for silence was a standing joke at Wahnfried.

Seidl also told us the "fish story" which he related to Mr. H. T. Finck [1] as an instance of Wagner's love of animals, with the additional information that this quaint encounter with the old fishwoman at the Bayreuth railway station was the immediate cause of the famous diatribe which the sensitive composer penned against the practice of vivisection. Another anecdote narrated by Seidl, and possessing an even wider interest, is worth setting down here at length.

Early in December, 1878, Wagner made up his mind that his wife should be serenaded on her birthday at Christmas with the strains of the "Vorspiel" to "Parsifal," of which work he had then completed the first act. The only question was how to obtain an orchestra. After some reflec-

[1] "Wagner and his Works," by H. T. Finck, Vol. II, p. 203.

tion, Wagner determined to procure the services of the celebrated Meiningen performers, but of course without their conductor, then no other than Dr. Hans von Bülow, Frau Cosima Wagner's first husband. The project was kept a profound secret, and young Anton Seidl was forthwith despatched to Meiningen to arrange matters with the band. He arrived there early in the morning, and went direct to the hotel at which von Bülow was staying. The worthy doctor was practising, and, being unacquainted with Seidl, sent out word that he could not see him until eleven o'clock. Accordingly, at that hour he presented himself at the great pianist's apartment and was duly ushered into his presence. At the first mention of Wagner's name von Bülow drew himself up and inquired in an icy tone what it was that Herr Wagner wanted. Seidl explained the object of his mission.

"Well," replied the doctor, "you must permit me to inform you that I do not occupy myself at all with the engagements of my orchestra. If Herr Wagner requires their services, his ambassador must be good enough to address himself to my Conzertmeister. Good morning." And with that he stiffly bowed Seidl out.

The "ambassador" quickly found the leader of the band, and, the Duke of Meiningen's permission being readily granted, it was arranged that the men should be at Bayreuth by a certain evening. They assembled in good time at the Sonne Hotel, where Wagner met them and conducted a rehearsal of the "Vorspiel." Early next morning, while Frau Cosima was still asleep, the heavier instruments were conveyed to Wahnfried, and the players quietly stationed themselves at their desks in the vestibule and upon the staircase. When all was ready, Wagner gave the signal, and his much-honored wife awoke from her slumbers to hear for the first time the mystic phrases of the prelude to "Parsifal."

In 1895, for the first time for eight years, there was a London opera season without the coöperation of Jean de Reszke. This was the year of Mme. Patti's return to the stage of Covent Garden, an event to which reference has already been made. Prior to her rentrée the diva sang at a Philharmonic concert, and was presented on that occasion with the society's gold medal—an honor bestowed upon only sixteen musicians before her. Her six appearances at the Opera (as *Violetta* and *Rosina*) resulted in a splendid and unparalleled triumph for herself and a handsome profit for her old friend Augustus Harris. Another welcome return was that of Marcella Sembrich, who had not sung in London since 1884, and was now a greater artist than ever. The *prime donne* further included Melba, Calvé, Albani, Emma Eames, Marie Engle, and Marguerite Macintyre—altogether a rare galaxy of soprano talent; so that, with Tamagno, De Lucia, and Alvarez dividing the principal tenor work, the absence of the distinguished Pole was less felt than it otherwise would have been. The principal débutante was Gemma Bellincioni, but her lack of vocal charm was fatal to the chance of the original *Santuzza* winning favor in England.

The only important novelty was Frederic Cowen's "Harold," a four-act dramatic opera, composed to a weak libretto by Sir Edward Malet, and, *mirabile dictu,* sung in English before a Covent Garden audience in mid-season! The fine music of this work deserved more enduring success. The cast comprised Mme. Albani, Miss Meisslinger, Philip Brozel, David Bispham, and Richard Green; but, unluckily, there was a lack of distinction (and distinctness) about the general rendering that was scarcely calculated to engender in aristocratic auditors any particular love of opera in the vernacular. Anyhow, the English experiment was never repeated; while, on the other hand, a performance of "Tannhäuser" in French, given later in the summer, was hailed with positive delight. Concurrently with the regular Covent Garden enterprises, the stock company from the ducal theatre at Coburg appeared at Drury Lane in a series of light German operas comprising "Der Vogelhändler," "Die Fledermaus," and "Die verkaufte Braut." These admirable representations were thoroughly appreciated.

It is timely here to note the gradual advent of the new generation of modern pianists, filling in the gaps left by the decease of favorites like Mme. Schumann, Anton Rubinstein, Hans von Bülow, and Sir Charles Hallé, all of whom died between

EUGEN D'ALBERT

From a photograph by Sarony, N. Y.

ARTHUR CHAPPELL

From a photograph by J. E. Mayall, London

1894 and 1896. The predominant position of Paderewski had long since been assured; now, however, came Moritz Rosenthal and Eugen d'Albert, seeking a London indorsement of the reputations they had already won on the Continent and in America. In each case the general verdict was emphatically ratified. Moritz Rosenthal's début at the Richter concerts (June 10, 1895), when he played the Liszt concerto in E flat, created a genuine sensation; and his subsequent recitals confirmed the opinion that he possessed the most phenomenal technique of any living pianist.

Eugen d'Albert was regarded in the light of a "prodigal." A native of Glasgow and educated at the National Training School for Music in London, he might with all fairness have been termed a British product. He preferred, however, to call himself a German, and had not stood upon an English concert platform since boyhood till he appeared at Queen's Hall under Felix Mottl (April 28, 1896), and gave a magnificent performance of Beethoven's E flat or "Emperor" concerto. He had a cold reception, but after he had played it became evident that the old grievances had been forgotten in the presence of a legitimate virtuoso, of a true artist possessing the fire of unmistakable genius. Personally I admire his playing immensely; and as an interpreter of Beethoven, it is upon the shoulders of d'Albert that the mantle of Rubinstein, to my thinking, has fallen. His place as a composer will have to be decided by a future generation.

Among other native pianists now coming to the fore were Frederic Lamond and Frederick Dawson, natives of Scotland and Lancashire, respectively. Ilona Eibenschütz, a pupil of Mme. Schumann, had become quite a favorite; and the romantic school had also a gifted and popular exponent in the clever Hungarian artist Benno Schönberger. Also noteworthy were the débuts at about the same time of Emil Sauer, Ferrucio Busoni, and Ossip Gabrilowitsch.

CHAPTER XVIII

A visit to America—Jean de Reszke as a German singer—Nordica's triumph—A private recital of "Tristan"—The London season of 1896—Death of Sir Augustus Harris—Two funerals at St. Paul's—Edward Elgar—"In a Persian Garden"—Charles Salaman—Puccini's "La Bohème"—Operas and débuts in 1897—Opera at Windsor: the Queen's last "commands."

JEAN DE RESZKE'S first appearance as a German singer in Wagnerian opera was destined to take place, not in England, but in America. This was during the winter of 1895–96. My impatience to hear him sing in German was natural, for I had fully sympathized with his desire to escape from the trammels of the Italian translation, and had done my share toward paving the way for his mastery of the original text. Fortune was kind enough to afford me an earlier opportunity than I had anticipated of enjoying the fruit of this endeavor. It happened that at Easter, 1896, I paid my first visit to the United States for the purpose of attending the production of the comic opera "El Capitan," of which my brother, Charles Klein, was the author and John Philip Sousa the composer. Directly after that successful event I spent a week in New York, just when Mr. Grau's supplementary season at the Metropolitan Opera House was approaching its close.

I had hoped, before my return to England, to hear both "Lohengrin" and "Tristan" in German; but, as it turned out, I could not remain for the latter. My passage was booked for Saturday, and "Tristan" was not to be given until the following Monday. In vain did the warm-hearted Polish brothers endeavor to persuade me to stay and sail with them on Wednesday. I dared not delay my return by a single day. I should have to be content, therefore, with hearing "Lohengrin," and wait for "Tristan" until it was done at Covent Garden later in the spring. That is precisely what did occur; but my self-denial was first to receive compensation in the shape of a very rare, if not unparalleled compliment—one of those tributes of personal regard which we appreciate most when they are perfectly spontaneous and unpremeditated.

It was arranged that we were all to sup together in Mme. Nordica's apartments at the Savoy after the performance of "Lohengrin." Our hostess was, indeed, the heroine, in a special sense, of that representation; for after the bridal scene she was presented with a superb diamond tiara, which had been subscribed for by the leaders of New York society. The assemblage was one of the most brilliant and crowded of the season. It was the first time I ever saw the Metropolitan Opera House, and I was much struck with its handsome proportions. Then again, under Anton Seidl's magic wand, the

NORDICA
AS BRÜNNHILDE

performance touched at all points a very high level of excellence. Finally, I derived immense pleasure from the novel sensation of hearing Jean and Edouard de Reszke as exponents of Wagner's own text. Their conscientious enunciation of each syllable, their accurate diction, and their admirable accent seemed to impart an added dignity alike to the music and to their impersonations. Even the more cultivated listener might easily have imagined them to be native German singers. Mme. Nordica, too, handled the German words with remarkable facility and confidence. Altogether, it was a most meritorious achievement.

The subsequent reunion at the hotel found every one in the highest spirits. Beside the three artists, there were present Mme. Nordica's sister (Mrs. Walker) and Mr. Amherst Webber, the talented English *maestro al piano,* who had recently acted as accompanist to the brothers in their Wagnerian studies. After supper the conversation turned upon Bayreuth, and allusion was made to a certain half-promise given by Jean de Reszke to Frau Cosima, that he would one day sing *Tristan* and *Walther,* or perhaps even *Siegfried,* at the festival. I remarked that, after what I had heard that night, I entertained no doubts concerning the adequate quality of his accent. This only elicited a further request that I would stay in New York until I had heard how it sounded in "Tristan." Then the distinguished tenor turned to Mme. Nordica and proposed that, as I was evidently not to be made to alter my determination, the best thing they could do would be to "bring the mountain to Mohammed" and sing some "Tristan" to me there and then; and that between one and two in the morning, and after a heavy opera like "Lohengrin"! Surely it was not possible. But surprise and incredulity quickly changed to delight. For, without an instant's hesitation, Mme. Nordica consented; Mr. Webber went to the piano and played a few introductory bars; and, almost before I could realize what was being done, the two gifted artists were warbling the wondrous love scene from Wagner's immortal music-drama.

They did not spare themselves, either, these generous friends. They sang with full voice; they went through not only the scene with which they had started, but the duet of the first act as well; and, from beginning to end, the exquisite beauty of their phrasing, the blending of their voices in perfect intonation and unity of color, the significance of their supreme dramatic interpretation, constituted at once a marvel and a revelation. It was a strange experience, sitting at the supper-table (for none of us but Mr. Webber had moved from our seats) while for an hour or more those two famous singers reveled in the enjoyment of their self-imposed task—undertaken for the sole purpose of conferring pleasure upon an old friend. The picture of that night remains vividly imprinted upon my mind, even as its vocal spell lives fresh and fragrant among my most treasured memories.

I shall always be grateful for the privilege of having listened to some of the grandest pages of "Tristan" under such novel and interesting conditions.

A month later the de Reszkes were at Covent Garden, giving habitués a taste of their quality as German singers in "Lohengrin," "Tristan," and "Die Meistersinger." Their success was unqualified. In the new *Tristan* was hailed the beau-ideal—the perfect conception and the complete realization—of the noblest of Wagner's knightly heroes. The *König Marke* and the *Hans Sachs* of Edouard de Reszke won unstinted admiration. Also to be noted was the *Pogner* of Pol Plançon, an artist whose magnificent organ and supreme gifts alike as singer and as actor had by this time won him immense popularity in London. Unfortunately, Mme. Nordica did not come that season to share in the triumphs of the new German campaign. Albani sang *Elsa* and *Isolde;* Emma Eames was the *Eva*—and a delightful one, I remember. But the Gallic craze was still rampant, and in the midst of all this good work we were amazed at the spectacle of a performance of "Die Walküre" in French, with Alvarez (not Alvary, poor fellow!) as *Siegmund,* Lola Beeth as *Sieglinde,* Mantelli (*sic*) as *Brünnhilde,* Albers as *Wotan,* and Castelmary as *Hunding!* Little need to state that the absurd and useless proceeding was a dismal failure.

The most notable event of the season of 1896 was, alas! the death of Sir Augustus Harris. It was in the middle of June, at a moment when everything appeared bright and prosperous, that London was startled by the sudden illness and premature decease of its favorite manager. Only forty-four years of age, the universally popular "Gus" died amid general expressions of sorrow. Like Tom Bowling in the ballad, "his friends were many and true-hearted"; these mourned for the man. But countless were the numbers of those that had never known him, yet deplored the loss of the genial worker who had catered generously to their theatrical amusement, and had raised opera in England from a "moribund" state to its present flourishing condition. Harris did not realize the limit of his physical powers. Though his heart was only in two or three undertakings, his brain and hand were in a dozen. When death overtook him he was actually struggling to revive the languishing fortunes of the huge circus business known as Olympia!

"His genius was of that Napoleonic order which comes but rarely into existence and still more rarely finds its exact bent. His spirit moved with the times; it was *fin de siècle* in the most marked degree, and it brooked the interference of tradition only when by so doing it could secure the survival of the fittest. Where the public taste was concerned his instinct seldom erred; he knew precisely what his patrons wanted and how best to give it them. As impresario, manager, entrepreneur, dramatist, librettist, and stage manager, all rolled into one, he was absolutely unique; and it

MAURICE GRAU

Copyright by A. Dupont, N. Y.

PUCCINI

From a photograph by Alinari, Florence

may be taken for granted that we shall 'ne'er look upon his like again.' " These words are as true to-day as they were when I wrote them nearly seven years ago. Sir Augustus Harris was buried at Kensal Green Cemetery, in the presence of an assemblage numbering many thousands. The problem of carrying on his chief operatic concern was solved by the formation of the Covent Garden Syndicate, the capital for which was furnished by the leading subscribers. Of this body Earl de Grey and Mr. H. V. Higgins were appointed directors, while Mr. Maurice Grau undertook the duties of managing director, and Mr. Neil Forsyth those of secretary.

Many other notable figures disappeared from the scene in this same year—among them Mme. Clara Schumann, Sir Joseph Barnby, Ambroise Thomas, Frau Klafsky, Italo Campanini, Henry Leslie, and Lewis Thomas, the Welsh basso. Of these the most interesting to the English musical community in general were the two talented choral conductors, Joseph Barnby and Henry Leslie, the former remarkable as a trainer of large vocal bodies, as that at the Albert Hall; the latter well known as the founder and leader of the Leslie Choir, probably the most wonderful embodiment of a perfect choral ensemble that London ever possessed, not excepting even the Bach Choir in its best days. I knew both men well, but was more intimately acquainted with Sir Joseph Barnby, with whom, after he succeeded Weist Hill as principal of the Guildhall School of Music, I was brought into almost daily association. It was a pity he ever went to that institution. The work killed him, even as the disappointment of failing to secure the appointment killed his rival candidate, Sir William Cusins.

Barnby is now remembered more for his church music than for his deeds with the baton. Yet he told me once that his greatest ambition was to be an operatic conductor; and I quite believed that when he deprived me of my post as conductor of the opera class at the Guildhall School in order to fill it himself,—though necessarily in perfunctory fashion, for he could not really spare the time. Well, I bore him no grudge on that account. We were the best of friends to the end; and when he died (January 28, 1896) I readily complied with Lady Barnby's request to organize the arrangements for the funeral service, which was held in St. Paul's Cathedral. This I did in conjunction with my friend Mr. Alfred Littleton, and in order to obtain the requisite experience for directing so elaborate a function I attended the funeral of Lord Leighton, who was buried in the cathedral on the previous day. The crowds were enormous, and the difficulties of the Barnby ceremony were increased in that, after the service at St. Paul's, the coffin had to be taken away for interment at Norwood Cemetery. Five years later I was called upon to perform a similar mournful duty in connection with the funeral of Sir Arthur Sullivan, who, like Lord Leighton, was deemed worthy of a niche in the crypt of the cathedral. Neither light nor pleasant was the labor of arranging these solemn functions; yet they will remain always among the proudest and most notable events of my life.

I seldom attended the festivals of the Three Choirs. They rarely yielded music of an "epoch-making" character, and they always occurred at the beginning of September, just when I was enjoying my hard-earned holiday. I was warned, however, not to miss the Worcester Festival of 1896; and I am glad I did not. That was the meeting which lifted Edward Elgar out of his obscurity as a Malvern teacher and revealed him to his countrymen as a musician of high attainments and still higher promise. For once the "local man" turned out to be something better than your ordinary writer of "Kapellmeistermusik"; for once the dip in the local lottery-bag yielded a genuine prize.

Edward Elgar produced at this festival a short oratorio entitled "The Light of Life," founded upon the miracle of the healing of the blind man, related in the ninth chapter of St. John. Its originality, the sense of proportion and tone-color displayed in the choral and orchestral effects, the bold and masterful treatment of the leading themes, and the generally engrossing character of the music fairly took connoisseurs by surprise, and prepared them for the development which so rapidly placed Edward Elgar in the very forefront of contemporary British composers. From "The Light of Life" to "The Dream of Gerontius" represents an enormous stride, and every phase of the transition is replete with interest. It would be hard to say in which direction—orchestral or choral music—his genius shows the more powerful bent. In both it seems to me that his individuality and imaginative force are equally striking, his technical resources equally comprehensive; and, at the same time, fully on a par with his gifts as a musician are his modest and unassuming yet sterling qualities as a man.

One warm July night in 1896 I was present at a large musical party given by the late Mrs. Edward Goetz at her house in Hyde Park Terrace. Always enjoyable were the entertainments of this liberal and sympathetic patroness of the art, who was a daughter of Mr. J. M. Levy, the founder of the "Daily Telegraph," and sister of Sir Edward Lawson, the genial proprietor of that journal. This, however, was a noteworthy occasion, since it brought to a first hearing a composition which was destined to win popularity in every land where English song flourishes—I refer to Liza Lehmann's graceful and fascinating setting of lines from Omar Khayyám's "Rubáiyát" ("In a Persian Garden"). I shall not readily forget the mingled surprise and admiration awakened by the novel fragrance and charm of this music, remarkable at once for its sincerity of feeling and expression and the subtle beauty of its harmonic structure. The solos were finely rendered by Albani, Hilda Wilson, Ben Davies, and David Bisp-

SIR JOSEPH BARNBY

From a photograph by Marx, Frankfort

EDWARD ELGAR

From a photograph by Russell & Sons, London

ham; and the accompaniments were played by the composer, who, I may add, seemed to be not less astonished than delighted at the warmth of the compliments showered upon her.

During the following December "In a Persian Garden" was sung, for the first time in public, at one of the Popular Concerts, and with extraordinary success. Apart from its intrinsic worth, the new song-cycle was especially welcome to an audience that had long counted Liza Lehmann the vocalist among its particular favorites. In that capacity, indeed, the fair musician was just bidding farewell to the concert platform and creating a vacancy that might have remained long unfilled but for the timely début of Blanche Marchesi, the accomplished daughter of the famous Paris teacher. Very different in type were these two singers, nor can it be gainsaid that the art of Blanche Marchesi covers a wider intellectual grasp, a broader range of color, a greater depth of dramatic intensity than that which distinguished the English soprano. Yet both must be given a conspicuous place in the group of artists whose talent helped at this time to keep alive the fading glories of the "Pops." For, alas! the closing years of the nineteenth century were to witness a sad deterioration in the quality of these renowned concerts. The secession of Joachim and the death of Piatti eliminated the last links that held intact the chain of the old subscribers. The support fell away, and with the resignation of Arthur Chappell the institution finally lost the prestige and the value that had earned it renown for a period of over forty years.

Among the remarkable old men of music whose light died out with the expiring months of the last century was my dear friend Charles Kensington Salaman. His active labors as composer and teacher had long ceased; but his brain was ever alert and ever busy amid his storehouse of memories of a bygone age. He could tell of a visit to the famous singer Catalani (heard for the last time in England at the York Festival in 1828), and he could describe the sensations with which he had played duets with Liszt when the Weimar pianist first came to London as a boy of eleven. It was a rare pleasure to listen to Charles Salaman's anecdotes; to sit by him as he played with still wonderful facility and grace some quaint old show-piece; or to sing while he accompanied some such exquisite lyric as his lovely setting of Shelley's "I arise from dreams of thee." It was his habit always to celebrate his birthday by composing a new song to lines specially written by his son Malcolm, and not the least charming of these efforts was the "Love Song" which commemorated his eightieth birthday on March 3, 1894. He was visited on these occasions by some of the foremost musical and theatrical celebrities in the metropolis. But after keeping up the charter another two or three years his health gradually failed and he died amid universal regrets.

In the spring of 1897 Giacomo Puccini paid his

second visit to England, to superintend the production of his opera "La Bohème" by the Carl Rosa company at Manchester. The young Italian composer had achieved only a moderate success with his "Manon Lescaut" at Covent Garden three years before, and was anxious to add to his laurels. On joining him at Manchester the afternoon of the première, I found him in very low spirits. He was not satisfied with the Carl Rosa artists, and fully anticipated a fiasco for the English representation of "La Bohème." I assured him that Carl Rosa singers (as distinguished from Carl Rosa "directors") did not know the meaning of the word "fail"; the intelligence and ensemble of the company were bound to pull him through. And so it proved. Deficient as it was in many respects, there was, nevertheless, so much spirit and animation about the performance, such a flavor of Bohemian jollity, that the opera instantly won the favor of the Lancashire audience and paved the way for its subsequent London success.[1]

With the Covent Garden season of 1897 the work of the new régime fairly began. Mr. Maurice Grau made his entry upon the scene, nominally as the successor to Sir Augustus Harris; and he paid that impresario the highest compliment in his power

[1] The cast was as follows: *Rudolph,* Mr. Robert Cunningham; *Marcel,* Mr. William Paull; *Colline,* Mr. A. S. Winckworth; *Schaunard,* Mr. C. Tilbury; *Benoit,* Mr. Homer Lind; *Musetta,* Miss Bessie MacDonald; and *Mimi,* Miss Alice Esty. Mr. Claude Jaquinot conducted, and Mr. T. H. Friend was the stage manager.

by frankly pursuing the lines that had marked the previous managerial policy of the establishment. Not a single innovation worthy of the name had to be recorded. As in America, so in London, Mr. Grau found that it would be impossible for him to do better at the head of a big operatic concern than steer the exact course that had been followed during the preceding decade by Augustus Harris. The usual sixty-seven performances were given, and altogether eighteen operas were mounted; no fewer than half of these were sung in French. The novelties were "Der Evangelimann," a sentimental work by Wilhelm Kienzl, in which the tenor Van Dyck scored a great success; and "Inez Mendo," a meritorious opera from the pen of Frédéric d'Erlanger, wherein Mme. Frances Saville, a new soprano, and M. Renaud, the barytone from the Paris Opéra, sustained the principal parts. Other débutants of the season were Miss Susan Strong, Mlle. Pacary, Fräulein Sedlmair, Andreas Dippel, Salignac, Marcel Journet, Fugère, Lemprière Pringle, and Thomas Meux.

The brunt of more than two months' hard work was borne by Jean and Edouard de Reszke, together with Mme. Emma Eames and David Bispham, gifted American artists who notably strengthened their London reputations in the course of this season. Mme. Melba appeared in a round of familiar impersonations, while the sterling qualities of MM. Alvarez and Plançon now began to earn for those singers a wider circle of admirers. From the be-

SCHUMANN-HEINK
AS ORTRUD

ginning of the season until the end of June the German operas were conducted by the late Anton Seidl, and the memory of this, his last appearance at Covent Garden, is associated with some exceedingly fine performances.

Among the visitors to London during the latter part of the year were Edvard Grieg and his wife, and the clever composer of "Hänsel und Gretel," Engelbert Humperdinck. The former appeared at the Popular and other concerts, beside paying a visit to the Queen at Windsor; while Humperdinck made his début, under the auspices of the Philharmonic Society, at the last of an autumn series of concerts and conducted some excerpts from his operas with signal success. Yet another distinguished composer, Moritz Moskowski, appeared at the Philharmonic during the same series, after an absence from London of over eleven years. He brought nothing new, but conducted with much spirit his violin concerto (played by M. Gregorowitsch) and three movements from his opera "Boabdil"; a contralto air, also from the latter work, was rendered by Mlle. Olitzka.

The début of a son-in-law of Queen Victoria in the capacity of operatic librettist was an interesting feature of the Carl Rosa season held at Covent Garden during the autumn of 1897, the year of Her Majesty's "Diamond Jubilee." Twenty years previous a cousin of the Queen, the then reigning Grand Duke Ernest of Saxe Coburg-Gotha, had figured upon the same scene as the composer of an opera called "Santa Chiara." In the present instance it was the Marquis of Lorne (now the Duke of Argyll), husband of that amiable and accomplished lady, the Princess Louise, who was responsible for the text of Hamish MacCunn's romantic opera "Diarmid"; and such was the striking all-round merit of this work that, but for the weakness of the dénouement and an unfortunate resemblance to the plot of "Tristan und Isolde," which evoked inevitable comparisons, it might have earned enduring success. As it was, I fancy the Marquis derived his principal reward from the amusement of attending the rehearsals, which he did regularly, in company with the Princess, who would watch the proceedings from the corner of a private box.

The Queen's love of music was at no period more strongly evinced than during the last few years of her life. She turned to it for solace and comfort in her old age, and derived the keenest pleasure from the performances of the various artists who were invited in quick succession to labor for her enjoyment. Her devoted daughters, Princess Christian and Princess Henry of Battenberg, were ever on the alert to procure talent for this purpose; scarcely a week passed but that some artist of note played or sang in the royal drawing-rooms at Windsor, Osborne, or Balmoral. Lengthy, indeed, must be the list of those, from the diva downward, who can point with pride to their jeweled brooch or pin bearing the familiar monogram "V. R. I.";

while many, too, can display even costlier gifts that were received, after repeated visits, as tokens of Her Majesty's grateful appreciation. A select few had bestowed upon them the insignia of the Royal Victoria Order; and the first musician to be thus honored, after Sir Arthur Sullivan and Signor Tosti, was M. Jean de Reszke, who received the cross of the "R. V. O." (fourth class) after a performance of "Lohengrin" at Windsor Castle on the Queen's eightieth birthday, May 24, 1899. His brother was similarly decorated fourteen months later, after a representation of "Faust"—the last occasion on which Queen Victoria ever listened to an opera.

The birthday celebration was marked by one or two curious incidents. To begin with, only the first and third acts of "Lohengrin" could be given. There was hardly time to include the second, as these royal functions do not commence until nearly ten o'clock at night. The plot, however, was fully explained to the Queen, who had never heard Wagner's opera, and the temptation of *Elsa* (Mme. Nordica) by the perfidious *Ortrud* (Mme. Schumann-Heink) and her spouse (David Bispham) was easily "taken as read." Mancinelli conducted, and everything went capitally until the fall of the curtain. Her Majesty then retired to one of the drawing-rooms and requested that the principal artists be presented to her, together with Mr. Maurice Grau as managing director of the Royal Opera.

The awful discovery was then made that neither

Jean nor Edouard de Reszke had with him any but the operatic garments in which they stood. It was the first time that the brothers had ever appeared in opera before the Queen, and, not knowing that it was usual to don evening dress for the subsequent presentation, they had clothed themselves as *Lohengrin* and *Heinrich der Vogler* before leaving London, and had traveled to Windsor in dark cloaks of sufficient amplitude to conceal themselves from the gaze of an inquisitive Cockney crowd. The situation was duly explained to Her Majesty, who laughingly declared that it did not matter in the least; for once court etiquette should be disregarded, and the two artists brought before her in their picturesque stage attire. The command was forthwith obeyed, and the Queen, in course of conversation with the brothers, "expressed the delight that it had afforded her at last to hear them in opera and listen to the beautiful music of Wagner's work."

Queen Victoria never heard Jean de Reszke again. In the summer of 1900, when "Faust" was given at Windsor, he was not well enough to sing, and a substitute was forthcoming in the new French tenor Saléza. I accompanied Edouard de Reszke to the castle and was present at the performance. The *Marguerite* was that sympathetic artist Mme. Suzanne Adams, to whom, afterward, Her Majesty personally handed a handsome sapphire and diamond bracelet. Philippe Flon was the conductor, and the cast further included Mlle. Bauermeister,

FRITZI SCHEFF

AS NEDDA

Copyright by A. Dupont, N. Y.

MARIE BREMA

AS AMNERIS

Copyright by A. Dupont, N. Y.

Mlle. Maubourg, and M. Declery, with M. Almanz as *régisseur*. The remarkable feature of that evening was the mental and physical endurance shown by the aged sovereign, who was now so near to the close of her august career. It was a hot, sultry July night, and although several cuts were made, the opera was not over until nearly twelve o'clock. From the beginning to the end the Queen remained deeply interested, and never stirred from her chair upon the dais. It was only as she walked down the inclined gangway, passing within a yard of where I stood, and leaning heavily upon the arm of her Indian attendant, that I perceived how intensely fatigued Her Majesty was. Her face bore a look of exhaustion that indicated actual suffering. Yet there was no suggestion of dispensing with the customary reception. From the door of the Waterloo Chamber the Queen's chair was wheeled through St. George's Hall to the Green Drawing-room, and quite forty minutes more must have elapsed ere the ceremony of receiving the artists and giving them their presents was over. Whether work or pleasure was involved, Victoria the Good never sought to spare herself in the rendering of those courtesies which she thought she owed to others. It was just six months after witnessing this "Faust" performance that Her Majesty breathed her last at Osborne House.

CHAPTER XIX

Operatic retrogression—The seasons of 1898, 1899, and 1900—Purchase of the Covent Garden lease—The "Perosi craze"—Final remarks on the Harris régime—Death of Sims Reeves—Edward Lloyd's retirement—English singers and English festivals: a concluding retrospect.

EVERY period of change and reform gives place to a corresponding spell of plodding, mechanical labor upon the lines that public appreciation has indorsed. By comparison with the decade extending from 1887 to 1897, the story of operatic progress during the succeeding five years is dull and uninteresting. That is an excellent reason for treating it with brevity, if not, indeed, for bringing it to a conclusion, as far as these pages are concerned, with all convenient speed. The spirit of innovation died when Sir Augustus Harris "shuffled off this mortal [operatic] coil." The temporary association of Mr. Maurice Grau with the management of Covent Garden only tended to crystallize the identical systems of supply and demand which had already distinguished the leading lyric theatres of London and New York. The dead impresario's successors contented themselves with a mild imitation of the Harris policy, plus a creditable endeavor to ameliorate the *matériel*—they could not well improve the *personnel*—of their establishment. Beyond that, there has been neither initial energy nor imagination to widen the scope and elevate the character of this important enterprise.

The last two or three seasons of the nineteenth century may be very briefly dismissed. In 1898 the novelties at Covent Garden were Saint-Saëns's "Henry VIII" and Mancinelli's "Ero e Leandro." In the former, Mme. Héglon made her début as *Anne Boleyn,* and M. Renaud gave an extremely picturesque embodiment of "bluff King Hal" as viewed through a pair of French pince-nez. The chief parts in Mancinelli's opera [1] were created by Eames, Schumann-Heink, Saléza, and Plançon. Another noteworthy feature was the revival of "Der Ring des Nibelungen" under Felix Mottl. In this Jean de Reszke made his first appearance in the rôle of *Siegfried,* and a splendid series of casts included, among others, Nordica, Ternina, Eames, Schumann-Heink, Marie Brema, Von Artner, Meisslinger, Van Dyck, Dippel, Van Rooy, and Edouard de Reszke. The general troupe further comprised Melba, Calvé, Zélie de Lussan, Frances Saville, Suzanne Adams, Saléza, and Campanari, of whom the last three then sang in London for the first time. The success of the young American débutante, who subsequently became the wife of Mr. Leo Stern, the violoncellist, was especially marked.

[1] Originally produced as a cantata at the Norwich Festival of 1896.

The profits in 1898 and 1899 were larger than during any like period since the operatic renaissance began; but from an artistic standpoint progress was no longer reflected in the deeds of the Covent Garden management. The season of 1899 yielded but a single novelty, namely, Isidore de Lara's "Messaline." True, this was the work of an Englishman; but it was composed to a French libretto and performed by French artists, and it owed its hearing exclusively to foreign influence. Its success, despite the glamour of its picturesque Roman setting, and notwithstanding the art of Héglon, Alvarez, and Renaud, must perforce be described as equivocal. The story at best is revolting; and the music combines with a few fine moments many dull *quarts d'heure.* Wagner again played a prominent part, his works furnishing just one third of the seventy-one representations that made up the season. These were directed, with two exceptions, by Dr. Muck, one of the conductors of the Berlin Hof-Oper. Conspicuous therein were some magnificent impersonations by Mme. Lilli Lehmann, who had not been heard in London for many years, and by Mme. Gadski, who now made her début at Covent Garden and at once earned the favor due to an artist of rare vocal and histrionic attainments. Of the other new-comers neither Mlle. Lucienne Bréval nor Mlle. Litvinne did herself complete justice; but Mme. Louise Homer created a satisfactory impression, and a posi-

LILLI LEHMANN
AS ISOLDE

tive hit was scored by Signor Scotti, one of the most versatile and accomplished barytones that Italy has sent forth in recent years. Jean de Reszke sang only nine nights and was then compelled by illness to seek rest; in the following winter, however, he was singing in America with all his wonted vigor and charm.

Early in 1899 the inheritor of the Covent Garden lease, Mr. G. F. Faber, disposed of the theatre to the Grand Opera Syndicate, for the remainder of his term, for the sum of £110,000. This desirable consummation, which was brought about through the efforts of Mr. Alfred de Rothschild, had the effect of placing the entire concern upon a sound and solid footing. The syndicate was formed into a limited liability company, the list of shareholders being headed by the Prince of Wales (now King Edward VII) and composed very largely of the opera subscribers, who thus became directly interested in the financial prosperity of the general undertaking. The direction of the company remained in the same hands, but Mr. Grau did not long continue the heavy labors involved in his double impresarioship. Another couple of years of fruitful toil, and then he relinquished his London duties altogether, so far as opera was concerned, thenceforth devoting himself with increased energy to the sister enterprise in New York. He was succeeded as artistic director at Covent Garden by M. André Messager, the composer of

''La Basoche'' and other works, whose experience as conductor and joint manager of the Paris Opéra-Comique eminently fitted him for the post.

This same year, by the way, witnessed the brief ''Perosi craze.'' How that purely artificial vogue ever came to extend beyond the walls of the Italian churches no one knows. At least it should have stopped short at Paris, which was as far as the youthful abbé himself contrived to get on his road to London. But for a time the ''craze'' raged in England with the virulence of an epidemic, and many sane musicians persuaded themselves that the new oratorio composer was a genius of the first magnitude. His ''Transfiguration,'' his ''Raising of Lazarus,'' and his ''Resurrection of Christ'' were all performed at the London Musical Festival which Robert Newman started at Queen's Hall in May; while his ''Passion of Christ'' was given at the Norwich Festival in the autumn. In each instance, however, there was felt a keen sense of disappointment. At best Perosi's works could appeal only to the ear amid ecclesiastical surroundings, and even there their woeful lack of originality was bound to irritate the critical listener. Far more interesting as choral events were the first performances in England (at the Gloucester Festival) of Professor Horatio Parker's ''Hora Novissima''; the revival (at Albert Hall) of Wagner's scriptural scene for male voices and orchestra, ''The Last Supper of the Apostles''; and the restoration, by the Royal Choral Society under Sir Frederick

Bridge, of the original accompaniments to Handel's "Messiah."

The opera season of 1900, the last touched upon in this chronicle, offered to a contented public practically the same company, the same repertory, the same familiar commingling of brilliant individual efforts and unsurpassable artistic resources, together, alas! with a growing roughness of ensemble and a lamentable mediocrity of *mise en scène*. It was the last London opera season in which Jean de Reszke had thus far taken part; and even that appearance was attended by a "partial eclipse," the climate of the British metropolis once more proving so seriously detrimental to the vocal organs of the famous tenor that he was unable to complete his engagement. Two cycles of the "Ring" were given, and among the new members of the cast were Frau Gulbranson, Miss Edyth Walker, Fräulein Hieser, Herr Ernst Kraus, Herr Briesemeister, Herr Slezák, Herr Bertram, and Herr Klopfer. In the direction of the German operas, Felix Mottl was assisted by that admirable conductor Emil Paur, who made a highly satisfactory impression. Distinct hits were achieved also by the clever young light soprano, Fräulein Fritzi Scheff; by Signor Bonci, a sympathetic Italian tenor of the old school; and by Mr. Blass, an American basso of German parentage and training.

Puccini's "Tosca" was the solitary new opera produced in 1900, and, thanks to the genius of Fräulein Ternina, its many beauties were at once made patent to all who were willing to perceive them. That artist's superb assumption of *Floria Tosca,* coming as it did on top of a series of triumphs in such rôles as *Brünnhilde, Sieglinde, Elsa, Elisabeth,* and *Leonora,* was but another revelation of her versatility and of her vocal and histrionic charm. This was Ternina's first essay as the heroine of Puccini's picturesque work, and she received excellent support from De Lucia as *Pietro Cavaradossi,* and from Scotti as *Scarpia*—this last a creation which has won universal recognition as an ideal presentment of one of the most subtle and malevolent figures in modern opera. Altogether it was a splendid performance, and Luigi Mancinelli conducted it in his most masterly manner. In the German operas the increasing success of Mme. Gadski became conspicuously characteristic; while Mme. Melba extended her repertory with a piquant impersonation of *Rosina* in "Il Barbiere." Mme. Calvé was content to travel within the limited circle of her old round of parts.

The following table indicates roughly the extent of the work accomplished during the regular London season, by the late Sir Augustus Harris and his successors, during the thirteen years that came after the tentative Drury Lane season of 1887:

	Weeks	Operas	Representations
1888........	10	19	48
1889........	10	16	53
1890........	10	18	60
1891........	16	20	94

DIPPEL

AS SIEGFRIED

Copyright, 1898, by A. Dupont, N. Y.

SCOTTI

AS DON GIOVANNI

From a photograph by A. Dupont, N. Y.

	Weeks	Operas	Representations
1892........	10	25	88
1893........	11	25	89
1894........	11	27	92
1895........	11	25	77
1896........	11	23	67
1897........	11	18	67
1898........	11	24	67
1899........	11	22	71
1900........	11	21	67

A casual glance at these figures will suffice to show how curiously in the nature of an "arc" are the rise and fall in the labor and energy which evolved them. In 1894, exactly half way between 1888 and 1900, was reached the high-water mark of activity under the Harris régime. I disregard the sudden "bulge" of 1891, because in that year the season was unduly extended, and there were then but twenty operas in the repertory. Three years later it attained the remarkable total of twenty-seven operas, an achievement never even equaled, much less surpassed, in subsequent seasons. But it is not altogether by aggregate results that the value of Augustus Harris's operatic work can be reckoned; it lies in the fact that opera, both in London and in New York, is to-day a living thing—a prosperous, not a "moribund" institution. Nay, more: instead of being the "Italian Opera" of our fathers, with all its miserable limitations and inartistic conventionalities, it is an opera that combines the three great schools of the art in one organization, and presents their masterpieces in the languages in which they were written. To render the system perfect it needs to be less wholly dependent upon the social equation; but that desirable result never will be accomplished, either in England or in America, until opera has been released from the shackles of the foreign tongue and driven right home to the hearts of the people through the medium of their own good Anglo-Saxon vernacular.

Strange was it that the closing weeks of the century were to see the English concert-room deprived of its two greatest tenors. In October, 1900, Sims Reeves died at the ripe old age of eighty-two; two months later Edward Lloyd went into retirement after giving a memorable farewell concert at the Royal Albert Hall. It may not be uninteresting to compare these two supreme artists. In many ways, notably as to character of voice and method, they were as unlike as two singers could be; but each in his own fashion exemplified the purest attributes of the *bel canto* and upheld the best traditions of the British oratorio school. Sims Reeves in the original instance was an opera-singer. I once heard him in opera, but he was then nearly sixty, and had long abandoned his stage career. I first heard him sing at the Norwich Festival of 1866, when he took part in Costa's oratorio "Naaman." His voice was then still in its prime. A more exquisite illustration of what is termed the true Italian tenor quality it would be impossible to imagine; and this delicious sweetness, this rare combination of "velvety" richness with ringing timbre, he retained in diminishing volume almost to the last.

It is probable that Sims Reeves lost more money through unfulfilled engagements than any other singer that ever lived. He himself computed the total amount thus eliminated from his banking account, during a career of half a century, at £80,000 ($400,000). An eighth of this sum would have sufficed to spare him the rigid economy and the necessity for music-hall work which marred the closing years of his existence. In the early "nineties" he took up teaching and accepted a professorship at the Guildhall School, where we frequently came in contact. I asked him once whether there had always been good and sufficient cause for his disappointing the public so frequently.

"Well, perhaps not always," replied the veteran tenor. "That is to say, I have no doubt it would have been possible very often for me to have sung, if I had made the effort. But the very fact that it would have required an effort was enough to prevent me from trying. You see, my throat has always been delicate, and at the slightest sign of hoarseness I have been afraid to sing, lest I should impose a strain upon my vocal cords. If I had not been so careful, who knows but that my voice would have given out long ago, instead of being as fresh and strong to-day as at any time these twenty years?" That may have been absolutely true. As it was, Sims Reeves was unquestionably the best-preserved male singer of his time. To hear him, long after he had passed the age of seventy, sing "Adelaide" or "Deeper and deeper still" or "The Message" was an exposition of breath control, of tone-coloring, of phrasing and expression, that may truly be described as unique.

Edward Lloyd, both as a man and a singer, was of quite a different calibre. Hardy of constitution, fond of exercise and open-air sports, the possessor of a strong, healthy throat, it was the rarest imaginable occurrence for him to be compelled to forego an engagement in consequence of indisposition. Moreover, he had no weakness for luxuries, and never spent his money extravagantly. On the contrary, he knew how to save it and how to invest it to good advantage. Therefore it came about that, after a public career of some thirty years, Edward Lloyd was in a position to indulge his longing for *otium cum dignitate;* and when he retired from active service, in the plenitude of his vocal powers, he was a tolerably wealthy man —though, truth to tell, that farewell came all too soon for the liking of the British public. There was no one to take Lloyd's place, and even now it remains practically unfilled. Ben Davies has in his voice some notes of beautiful quality, and he is an artist of undoubted taste and distinction. Nevertheless, to place him wholly upon the same artistic level with his gifted predecessor might be to imitate the *Player Queen* in "Hamlet" and "protest too much."

GADSKI
AS ELISABETH

As these lines are penned Edward Lloyd is contemplating a farewell tour of the world; so, happily, there is no necessity yet to speak of him altogether in the past tense. He has promised, too, from time to time to reappear in the concert-room in England, as compliment or charity may demand. Edward Lloyd's is one of those pure, natural voices that never lose their sweetness, but preserve their charm so long as there are breath and power to sustain them. His method is, to my thinking, irreproachable and his style absolutely inimitable. His versatility was greater than that of Sims Reeves, even though he was never a stage tenor; for he was equally at home in music of every period and of every school. In Bach and Handel, in modern oratorio, in the Italian aria, in Lied, romance, or ballad, he was equally capable of arousing genuine admiration; and, when he had finished with all of these, he could declaim Wagner with a beauty of tone, a fullness of dramatic expression, and a clarity of enunciation that used to make his German audiences in London shout for very wonder and delight. Hans Richter was wont to declare that Edward Lloyd was the first tenor to bring out in all its fascinating loveliness the exquisite vocal charm of the "Preislied." That thought occurred to me when he was singing it at his farewell concert at the Albert Hall in December, 1900; and I was fain to admit that upon the operatic boards only Jean de Reszke had accomplished with this inspired melody what Edward Lloyd had done with it upon the concert platform.

Another great English singer who yet lingers upon the field of his former successes is Charles Santley. For his years, his voice is wonderfully preserved, and no "old man eloquent" could throw into his efforts a more remarkable measure of energy, vigor, and feeling. Like Reeves, he made his name first as an opera-singer; there are many still living who, like myself, entertain a vivid recollection of his sympathetic and dramatic delineation of *Valentine* in "Faust" and the *Conte di Luna* in "Il Trovatore" years before the appearance with the Carl Rosa Company to which allusion has already been made in these pages. But of late years the voice has lost its haunting beauty of timbre, and the charm of Santley's singing, save that which survives in his perfect phrasing, is no longer aught but a memory.

England's leading vocalists, at the dawn of the twentieth century, comprised many artists of genuine excellence. The time when there were "giants in the land" might be past and gone; the advent of a great English soprano might seem as far off as ever. But the average singing heard in the concert-room was often distinguished by fine musical feeling and intelligence. A busy career of nearly thirty years had not yet made serious inroads on the thrilling tones of Emma Albani. The "Queen of the British Musical Festival" was still the most reliable and conscientious of interpreters, the most industrious of artists. Marguerite Macintyre, despite her stronger penchant for opera, was nevertheless best known to her home public as a concert soprano; and the same statement applies with equal appropriateness to Ella Russell, who, American by birth, English by adoption, and Italian by marriage, was the dramatic soprano *par excellence* of the concert platform, a singer always sincere, thorough, and convincing in her work. Another acclimatized American of tried ability alike in opera- and concert-work was Lucile Hill; while yet another (who, however, had not yet trodden the lyric boards) was Lillian Blauvelt, a refined and highly cultivated singer with talents equally appreciated on both sides of the Atlantic.

But where, among the leading women singers, were the English-born artists? To find them one had to turn to the contraltos—to Clara Butt, with her glorious wealth of tone and Gallic grace of delivery; to Marie Brema (who, however, would be more correctly classified as a mezzo-soprano), with her admirable command of tone-color, her faultless diction, her infinitely varied shades of impassioned poetic expression; and to Kirkby Lunn, with her warm, rich notes of true contralto quality, a singer full of talent and an observant, persevering artist. The foremost contralto group would not be complete, however, without the name of the talented Australian, Ada Crossley, whose popularity, rapidly and surely earned, was due almost as much to winning charm of style as to sheer force of tonal beauty.

The mantle of Braham and Sims Reeves, as

worthily borne by Edward Lloyd, was resting more or less easily upon the shoulders of Ben Davies, a singer whose rare musical instinct and intelligence have always partially atoned for his uneven scale and his lack of ringing head-notes. Among the tenors who had made their mark, Joseph O'Mara must not be forgotten, nor William Green, the somewhat Italian quality of whose organ gave promise of rich development with greater freedom of emission and growth of temperament. At the head of the barytones stood Andrew Black, one of the best male singers that Scotland has ever produced, the possessor of a superbly resonant voice, and notably impressive in music calling for pathetic sentiment and declamatory vigor. Artistic singers were Kennerley Rumford and Denham Price, while as a "safe" oratorio bass Watkin Mills fully deserved his position. To complete the list there only remains to mention Plunket Greene, who, had his vocal attributes only been on a par with his interpretative powers, might fairly have been described as one of the finest concert vocalists of his time.

And so I conclude these recollections, as I began them, with reflections upon English Festival artists and English Festival singing. The festival, indeed, lives and flourishes, and remains perhaps the most characteristic feature of musical progress in the United Kingdom. It is the institution which continues to compare most favorably with what it was at the beginning of the thirty years traversed

CLARA BUTT

From a photograph by Messrs. Bassano, London

SIMS REEVES

From a photograph by Rockwood, N. Y.

by these pages. There were greater singers in the "seventies"—greater, maybe, than ever will be heard at a festival again. On the other hand, there were not then finer choirs than can be heard to-day at Leeds, Birmingham, Norwich, and Sheffield; nor were there splendid orchestras available then, as now, for the adequate rendering of something more than choral accompaniments and easy symphonies by Haydn or Mozart. Moreover, thanks to superior executive means and a higher order of musical appreciation, there has been a manifest improvement in the tone of festival programmes. A spirit of eclecticism dominates the choice of works and reflects a catholicity of taste that nowhere could be surpassed. Indeed, as regards the future of the art in England, it is the great provincial centres that display the promise to be sought for in vain amid the invertebrate elements which constitute musical life in the huge, overgrown metropolis of the British Empire.

INDEX

Index

Index

Index

Index

Index

Index

Index

Index

Printed by
BALLANTYNE, HANSON & Co
London & Edinburgh